The Tower
and
The Cloud

*Higher Education
in the Age of
Cloud Computing*

Printed in the United States of America on recycled paper.

Cover and interior paintings by Elizabeth Black
Book design and production by Anita Kocourek

Illustrations:
Campanile, University of California, Berkeley, cover, p. iv
King's College, Cambridge, p. xxii
Cairo University, p. 62
Trinity College, Dublin, p. 88
Rajabai Clock Tower, University of Mumbai, p. 106
University of Melbourne, p. 138
Cathedral of Learning, University of Pittsburgh, p. 170

EDUCAUSE

To Julia A. Rudy, extraordinary editor, colleague, and friend

Campanile, University of California, Berkeley

The Tower and The Cloud

Higher Education in the Age of Cloud Computing

Richard N. Katz

Editor

EDUCAUSE

Table of Contents

Foreword

By now, we've all heard, read, or said enough about the rapid pace of technological change for it to become cliché. We may have grown numb to the recitation of Moore's law and the sweeping social and economic impact of technological advances. Continuous, rapid, technology-based change, along with persistent, simultaneous efforts within the academy to both embrace and combat it, has become an assumed feature of our universe—like the existence of the university.

However, in *The Tower and the Cloud*, Richard Katz and his fellow authors remind us that the emergence of this technology "cloud" and its ever-increasing impact on us—individually and collectively—has significant implications for higher education as we know it. Only by looking past the cliché and carefully reflecting on the truth behind it can we appreciate the potential shape and direction of the change colleges and universities face. *The Tower and the Cloud* tackles questions such as "How are 'cloud' technologies and applications already affecting us?" "What does that say about how they are likely to evolve and impact us in the future?" "What might colleges, universities, and higher education overall look like as a result?"

The book explores a wide range of topics, beginning with the interplay of history, tradition, and technology that defines the modern academy—the "tower." Authors address what the academy must do to maintain the coherence of its mission—if not necessarily all of the forms through which it pursues that mission—as it moves forward. Given the geographically unbounded nature of the cloud, the discussion turns to the promise and challenge of the truly global higher education community—and market—which the network increasingly makes possible.

In the face of these trends, institutions must also cope with rising demands for accountability, even as the cloud affects the nature and meaning of the relationships among institutions, faculty, students, alumni, and government. *The Tower and the Cloud* looks at those issues in light of institutional capacities and asks, "What role should technology play in meeting these shifting demands?" It posits at least part of the answer through essays that take a fresh look at institutional governance of IT and encourage realignment of those structures with the reality of a networked world (and institution).

The collection then turns to the heart of the academy—scholarship and teaching, and the principle of openness that underlies them both. The open source and open educational resources movements are examined to illustrate how higher education's core commitment to the free exchange of ideas and information is finding renewed expression in the cloud environment. By leveraging the ease of collaboration, publication, and distribution that digital networks make possible, these movements are allowing communities of scholars, technology professionals, and institutions to come together to more effectively meet their needs and the needs of their students while contributing to the greater good.

The concluding essays highlight a diverse array of ways in which teaching, learning, and scholarship might evolve as a result of the cloud's impact. For example, digital media and broadband networks continue to change the form and amount of knowledge institutions can store and share, as well as who they can share them with. Yet the rapid evolution of digital media raises concerns about sustaining access—and the cost of doing so—over the long term. The cloud raises other questions, such as what impact the breathtaking rise of online social networking will have for building and sustaining community in higher education. As teaching, learning, and scholarship come to increasingly rely on networked services and resources beyond the institution's physical (and virtual) walls, how must IT leadership change to guide institutions through new realities while safeguarding the community's varied (and sometimes conflicting) interests?

These are just some of the major issues *The Tower and the Cloud* addresses as it illustrates the promise, pitfalls, and potential evolution of the academy in a network-based world. While not offering a crystal ball, it does provide a series of reasoned, analytical perspectives on how current trends may unfold, altering our institutions and the higher education landscape in a future that may arrive faster than we expect. In reading it, we are all challenged to move beyond acknowledging the pace of technological change to envisioning all that the tower can be if we embrace the cloud.

Diana G. Oblinger
President, EDUCAUSE

Preface

As I approach my 30th year of employment in higher education, I continue to feel as if I am in Wonderland. The life of the mind is, of course, always filled with wonder, and higher education enjoys proximity to two renewable sources of wonder: young people and a mission of discovery. Immersion in higher education IT adds even more to the wonder: I suspect that careers in IT in higher education leave many of us feeling like we have tumbled down Alice's tunnel to a pool of tears, the queen's croquet grounds, or a mad tea party.[1]

My fascination with technology was kindled as a graduate student by a reading of Professor David Landes's *The Unbound Prometheus*, a history of technological change and industrial development in Western Europe from 1750. Landes described how changes in technology and in process occur hand in hand, leading to new forms of industrial organization.[2] Since that reading, I have been consumed with the desire to understand the historical and institutional context for IT—in higher education. More recently, my understanding was deepened by Professor Martin Trow, who argued that:

> IT is embedded in and used by institutions that have a history. The historically shaped characteristics of colleges and universities are highly relevant to the ways IT will be used by (and over time transform) the existing structures of higher education. It is also likely that IT will cut its own channels, leading to the creation of institutions that differ from those of today, institutions where the weight of history does not condition and constrain IT's use.[3]

Professor Trow was most certainly right. With respect to higher education's administrative and teaching activities, IT has perhaps not fulfilled its promise to the extent witnessed in some other sectors of the economy. Here, the handicraft traditions of teaching and learning in the academy have, as Trow suggests, conditioned and constrained IT's use. Indeed, at some colleges and universities, good instructional technology is viewed as a barrier—or even antithetical—to good instruction. Change is slow.

In scientific research, however, and increasingly in social science and humanities research, IT's role has been transformational. Our ability to simulate and model physical phenomena, living systems, weather, traffic flows, and the economy through IT has placed IT on the same footing as experimentation and theory, as one of the pillars of research method. And Trow, too, was right about IT's capacity to cut its own channels. Today, so-called "open universities" serve hundreds of thousands of distant degree seekers worldwide through a variety of technologies, and in the time since Trow's essay was written, for-profit postsecondary school revenues have grown at a nearly 19 percent compound annual growth rate to nearly 6 percent of all postsecondary education spending. These institutions, which are expected to comprise nearly 8 percent of U.S. higher education by 2011, are certainly unconstrained by the weight of history.[4]

Lastly, teaching and learning are changing—albeit more slowly— under the influence of IT. More and more courses offer hybrid forms of instruction that are made possible by the networks and various computing and communications platforms that are being placed at students' disposal. At the same time, more and more students are supplementing—or replacing—lectures, seminars, and course materials with resources they uncover on the web.

As we slide farther and farther down the rabbit hole, we stare at or interact in wonder with grids, semantic webs, wikis, podcasts, open education resources, social networks, and other destinations. IT leads us not to a pool of tears, but to "peaks of inflated expectations" or to "troughs of disillusionment."[5]

Amidst our wonder is confusion. This volume is born of my confusion over where IT is moving and what channels it may begin to cut now in our historical institutions of higher education. This volume, too, is born of the confusion of college and university IT leaders throughout the world who need to make some sense of a chaotic and fast-changing environment long enough to guide institutional investments and to operate needed services for students, faculty, staff, and others. The volume is, if you will, a periodic measurement. It is an ice core from 2008; an assessment of where IT and social behaviors related to IT appear to be headed and of channels they may cut through our historical institutions. This volume is offered as an opportunity for very busy people to reflect on and assimilate the *meaning* of IT to higher education purposes and methods. The contributors to this volume strive to separate those torrents that may cut large and potentially disruptive channels in higher education from those smaller channels that may beautify our institutions or simply disappear without a trace. Creating this volume reflects the belief that educators and technologists need context for our actions and that we need to recalibrate this changing context more and more often. We need to think visions, not vision. We need to think of possibilities, predispositions, and probabilities, not of certainties. We need to think of directions and not fixities.

This volume—in my thinking—really represents the third volume in a visioning and context-setting exercise that began with the writing in 1992 of *Sustaining Excellence in the 21st Century* and continued in 1999 with *Dancing with the Devil.*[6]

Sustaining Excellence chronicled the emergence of the campus network and its capacity to link what we then called the campus technology archipelago. This report forecast the flattening of college and university organizations as access to resources on the network made it possible for members of the organizational community to make decisions without a dependence on formal hierarchies. *Sustaining Excellence* forecast, as well, the federation of central campus systems with local and personal systems, unified via a network and a common user interface.

Dancing with the Devil looked outside the walls of the university as the potential for the Internet and the new World Wide Web created simultaneously (1) the capacity to expand the college or university's presence, (2) unprecedented access to scholarly information resources, (3) the capacity to deliver core academic services at a distance, and (4) the opportunity for profit-oriented newcomers to enter higher education's market. The notion of empowerment permeates both of these volumes.

It Is Still about Empowerment

The theme of empowerment continues to pervade my thinking and the thinking of many of my colleagues. Looking back, I am pleased that I recognized this strand nearly 20 years ago, but I chuckle at my naïveté. In 1992, my colleagues and I at the University of California recognized that the network would draw power from the center of the administration to the myriad departments, schools, and colleges where the real mission of the university is discharged. This group of gifted and visionary central administrators welcomed this new sharing of responsibility. But we all believed that we could control the flow of power and that networks would foster shifts of power—among organizations! We did not understand—like Martin Trow—that IT was a force that would cut its own channels. Today, many writers refer to this empowerment as "consumerization."

Most futurists overstate the proximity of change and understate its magnitude. The premise of this volume is that the spectacular success of the network, the persistent interconnection of billions of people, the emergence of English as the global language of commerce, and other forces are empowering individuals. This empowerment has the potential to cut imaginable channels in our existing institutions and to make room for new institutions.

One colleague recently asked: Does the emergence of the network, unimaginable resources, and of virtual worlds now make it possible to liberate higher education from economics that are dominated by the cost of maintaining physical environments? Can we provide meaningful and cost-effective learning environments for 100 students? Can we imagine a return to the School of Athens? One need not look far to uncover the impact of IT on neighborhood banks, travel agencies, encyclopedias, libraries, political campaigns, and other institutions. The question remains: How can information technology change historical institutions of higher education? Perhaps in 2008 the question is: What is the role of the *institution* in a world where *individuals* are empowered to seek solutions anywhere in the network cloud?

To understand the possible impacts of IT on institutions, it makes sense to separate the idea of the university from its corporeal form. Western higher education traces its roots to Plato's academy of skeptics nearly 2,500 years ago. This history is dominated by adaptability. Colleges and universities rank among the world's most persistent institutions. Many have survived—in recognizable form—for more than a millennium, despite war, regime charge, recession, revolution, and other upheavals.

Universities and colleges have themselves been empowered. Colleges and universities were chartered originally by popes and kings as *places* where *elites* and *experts* were sequestered. Over time, their governance evolved and the dominion of priests and clerics, or that of government ministers, yielded to *shared governance* by rectors and academics. Fueled by the Renaissance, the invention of movable type, the Protestant reformation, democratic egalitarianism, and the Industrial Revolution, colleges and universities grew in number, size, and influence and were largely empowered to govern themselves as perpetuities.

The themes that pervade this history until the 20th century are skepticism, expertise, physicality, expansion, influence, resiliency, empowerment (self-governance), place, and craft. The history of the university has also long been characterized by autonomy and by the separation of utilitarian and nonutilitarian education.[7] The metaphors of the ivory tower, gated city, sheltered grove, and city-on-the-hill continue to find substance in campus plans and architecture. Finally, and more recently, the university mission and organization were enlarged to recognize the intimate and complex interplay of instruction and research.

Along the way, higher education's gates were swung wide open as societies and individuals came to understand the importance of knowledge in the production of national wealth and social mobility. While the modern college and university retains certain medieval

Table 1. Kant's Polarities Updated: New Conflicts

FROM	TO
Elite	Popular
Pure	Applied
Not-for-Profit	For-Profit
Education	Marketplace
Ivory Tower	Real World

Source: Reprinted with permission from Mark C. Taylor, "Useful Devils," *EDUCAUSE Review*, July/August 2000, 44.

aspects and forms, its adaptability and persistence do not arise out of inflexibility. Professor Mark C. Taylor traces higher education's evolution as shown in Table 1.

This evolutionary sweep is a work in process and today's higher education remains defined by the continued creative tension and debate between utilitarian and nonutilitarian values. Increasingly, I believe, the challenge for higher education is to understand how technology and changing human behavior influence skepticism, expertise, physicality, expansion, influence, resiliency, empowerment (self-governance), place, and craft.

Issues Raised in This Volume

The essays in this volume span a wide variety of topics. The contributing authors are among the best thinkers and practitioners in their fields. In the main, this volume examines issues such as the virtualization of service delivery, the "opening" of software and academic course content, and globalization through the lens of the empowered individual. The contributors raise, but rarely answer, questions about the roles of place, expertise, the library, and governance in the virtualized and distributed world of the network cloud.

The elephant in the room is the question: If a 300-year-old institution like *Encyclopedia Brittanica* can be threatened in five years by *Wikipedia*, can other aggregators of expertise (aka colleges and universities) be similarly challenged? Similarly, if knowledge and talent are now globally understood to be the *sine qua non* of the Information Age, then can colleges and universities lever their communities, reputations, credentials, and presence globally? And, finally, how does the new channel cut by information technology change scholarship? Does the existence or accessibility of new tools, instruments, and resources change academic practice, and how do changes—or constancies—get socialized?

Acknowledgments

This volume reflects a collaboration of many, many people. Brian Hawkins, president emeritus of EDUCAUSE, initially encouraged me to pursue this work. My colleagues Cynthia Golden, Mark Luker, and Diana Oblinger have both been intellectually indispensable and kept me going through their encouragement. The Fellows of the EDUCAUSE Center for Applied Research (ECAR) are extraordinary. Whatever good there is in the framing of the questions and the reasoning in this volume is their doing. Here I specifically thank Robert Albrecht, Judy Caruso, Phil Goldstein, Jack McCredie, Mark Nelson, Gail Salaway, Mark Sheehan, Toby Sitko, Don Spicer, and Ron Yanosky, who participated in two of the most provocative and forward-thinking meetings of my career. They are an extraordinary resource for higher education. I also had the pleasure of traveling for eight months with Ted Dodds, CIO of the University of British Columbia. Ted was a constant source of ideas, an ardent supporter, and a gentle but effective critic.

I was also able to tap—perhaps to excess—the time, talent, and goodwill of members of the EDUCAUSE Advisory Group on Enterprise Information Systems and Services (AGEISS). Nadine Stern of The College of New Jersey and Colin Currie of Princeton University chaired this group during the past 18 months and deserve special thanks. Special thanks as well to Roberta Ambur of the University of South Dakota, Mark Askren of UC Irvine, Kathryn Gates of the University of Mississippi, Ron Kraemer of the University of Wisconsin–Madison, Tracy Shroeder of the University of San Francisco, Mary Stephens of CSU–Long Beach, Niran Subramaniam of the University of Warwick, David Trevvett of the University of Chicago, Walter Weir of the University of Nebraska, and Khalil Yazdi of the University of Mary Washington.

If authors are the architects of books, then the editorial and production staff are the engineers that render the words clear, usable, and maybe occasionally inspiring. At EDUCAUSE we are actively trying to experiment and model behaviors that promote openness and that is especially important for a volume like this. This inclination means that we depend on EDUCAUSE staff and contractors for a wide range of editorial, art design, book design, layout, printing, and distribution services. Nancy Hays of EDUCAUSE coordinated the efforts of a large cast of very talented characters. Elizabeth Black, whose paintings I collect, was intrigued enough to produce the towers and clouds that appear occasionally in the volume. She is a gifted artist. Anita Kocourek has done graphic design, layout, presentations, and all things graphic for me for nearly 20 years. She has that rare ability to take my scribbles on napkins and render them into beautiful and meaningful illustrations. Catherine Yang is a trusted and valued colleague who is one of the best strategic thinkers I know. She provided senior leadership to the editorial, art, and production team. Her kindness and good nature, too, always kept this project of many parts on track. Lorretta Palagi provided expert editorial support.

This volume might not have come to fruition without the encouragement and financial support of my friends and colleagues at SunGard Higher Education. It's been my honor to work with the leadership of this organization for more than a decade. They have been unstinting supporters of EDUCAUSE and care deeply about higher education

Finally, and not at all least, Julia Rudy again worked as my editorial alter ego. Julie began as my editor more than 15 years ago when I was at the University of California and she was at CAUSE. She lured me to CAUSE, then EDUCAUSE, and is not only the best editor I know, she is a friend. Julie postponed retirement to have this last ride with me. It has been a pleasure and honor to work with her and I dedicate this volume to her, just as she dedicated her life to the higher education IT community.

Richard N. Katz
Boulder, Colorado

Endnotes

1. Lewis Carroll, *Alice's Adventures in Wonderland* (London: Macmillan Publishers, 1865).

2. David S. Landes, *The Unbound Prometheus* (Cambridge, England: Cambridge University Press, 1969).

3. Martin Trow, "The Development of Information Technology in U.S. Higher Education," *Daedalus* (Fall 1997): 294.

4. From Jeffrey M. Silber's study, *Education and Training*, published by Equity Research: BMO Capital Markets–U.S. (September 2007): 85–86.

5. From Gartner Hype Cycles, developed by Gartner, Inc., to represent the maturity, adoption, and business application of specific technologies, http://www.gartner.com/pages/story.php.id.8795.s.8.jsp.

6. R. N. Katz and R. P. West, *Sustaining Excellence in the 21st Century: A Vision and Strategies for University Administration* (Boulder, CO: CAUSE, 1992); and R. N. Katz and Associates, *Dancing with the Devil: IT and Higher Education* (San Francisco: Jossey-Bass, 1999).

7. See Mark C. Taylor's summary of Immanuel Kant's *The Conflict of the Faculties* in "Useful Devils," *EDUCAUSE Review* (July/August 2000): 42.

Bibliography

Carroll, Lewis. *Alice's Adventures in Wonderland*. London: Macmillan Publishers, 1865.

Katz, R. N., and R. P. West. *Sustaining Excellence in the 21st Century: A Vision and Strategies for University Administration*. Boulder, CO: CAUSE, 1992.

Katz, R. N., and Associates. *Dancing with the Devil: IT and Higher Education*. San Francisco: Jossey-Bass, 1999.

Landes, David S. *The Unbound Prometheus*. Cambridge, England: Cambridge University Press, 1969.

Silber, Jeffrey M. *Education and Training*. Equity Research: BMO Capital Markets–U.S. (September 2007).

Taylor, Mark C. "Useful Devils." *EDUCAUSE Review* (July/August 2000): 38–46.

Trow, Martin. "The Development of Information Technology in U.S. Higher Education." *Daedalus* (Fall 1997): 293–314.

About the Authors

BRYAN ALEXANDER is Director of Research for the National Institute for Technology and Liberal Education. He was an English professor at Centenary College of Louisiana.

DAVID A. ATTIS is a Senior Consultant in the higher education practice at the Advisory Board Company. He was a senior policy consultant at the Council on Competitiveness.

YOCHAI BENKLER is the Jack N. and Lillian R. Berkman Professor for Entrepreneurial Legal Studies at Harvard Law School and the author of *The Wealth of Networks* and the paper "Coase's Penguin." He is also Codirector of the Berkman Center for Internet and Society at Harvard University.

ANDY COOLEY, senior vice president of marketing at SunGard Higher Education, works with customers to help SunGard Higher Education understand and respond to emerging technology trends and institutional needs. He holds degrees from the University of Utah and Harvard University.

PAUL N. COURANT is University Librarian and Dean of Libraries, the Harold T. Shapiro Collegiate Professor of Public Policy, and the Arthur F. Thurnau Professor of Economics and of Information at the University of Michigan. He has also served as Provost and Executive Vice President for Academic Affairs at Michigan.

JIM DAVIS is Associate Vice Chancellor and CIO and professor in the Chemical and Biomolecular Engineering Department at UCLA. He instituted the first offices of the CIO at The Ohio State University and UCLA.

GLYN DAVIS is Vice-Chancellor and Chief Executive Officer of the University of Melbourne, Australia. He is a professor of political science in the university, fellow of the Academy of Social Sciences in Australia, and a Companion in the Order of Australia.

LARRY R. FAULKNER is President of Houston Endowment Inc. and President Emeritus of The University of Texas at Austin.

IRA FUCHS is Vice President of Research in Information Technology at the Andrew W. Mellon Foundation. He was Vice President for Computing and IT at Princeton University. Fuchs was a founding director and chief scientist of JSTOR and founded BITNET. He was President of the Corporation for Research and Educational Networking for 25 years.

PAUL B. GANDEL is the Vice President for Information Technology and CIO at Syracuse University (SU). He also holds an appointment as professor in the School of Information Studies at SU.

CHRISTINE GEITH is Executive Director of MSUglobal and Assistant Provost at Michigan State University. She is a founding partner in several entrepreneurial e-learning ventures including Learn2Grow.com, the Global Community Security Institute, and AmericanCitizenPlanner.com.

PHIL GOLDSTEIN is the President of Goldstein & Associates, an independent consulting firm specializing in higher education strategy, management, and information technology, and a fellow with the EDUCAUSE Center for Applied Research. He was formerly a partner at PricewaterhouseCoopers Consulting.

BRIAN L. HAWKINS is President Emeritus of EDUCAUSE and was the founding President and CEO of that organization. He was formerly Senior Vice President of Brown University.

RICHARD N. KATZ is Vice President of EDUCAUSE and the coauthor of *Dancing with the Devil* and six other books on information technology's role in higher education. He is founding director of the EDUCAUSE Center for Applied Research.

ANDY LANE is Director of OpenLearn, an open educational resources website for The Open University in the United Kingdom. He is a professor in the university and an elected board member of the Open Courseware Consortium.

CLIFFORD LYNCH is the Executive Director of the Coalition for Networked Information and an adjunct professor at the School of Information at the University of California, Berkeley.

MARY MARLINO is the Director of the National Center for Atmospheric Research Library. She was also the principal investigator for the Digital Library for Earth System Education and was one of the original principal investigators for the National Science Digital Library.

PATRICIA MCLEAN is Director of Academic Enrichment Services at the University of Melbourne, Australia. She was seconded to manage the strategy office responsible for overseeing implementation of the university's Growing Esteem strategy.

DIANA OBLINGER is President of EDUCAUSE. She served as Vice President and CIO at the University of North Carolina system and in faculty and administrative positions at Michigan State University and the University of Missouri–Columbia. Oblinger was Director of the Institute for Academic Technology for IBM and Executive Director of Higher Education for Microsoft.

LINDA O'BRIEN is Vice Principal, Information, and CIO at the University of Melbourne, Australia. She is responsible for the university's scholarly and corporate information strategy and the information services, systems, and infrastructure that underpin this.

MALCOLM READ is the Executive Secretary of the Joint Information Systems Committee of the United Kingdom, whose mission is to provide world-class leadership in the innovative use of ICT to support education and research.

TAMARA SUMNER is Executive Director of Digital Learning Sciences. She is also an associate professor at the University of Colorado with a joint appointment in computer and cognitive science.

JOHN UNSWORTH is Dean and professor at the Graduate School of Library and Information Science, University of Illinois, Urbana–Champaign. He chaired the American Council of Learned Societies' recent national commission on cyberinfrastructure for humanities and social sciences, and he is currently coordinator of the I-Schools Caucus.

BRADLEY C. WHEELER is the Vice President of Information Technology and CIO for Indiana University and co-founder of the Sakai and Kuali Foundations. He is also a professor of information systems at the Kelley School of Business.

KRISTINA WOOLSEY is a Learning Experience Designer at the Exploratorium and chair of the Advisory Group of the Learning, Design and Technology program at Stanford University. She was formerly the director of the Apple Multimedia Lab.

RONALD YANOSKY is Deputy Director and Senior Fellow of the EDUCAUSE Center for Applied Research (ECAR). Before joining ECAR, Yanosky was principal analyst at Gartner, Inc., and assistant professor of history at Harvard University.

King's College, Cambridge

Higher Education
and
Information Technology

The Gathering Cloud:
Is This the End of the Middle?

Richard N. Katz

"… it is clear that technology allows institutions to blur, if not erase, institutional boundaries once clear and distinct."

—*Steven Crow, former president, Higher Learning Commission
of the North Central Association of Colleges and Schools*

H. G. Wells described human history as a race between education and catastrophe. If this is so, higher education has played a major role in safeguarding the world. In the West, educators often trace their professional origins to Plato's academy, where skeptics reasoned and reflected on goodness and knowledge. Platonic education was personal, eschewing even the written word. Socrates described writing as an "invention [that] will produce forgetfulness in the souls of those who have learned it."[1] In early modern Europe, itinerant educators traveled to students who pooled resources to pay for their tuition.[2]

The 11th and 12th centuries represent a turning point in the history of higher education, with the founding of the College de Sorbonne, Oxford University, the University of Salamanca, the University of Bologna, and the University of Modena and Reggio Emilia. Universities in the West assumed the physical form that we recognize today and operated under papal or royal charters. The Western form of universities and colleges is resilient. Many institutions have served their societies through natural disasters, times of war, revolution, economic turmoil, and political upheaval. In many cases, our oldest universities have persisted longer than the nation states, forms of government, and royal houses that chartered them. They have grown in number, size, and influence, bearing witness to Wells's lament."[3]

Fiat Lux

Ten threads have influenced the makeup of Western higher education's tapestry in this millennium.

1. *The academy is an artisan community.* The Western university and college is a clear outgrowth of medieval monastic and guild life. Like guilds and monasteries, the modern academy consists of communities that "comprise the enduring interpersonal relations that form around shared practices."[4] Brown and Duguid argue that successful academic communities are inhabited by people who share common tasks, obligations, and goals.[5] As with medieval guilds, modern professors enculturate their students to the language, syntax, methods, and resources of an academic discipline as well as connect students with other scholars in the community. Students (apprentices), like their medieval guild counterparts, look to older students (journeymen) for instruction, to peers for edification and affirmation of practice, and to professors (masters) for endorsement and acceptance. The craft origins of higher education are evident in our cottage-industry modes of research and instructional production. To a very great extent, research funding flows to individual researchers from sponsors outside the academy's walls, and the key decisions about the scope, methods, time frames, and goals of research are set and enforced by individual investigators. In instruction, academic courses are typically crafted by individual instructors and are rarely shared among other academics who share similar—or even identical—responsibilities.

2. *Academic practice is organized around scarcity.* The modern Western university and college evolved to a great extent from the libraries and *scriptoria* of the 6th century, which served to select, collect, copy, preserve, and protect the textual record of European life. The crafts of writing and illuminating manuscripts and written materials themselves were rare, and early academic institutions were designed to protect and preserve scarce people and objects and to mediate access to scarce resources. Early institutions operated more as knowledge and learning filters than as pumps. Books were chained and locked away in towers. Higher education's emphasis today on openness reflects both the growing abundance of knowledge and knowledge work and a relatively recent understanding that widespread education is an engine of progress and human development.

3. *The academy is a place.* Since the 12th century, higher education has been a place. Students "go to college." Scarcity drove the early need for space and early colleges and universities were built as a means of attracting scarce people of intellect to one another and to the scarce raw materials of scholarship (books, laboratories, surgical theaters). These were not humble beginnings. In keeping with their papal or royal charters, early univer-

sities were often beautiful places. The medieval idea of the university as
a majestic and cloistered place designed to foster fellowship, collegiality,
reflection, and independence is deep seated. It is reinforced in literary and
film treatments of higher education and has influenced generations of
architects and campus planners. Even campuses in virtual worlds such as
Second Life and elsewhere draw inspiration from the medieval idea of a city
of intellect featuring sacred gardens and other spaces to be secured by walls,
gates, and towers. Medieval universities—and many modern ones—were
designed to be places apart from the rude and cacophonous rabble, places
of quiet and beauty, ripe for reflection, discussion, inquiry, and discovery.

4. *Academic governance has devolved.* Before colleges and universities
were chartered by civil or ecclesiastical powers, students pooled their
financial resources to bring learned men to their cities and towns. By the
11th century, place-based institutions largely displaced these practices. The
power and influence of the student guild declined. Over time, authority
over many universities passed to local authorities, and ultimately universities became self-governing corporations. A unique aspect of university
self-governance is the division of responsibilities among administrators for
the material sustenance of the institution and among the academics for
the intellectual welfare of the academy and its citizens. Student opinion
continues to play a role in college and university decision making, but not
to the extent found before the construction of the great universities.

5. *Academic activities are bundled.* Colleges and universities approach
learning holistically. We speak of academic programs and of courses of
instruction. We distinguish an educational experience from a training
experience. Institutions strive not only to impart knowledge but to prepare
enlightened citizens, engage members of their communities in the "life of
the mind," and enhance "every individual's particular gifts, and voice, and
promise."[6] Thomas Jefferson argued that "light and liberty go together."[7]
Colleges and universities issue credentials designed to signal others about
one's standing as an educated apprentice, journeyman, or master in a
domain of knowledge and practice. The holistic approach to education is a
practical one. Modern academies seek wherever possible to leverage their
faculty, libraries, and other resources. Bundling academic offerings into
programs and courses of instruction enables (and masks) a complex system
of cross subsidies that make it possible for institutions to provide for study
in those disciplines that may be impractical or out of favor. This insulates
colleges and universities to an extent from pressures to be fashionable.
From a narrower consumer perspective, bundling allows these institutions
to offer—or even require students to take—instruction they have available
rather than instruction that students (or employers) may want.

6. *The academic mission has three parts.* From their inception, universities and colleges have mixed three missions. Instruction, research, and service have always been intertwined. Early academies featured surgical theaters, translation centers, clinics, and astronomical observatories. These institutions not only served the community of scholars but were important in spreading knowledge, in food production, in nautical exploration, in diplomacy, and in military applications such as ballistics. Research and service to society and to the institution's political patrons have always been intertwined. Most academics believe that the elements that comprise higher education's mission mutually reinforce each other.[8]

7. *The academy has become more accessible.* Ideas about enlightenment and citizenship fueled significant growth in colleges and universities in the 18th century, and access widened even more in the 19th century as the commercial application of scientific discoveries further enhanced the standing of higher education. Thomas Jefferson reflected that an aristocracy of virtue and talent would be essential to the functioning of a well ordered republic.[9] In the United States, secondary school enrollments rose from 297,894 to 824,447 between 1890 and 1906 as a reflection of the rise in education's perceived value.[10] This expansion was echoed in higher education as U.S. postsecondary enrollments rose from 200,000 at the turn of the 20th century to more than 18 million today.[11] As the wealth of nations and citizen prosperity have become closely associated with higher levels of educational attainment, many nations have opened higher education's gates wider. Women, long denied access, now outnumber men in higher education throughout much of the developed world, and institutions such as the Open University and the University of Phoenix enroll more than 100,000 students, spanning multiple state and national jurisdictions. Colleges and universities no longer serve only elite populations and increasingly serve students of all ages and backgrounds.

8. *Openness pervades academic inquiry.* The history of Western higher education is a history of increasingly open inquiry. Early universities regulated as well as preserved knowledge. As colleges and universities won self-governance, academic freedom and openness have become values that are shared widely among members of the academy. Open inquiry is at the heart of scientific method, which makes sense of the world by making observations, forming and testing possible explanations of those observations, and repeating experiments over and over again. The process of structured scientific inquiry depends on an open and increasingly public iteration between observations and interpretations. Patterns of observations are socialized by the academic community and can thus suggest possible general principles that in turn are used to generate predictions about future

observations. Openness is central to others' ability to reproduce experimental results, and reproducibility is central to scientific research. To a great extent, academic scholarship is less about finding "truth" than it is a process of continual and open inquiry informed by curiosity, and skepticism.

9. *The academy's range is growing geographically.* Colleges and universities have extended their geographic presence, influence, and footprint. By 2007, nearly 600,000 non-U.S. students enrolled in U.S. colleges and universities.[12] U.S., British, and Australian universities have opened significant academic operations in the Middle East, India, Singapore, and elsewhere. A decade ago, Australia made exporting Australian higher education to international students a cornerstone of its education and trade policy. The importance of higher education has become widely understood throughout the world.[13] The emergence of robust networks, collaborative tools, and rich digital stores of scholarly materials is making it possible to extend higher education to more and more people. As Thomas Friedman put it, "We are now in the process of connecting all the knowledge pools in the world together ... anyone with smarts, access to Google, and a cheap wireless laptop can join the innovation fray."[14]

10. *Scientific research is a catalyst of accelerating change.* While the academy's instructional mission is discharged today in ways that can be traced to medieval monastic or guild traditions, the organization and conduct of research—particularly scientific research—can be barely recognized from that of 100 years ago. Teams of researchers that extend across domains of expertise and national borders organize experiments using instruments of unimaginable size, power, and expense. The time scale from problem conception to experimentation to commercialization has collapsed. New fields of inquiry are born regularly, often requiring the emergence of new methods, a new language of description, and new conventions. Research output is breathtaking. In 2003 and 2004 there were more than 7,500 scientific journals, and the number of articles appearing in the top 16 of those journals alone in 2002 and 2003 was 6,911.[15] Table 1 summarizes some of the key trends that can be traced in the history of Western higher education.

The Gathering Cloud

While it took 1,000 years to raise the tower of higher education, it has taken only 60 years to launch the digital computing and communications revolution. And while the history of computing and communications is faster moving and more boisterous than the history of higher education, it is less subtle and therefore easier to tell. At the most fundamental level,

Table 1. Key Trends in the History of Western Higher Education

FROM	TO
Teaching is a small-scale craft and learning is personalized.	Instruction is a scalable craft and can be standardized, personalized, or self-guided.
The governing power of colleges and universities is derived from church or state.	Colleges and universities are largely self-governing.
The academy is isolated from society.	The academy is enmeshed in communities served.
College or university education is accessible to an elite student body.	College or university education is accessible to all capable.
The college and university service base is local.	The college or university service base can be local, regional, national, or global.
The college or university is a place.	The college or university is situated in a place and virtually enhanced.
Scholars and academic resources are scarce and inaccessible.	Scholars and academic resources are plentiful and easily accessible.
Colleges and universities are purveyors and collectors of knowledge.	Colleges and universities are creators of knowledge.
Colleges and universities are local.	Colleges and universities are increasingly global.

the story of information and communication technology is that of a quest to put thinking and communicating power everywhere and in everything and to connect it all. This is being accomplished by making computers faster, cheaper, better, more reliable, smaller, and more personal; by making communication ubiquitous and fast; and by making connections persistent.

The fuller story is a rich tale of five eras of innovation, economics dominated by Moore's law, and exponential improvements in performance.

Mainframe Computing

The mainframe era was launched in the 1940s with the appearance of computing behemoths named Mark I, ENIAC, EDVAC, and Manchester's Baby. They were developed and housed in major research universities such as MIT, Harvard, the University of Pennsylvania, and the University of Manchester. These machines were enormous, cumbersome, and specialized. They were used chiefly for computationally intensive military applications such as ballistics.

The replacement of vacuum tubes with transistors in 1947 and the introduction of semiconductors in 1958 enabled cost-effective miniaturization, the proliferation of devices, and decreases in cost. Third-generation programming languages such as C, Basic, FORTRAN, ALGOL, and COBOL made it possible for computers to support an increasingly wide range of scientific and accounting functions. Large-scale computing is inherently expensive and complex and tends toward centralized management. Large computers, computer clusters, and associated storage devices require power, space, cooling, scientific and technical expertise, and physical security. Computation of this kind was expensive and therefore tightly controlled. And, of course, the mainframe—and later the minicomputer—was an island. While multiple monitors were multiplexed to mainframe computers in the 1950s, allowing more than one user to make use of a mainframe, this practice did not become commonplace until time sharing was successfully commercialized at Dartmouth in 1964.

Personal Computing

While the economics of semiconductors made it possible to develop relatively inexpensive minicomputers such as Digital Equipment Corporation's PDP-8 (1965), the development of the home computer by Apple in 1977 and the personal computer by IBM in 1981 ushered in a new age of computing. These developments led *Time Magazine* to name the computer as its "Man of the Year" in December 1982.

The shift from large-scale to personal computing was revolutionary. In this era, Microsoft acquired QDOS and emerged as the dominant supplier of operating systems for computers of this kind. Within a year, the text and keyboard command-driven MS-DOS operating system were under pressure from graphical user interfaces (GUI) such as those demonstrated on the Apple Lisa. In 1983, Apple released the Macintosh along with the Orwellian Super Bowl television commercial suggesting the coming of a new age in computing. By late 1983, Microsoft announced Windows, an operating system that featured GUI and a multitasking environment for the IBM PC.

In higher education, the PC and its evolving operating system liberated computing from the data processing department in an unplanned fashion. Decentralized grant funding, in particular, resulted in a proliferation of personal computers throughout research universities and an associated proliferation of software applications, support organizations, and so forth. This unplanned technology archipelago gave rise to persistent IT governance challenges, inefficiencies, and risks. Notwithstanding these challenges, the personal computer put incredible capabilities into many people's hands. Computers became the defining medium of work. And while early PCs were slow and cumbersome to use, they quickly became faster, easier to use, and more standardized and enjoyed the emergence of an extraordinary proliferation of software programs—many directed at improving professional productivity. IT research firm Gartner, Inc., predicts that there will be 2 billion computers in use worldwide by the year 2014—remarkable growth in less than 35 years.[16]

PCs in this era, like mainframes, were stand-alone devices, and early personal computing suffered from local suboptimization from the institutional perspective. Enterprise computing consisted of the financial system, the student system, and the payroll/personnel system. Research computing and most office work took place outside the gaze and purview of the campus IT organization.

Physical Connectivity

By 1969, host computers at UCLA, UC Santa Barbara, Stanford Research Institute, and the University of Utah were connected by a network developed by the Department of Defense (DOD). Over the next 15 years, ongoing innovations such as the development of Ethernet, Transmission Control Protocol (TCP), packet switching, and others resulted in the remarkable proliferation of networks and interconnection of computers and other devices. By 1971, 23 host computers were connected by networks, and by 1973, University College London became the first international host to be connected to the DOD's ARPAnet. By 1984, the increasing adoption of Internet Protocol (IP) and other innovations fueled the accelerating growth of the network. The number of network host computers broke 1,000 that year. With the evolution of the domain name system, e-mail, file transfer protocol, newsgroups, and other enabling communication innovations, the computer became a communication device. In 1986, the 56Kbs NSFnet succeeded the ARPAnet, fueling greater demand for computer connections and paving the way for the growth of supercomputer centers at Cornell, Pittsburgh, Princeton, San Diego, and Urbana-Champaign. By 1987, the NSFnet was commercialized and more than 10,000 host devices were connected. By 1989, more than 100,000 host devices were connected to the NSFnet. Networks in Canada, Denmark, France, Iceland, Norway, and Sweden were connected to the U.S. network. By 1990, more than 1 million hosts were connected to the network. The invention of the World Wide Web meant that digital resources of many kinds could now be linked and displayed in common and easy-to-use ways that were also graphically rich. This invention fueled a rush to post and link an unprecedented volume of information online that shows no signs of abating. Search engines emerged in 1995 to help make it possible for people to gain unprecedented access to a wide variety of information resources by using language that was natural to them. The computer was now a communication device and the Internet and web, a mass medium.

Logical Connectivity

The extraordinary proliferation of computers in the 50 years between their invention and the middle of the 1990s, and the emergence of a global data communication network linking hundreds of thousands of users, created the possibility of doing things "anytime and anywhere." In the United States, the NASDAQ stock exchange began trading over the Internet, lending legitimacy to business conducted over the network. By 1997, new standards (802.11) for connecting devices and networks wirelessly were approved and deployed over dedicated portions of the U.S. spectrum. At the same time, second-generation mobile telephone systems began to appear using TMDA and CMDA protocols. SMS messaging also emerged during this period. The message was clear— connectivity to networks was spreading like wildfire, and connectivity no longer depended on physically linking devices through wires or cables. These and subsequent innovations worked hand in hand with ongoing efforts to make intelligent devices smaller and faster, resulting in an explosion of intelligent and connected devices that were designed to travel with their owners. Computers no longer filled entire rooms; they fit inside pockets.

The connectivity associated with networks and the mobility associated with modern computing and storage devices have made "being digital" irresistible, and telephony, television, film, music, and video have raced to become part of an interconnected digital landscape that could only be characterized as a lifestyle. By 2000, wireless devices were in widespread use in Fortune 500 companies, and by this writing there are 220,000 wireless hot spots in the United States alone.[17] The rapid deployment of new Wi-Fi standards and the global adoption of third-generation standards for cellular communications herald an age when it will be possible to remain persistently and logically connected to the Internet anywhere in the world.

Embedded Connectivity

As video, voice, and text have become increasingly digital, the focus of attention is on ubiquitous access and persistent connection. In such an environment, everyone may be connected all the time to a network that is linked essentially to everything. That day has not arrived, but as of 2007, there were more than 1 billion people who used the Internet, and more than 100 million websites. Radio frequency identification (RFID) chips that communicate wirelessly are embedded routinely in everyday products. Computers regulate the performance of automobiles and other devices and track, transmit, and recount product history, performance, and anomalies to networks of automotive dealers and others. Sensors can be found in seismically active areas or in tornados tracking the intensity, direction, and forces associated with atmospheric, oceanic, or seismic movement. Intelligent and communicating devices can be found in the backpacks or bracelets that accompany Japanese children throughout their day, and they are now frequently implanted in our pets.

Technology has become standardized, personalized, miniaturized, economical, ubiquitous, and even friendly. Connection to the Internet is becoming persistent. Many people now routinely carry a multiplicity of devices whose power far outstrips that of ENIAC or Manchester's Baby. The evolution of context awareness, user interfaces (such as virtual worlds), and natural language processing will continue to erode the boundaries that separate our face-to-face presence from our presence in virtual spaces.

Finally, this period has seen the maturation of virtualization technology. Virtualization refers to the abstraction of computing resources and makes it possible to do things such as abstracting storage from networked storage devices, or hosting computer applications on alien hardware or software platforms. Virtualization makes it possible to optimize underused computing resources independent of their location. In the ideal, virtualization suggests the possibility of unifying a college or university's far flung collection of networked devices for the purposes of managing costs, conserving power consumption, applying security, promoting sound information practices, and enforcing institutional policies. These same capabilities, of course, will make it possible to reconsider the campus altogether as the locus of enterprise computing. Table 2 summarizes some of the key shifts in computing and communications that have occurred in this period.

A Confusing Cusp

So what can we conclude is happening? Somewhere between the stable, yet adaptable history of the tower and the boisterous and disruptive history of information technology, things have become unclear. Why has it become increasingly difficult to predict the channels that IT may cut in higher education? Is IT a tool that we control or will information and communications technologies profoundly influence and perhaps deeply disrupt higher education?[18] Have things become so murky that we can only predict the present or have we arrived at a moment of history when "change is so speeded up that we begin to see the present only when it is already disappearing"?[19]

Table 2. Key Shifts in Computing and Communications

FROM	TO
Computers are rare and expensive.	Computers are affordable and are nearly everywhere.
Computers and computing are isolated.	Computers are connected.
Computers are stationary.	Computers are mobile.
Networked computing is an enterprise-scale professional endeavor.	Networked computing is a widely held capability and activity that spans consumers of all ages and a wide range of personal and professional roles.
Computing, network, and data storage capacity are fixed and must be managed for growth.	Computing, network, and data storage capacity can be virtualized, shared, and increased or decreased on demand.
Information systems, resources, and services are organized, assembled, mediated by the enterprise.	Information systems, resources, and services can be organized, assembled, mediated anywhere and by anyone on the network.
Networked information resources are scarce.	Networked information resources are abundant.
Finding networked information requires end-user education and skills.	Finding network information is relatively natural and easy.
Standards are evolving and impede progress.	Many key standards are in place and standard-setting processes have themselves become standardized.
The physical form of information mediates access to information.	Policy and law mediate access to information.

We are in a time of emergence when the best advice is to observe and to be sensitive to areas from which change is emerging. Periods of emergence are characterized by hype, hope, rational and irrational exuberance, uncertainty, promises, panaceas, hyperbole, fear, risks, and opportunities.

This volume was intended to define the perimeters of this fluid and uncertain period. Not only is the *rate* of change accelerating, but the *form* that change is assuming is becoming indistinct. The form that change is assuming is that of a cloud. Cloudiness denotes heterogeneity, dynamism, shape shifting, indistinctness, and the capacity for expansion and reorganization. Cloudiness also denotes confusion and lack of clarity. We are at change's borders and we cannot fully envision the territory that lies ahead. We are at a cusp—an interregnum that separates innovation and socialization. We are making the leap from one innovation curve to another. We are changing regimes without really comprehending the new regime. We are letting go of a known and trusted toehold in favor of an uncertain one.

Our uncertainty makes sense. Technological changes typically outpace people's ability to socialize those changes. While innovations like the steam engine replaced the power of humans, animals, wind, or water with mechanical power in the 18th century, the reorganization of work itself changed very slowly and over a long period of time. Indeed, it was not until the 1918 opening of Henry Ford's Rouge River plant—the cathedral for the Industrial Revolution—that industrial work finally and fully embraced the capacity for change presented by the technologies of the industrial age. The gap between innovation and full realization took more than two centuries to disappear.

This interregnum, too, is unique. First, clouds do not get clearer as you approach them. Second, the acceleration caused in fact by our interconnectedness means that this interregnum will not take 200 years to play out. The socialization of IT is a drama being enacted simultaneously by 1 billion interconnected people, many of whom are adapting to change and assimilating new behaviors in real time, all the time. Third, *we* are becoming cloudy. Grant McCracken argues that like clouds, we are "an aggregation of interests, connections, and contacts, tagged in several ways, linked in all directions, changing in real time." This characterization of the self, groups, networks, and ideas stands in stark relief to Clifford Geertz's concept of Western man as a "bounded unique, more or less integrated … dynamic center of awareness, emotion, judgment and action organized into a distinctive whole." At its most philosophical, this particular cusp causes us to ask the most uncomfortable questions about the nature of enterprise, the nature of work, the nature of knowledge and ideas, and the nature of ourselves.[20]

The end of the middle, indeed.

Disruptions at the Cusp

So what is clear? It is clear that the history of higher education is one of persistence and adaptability. It is increasingly clear that core competency of universities "is not transferring knowledge, but developing it [through] intricate and robust networks and communities."[21]

It is reasonable to conclude that higher education's history is a history both of rising importance and accessibility and of continuity in instructional method. This history is partly defined by the tension between the academy's costly craft-based instructional preference—defined as "quality"—and the drive to provide affordable higher education to more and more people. Increasing access to higher education has for most come with increasing costs and at the expense of personalized instruction. Few educators can deliver personalized instruction affordably on a large scale, without endowments or other subsidies. The history of higher education is also a history of increasing openness. From the time of locked and guarded *scriptoria* and of chained books to the proliferation today of open repositories, open content, open source software, and open inquiry, the vector of change has been easy to discern.

The history of information technology is similarly a history that can be summarized by the increasing availability of IT, of IT-enabled services, and of information itself. Unlike higher education, the history of IT is one of increasing accessibility *with* increasing affordability and increasing personalization. This is due largely to the breathtaking effects of Moore's law, to near ubiquitous network access, and to the adoption of standards. And with IT, investment in personalization means ultimately that success is defined by making operations and learning so transparent and easy as to eliminate the need for human intervention. Most higher education offerings are predicated on the desirability of human intervention.

While so-called cloud computing remains an emergent concept and development and thus is subject to hype, definitional disputes, and inevitable fits and starts, it is clear that (1) open information content, software, and services, (2) service orientation and delivery, (3) server and storage virtualization, and (4) standardization of computing across the Internet are leading to what some describe as the democratization and industrialization of IT.[22]

Philosophizing about the cloud and the possible dematerialization of things can lead one to end-of-time ideas about the "big switch," the "digital enterprise," and the "end of corporate computing"[23] or to incapacitating confusion and inaction. This volume and essay are in fact organized to accent an important portion of the trends so that the practitioner can engage the institution in setting a broad agenda for action in the coming years. While the prospect of "end-of-the-middle" possibilities is quite real, there are more fascinating and more positive questions to be asked. In particular, can enabling our IT infrastructures for industrial-scale computing make it possible to defeat the historical tension between access to and personalization of education? Can we extend the footprint of our existing colleges and universities in ways that take advantage of scale economics, while maximizing the degrees of operating freedom enjoyed by our students, faculty, operating units, international affiliates, and so forth? In short, is mass personalization of higher education possible?

To answer these questions, we need to understand the nature of the disruptions that are likely to occur in the future. University of Virginia Vice President James Hilton makes a compelling case that "four disruptive forces are bearing down on higher education at this very moment: unbundling; demand-pull; ubiquitous access; and the rise of the pure property view of ideas."[24]

Unbundling

Unbundling, or disintermediation, makes it possible for the consumer to acquire only the blurb rather than the book, the cut rather than the album, or perhaps the course rather than the academic program. It is now possible for traditional colleges and universities to offer coursework in learning centers, on campuses, online, and in a variety of hybrid forms. It is also increasingly possible for new colleges and universities to do the same, and for institutions to sell unbundled educational offerings across traditional higher education jurisdictions. It is also possible for other "knowledge" and expertise businesses, such as *The New York Times*, to rebundle their human and information resources and reinvent themselves as educational enterprises, and for others to explore reconstructing the educational delivery model altogether. Just as one can unbundle a course from a catalog, one can unbundle course delivery from classrooms, and so forth.

Unbundling cuts both ways. Savvy education providers with strong brands will be able to enlarge their institutional footprint by organizing education and other institutional services for delivery to new students, customers, patrons, and fans. For others, the virtualization of services and the evolution of cloud-based services will likely add new competition for the mix. For still others, the availability of virtualized services will make it possible to rebundle elements of the educational infrastructure (tutors, library materials, assessments, and so forth) in ways that are experientially rich while being scalable and enjoying very different economics from their place-based alternatives. In an era of increasing concern about an institution's carbon footprint and energy costs, such virtualized service offerings may become especially appealing.

Hilton also reveals another aspect of unbundling—the unbundling and repackaging in the cloud that is embodied in the creed of ripping, mixing, and burning. Not only does the cloud enable the unbundling of higher education's service offerings, it facilitates a world of "mashed up" IT applications, expression, ideas, and scholarship. Ideas move through the cloud at the speed of light. They are mashed together with other ideas, commented on, transmuted, embedded, enlivened, debased as they circle the globe. Unbundling, in this regard, in its most positive light, presents the academic with unprecedented access to other interested scholars—and amateurs. In astronomy, for example, this is making it possible for theoretical astrophysicists to accelerate the pace of observational confirmation (or disconfirmation) by tapping into networks of amateurs. Every home can become part of a global observatory, meteorological data collection station, and so forth. In this same positive light, harnessing the talent and effort of the crowd can reduce the amount of time taken on an academic task and can simultaneously increase an institution's fee base while "maintaining links to the sort of practical expertise they often lack."[25]

Unbundling can disrupt an institution and industry so as to cause fragmentation. The potential to unbundle, for example, the offerings of the mainstream media has resulted in the likely permanent fragmentation of the mediascape. On one hand, citizen journalism is putting more news into more hands faster and faster without the overlay of corporate or governmental editorial policy. On the other hand, advances in technology have helped "turn each of us into producers, distributors, and editors of our own media diet."[26] While this is liberating, Farhad Manjoo reminds us that "while new technology eases connections between people, it also paradoxically facilitates a closeted view of the world, keeping us coiled tightly with those who share our ideas. In a world that lacks real gatekeepers and authority, and in which digital manipulation is so effortless, spin, conspiracy theories, myths, and outright lies may get the better of many of us."[27] The vision of higher education splitting into niches of scholars, students, amateurs, and others who are united by common biases and preexisting beliefs is an unnerving one. However this aspect of unbundling plays out, it is likely that unbundling and rebundling words from their authors represents what Professor Chris Dede calls "a seismic shift in epistemology."[28]

More narrowly, unbundling has real disruptive consequences for those of us who manage the institution's information, information services, and information resources. A great deal of the scholarly information resources of the planet are being digitized at the same time that unprecedented investments are being made in search engineering. These forces are unbundling the collection from the library. Similarly, markets for delivering core aspects of the IT infrastructure—compute cycles and data storage—are emerging and will likely mature quickly. Virtualized IT infrastructure and application services, such as mail, make it possible to increase or decrease the institution's IT consumption on demand, take better advantage of scale, and in some cases take advantage of providers' access to renewable energy sources. Commercially provided cloud services, in the long run, are also likely to feature better security and improved business availability. It is increasingly likely over the long term that core higher education processes will be available as cloud services.

Demand-Pull

If unbundling is a phenomenon that speaks to what producers do (or what happens to them), then demand-pull relates to the capabilities, preferences, and behaviors of consumers in a cloudy world. Just as the cloud is making it possible for producers to deconstruct and re-source their services, it is making it possible for consumers to assemble their world.

One student put it this way: "I don't look at it as 'getting on the Internet.' The Internet is a part of life. It is a lifestyle." Part of that lifestyle includes RSS feeds, social networks, portals, and other tools that make it possible for people to configure their social and informational worlds in cyberspace precisely to suit their needs and tastes.

In the context of higher education generally, the emergence of a robust tool set for configuring our world is enormously powerful and beneficial. We are able to consume more relevant information, faster, and share insights within purposeful communities more effectively than ever before. Because developing and transferring knowledge within communities is a part of our educational mission, an infrastructure that empowers us to configure and contextualize our world levers this mission. However, as with unbundling, the sword cuts both ways. Our students and other constituents, too, are using tools to arrange their worlds. Higher education, like many industries, is organized today in a producercentric fashion. We are *supply-push*–based institutions. We don't offer a course on the history of feudal Japan, but we have a raft of wonderful Byzantine history courses you can take. In an unbundled cloud in which the consumer has been fully empowered, we run the risk that students will lose confidence in our ability to construct curricula that meet their needs. Like their medieval counterparts, students will have the easy ability to use their social or scholarly networks to source the academic programming they want. In the extreme, faculty free agents—like the itinerant scholars before 1100—may find interesting niche opportunities among such bands of students. This massive customization or personalization of an education is no different from how students today organize and consume their news or organize their philanthropic or social agendas and communities.

Another interesting aspect of this potential disruption is the long-tail phenomenon. Chris Anderson argues that "the future of business is selling less of more. Infinite choice and lower costs to connect supply and demand is changing the nature of the market and will transform entire industries. Growth is in the long tail."[29] The long tail of demand may—in concert with an institution's course delivery system—provide ways for comprehensive universities to continue to offer instruction in rare and exotic fields while expanding student choice, either independently or at smaller institutions. The long tail of demand may express itself in efforts by smaller colleges to enlarge their footprints by importing parts of an expanded curriculum. Or students may simply customize their courses of instructions themselves.

For the college or university administrator and IT leader, the move to a demand-pull economy is similarly disruptive. Faculty will be presented with the opportunity to use cloud-based services to manage their grant activity and to organize a personalized e-research infrastructure in the cloud. Faculty will also be able to use their institutional platforms to launch extramural consulting, teaching, and other ventures.

When the forces of unbundling and demand-pull combine, the results are easy to visualize. The growing availability of low-cost, easy-to-use devices and cloud services makes it possible for today's student or new faculty member to arrive on campus with an intelligent phone, portable digital music player, laptop computer, router, social networks, e-mail accounts, network data storage, RSS reader, and perhaps open source office productivity tools and web development environment. The lament of tomorrow's IT provider could be: "There go my customers. And I must hurry to follow them. For I am their provider."[30] As the explosion of content continues along with the increasing maturity and availability of web-based academic services and applications, tomorrow's students will arrive on campus with their own IT architectures and service arrangements. These students—and tomorrow's faculty—will have little use for or patience with college or university offerings that underperform or force them to lose precious connections to people and processes that they have accumulated since childhood.

Ubiquitous Access

The first 50 years of the IT revolution were preparatory. In essence, the race to miniaturize computers, put them on desktops, make them portable, and connect them to networks met the preconditions for a networked information economy. The invention of the World Wide Web and the widespread adoption of search engines—and in particular Google—have made the Internet a transformative medium. As James Hilton puts it: "We are on the cusp of a world in which everyone will have access not only to online information but also to information that traditionally was accessible only by going into a library ... . Any information that one could desire will be but a click away."[31]

The importance of having more than 1 billion people and nearly all published information online cannot be overstated. Such milestones suggest the arrival at tipping points—in the roles played by traditional libraries and in the roles played by academics. In the near term, this is all liberating. No longer will information be rationed by the availability or scarcity of books, serials, government publications, and so forth. No longer will students and other researchers be constrained by search techniques that are confined to the small number of subject descriptors supplied long ago by catalogers.

The capacity to create or follow hypertext links creates opportunities to follow, develop, or abandon research trails at a rate that could not be imagined 10 years ago. Google, for example, is working with 20 major research university libraries worldwide to make their collections available over the Internet. Columbia University Librarian James Neal argues that "[Columbia's] participation in the Google Book Search Library Project will add significantly to the extensive digital resources the Libraries already deliver. It will enable the Libraries to make available more significant portions of its extraordinary archival and special collections to scholars and researchers worldwide in ways that will ultimately change the nature of scholarship."[32]

The nature of scholarship has changed and indeed must change in light of ubiquitous access. The emergence of the networked information economy has made information and knowledge central to human development and progress. The premium on information and knowledge—and on processes for creating and socializing this information and knowledge—carries with it the potential for colleges and universities to occupy places of increasing centrality. These vectors of change also create opportunities for others. As Hilton concludes, the function that colleges and universities have played as gateways to information will be gone: "If higher education remains synonymous with access to information in the eyes of the public, then it has a huge problem. There are many more efficient ways to get information than attending classes for four years."[33]

The Rise of the Pure Property View of Ideas

The very rich IT infrastructure that we have created has made it possible to deliver everything in digital form and thereby to code it, tag it, watermark it, track it, and extract rents from it. The long-standing calculus of copyright law and patent law—which strives to balance the limited rights of creators and inventors to enjoy compensation for their creative contributions and effort with the overarching public right and need to have, share, and develop ideas—is being revised in both directions.

On one hand, copyright and patent law "are moving aggressively in the direction of protecting owners and away from protecting access and learning. Even more important, our understanding of the nature of ideas is shifting."[34] Students are asking professors to sign nondisclosures to protect their rights to intellectual property in course assignments; the rights to alleged prior art obtained in open community discourse is at the heart of high-profile patent litigation and reexaminations; and so forth. The past few decades have witnessed the extension of copyright protection to all written works at the moment of their creation and this protection has been extended in duration.

At the same time a vigorous, if struggling, movement has arisen to liberate scholarly and other information from the strictures and constraints of copyright and patent law. Open source and community source software have become commonplace, if not clearly or comprehensively sustainable. Open courseware initiatives of varying intensity are under way at many colleges and universities. These efforts make available course content, instructional frameworks, syllabi, and in some cases textbooks and even limited access to instructors. These initiatives bear witness to three important observations. The first is that for some learners and some learning purposes, disembodied learning content that is well contextualized in a learning framework and supported by indicators of progress and self-administered assessments can be quite effective. The second is that some learners do not need mediation of course materials by experts, guides, and peers. The third observation is that giving away this wealth of material does not impoverish the donor. Indeed, the reputation enhancement alone of providing open course content suggests that these initiatives are net economic winners for their sponsors. These economics were understood in 1813 by Thomas Jefferson[35] and more recently by John Perry Barlow. Barlow argues:

> You take a piece of information and share it between two people and that same piece of information becomes more valuable, because it now has a context that automatically makes it more complex than it was before you shared it. It layers new forms of value onto itself with each iteration. You get a deeper understanding, a better strategy, a more finely tuned approach. This is a very different way of looking at the economy than the one we have been using, which is based on physical objects. Scarcity of physical items increases their value, which is not necessarily true of information. With information such as music or books, the better something is known, the more valuable it becomes. Most of the economic value now is coming out of the informational world, not the physical.[36]

And finally, consumers in many cases are taking matters into their own hands. The compelling and perhaps inexorable flow of information on the Internet is the free flow of information. Outside the civilized, if passionate, arguments for greater openness or more protection of rights, markets are operating. Network babies who have grown to adulthood accustomed to unimpeded movement across network environments are developing and socializing their own ideas and morality around intellectual property rights.

Whether rights holders can educate or sanction young people into confor-
mance with the pure property views of information or Net Gen citizens
grow up to reflect their own ideas in the workplace and ballot box remains
to be seen. In any case, it is not hyperbole to suggest that as digital delivery
of protected textual becomes the norm, this issue will divide higher
education as perhaps no other.

Toward a Cloudy Academy

Former Wellesley College President Diana Chapman Walsh and her
commissioners at Wellesley College argue persuasively that colleges and
universities operate increasingly in a fluid and uncertain environment.
Higher education in the future will need to come to grips with globalization and will be subject to worldwide competition. Long-standing
demographic trends are playing themselves out in ways that will reshape
the world. The populations of many leading nations are expected to
collapse in size within two or three decades, and much of the developed
world will need to meet the demands of large numbers of older citizens.

The ascendance of knowledge work places a premium on education
and presents the possibility of a new centrality and vitality in the role
and place of the college and university in society. This possibility is also
presented to other potential educators, and it is likely that the ongoing
progress of virtualized services, web standards, open information, and other
developments will make it increasingly possible to unbundle parts of the
higher education mission and thus to invite new competitors and forms of
competition. And despite our nearly ubiquitous access to each other and
to an increasingly complete digital record of human activity, the threats of
fragmentation and polarization are higher than ever before.

Walsh and her colleagues point out that "the Internet has provided
everyone with a voice, and the cacophony of clashing worldviews and faith
systems [that are] overlaid with political and social agendas ... ."[37] They also
point out that another critical aspect of this uncertain environment is the
climate of ferment in higher education, a growing view that "the system [of
U.S. higher education] has serious enough deficiencies in access, quality, and
costs as to raise concern about the nation's long term prospects of sustaining
its standard of living in a newly-competitive global economy."[38]

The emergence of new technological capabilities, of the disruptive
socialization of these capabilities, and of this fluid and uncertain
environment suggests a plan of action and a set of priorities for colleges
and universities. In many ways, the emergence of the cloud presents yet

Figure 1. The Cloudy Academy?

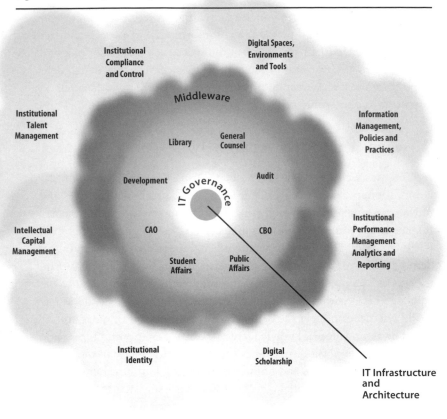

another opportunity to visit what John Henry Newman called "the idea of a university."[39] This essay and this volume suggest an agenda for discussion, debate, and eventual decision as colleges and universities work toward a cloudy academy. This agenda for action is described in Figure 1.

Develop a Cloud Strategy

Whether or not the cloud metaphor is right, it is clear that the capacity to dial up IT infrastructure and to invoke services over the network is evolving. This evolution presents enormous opportunity and risk. We can leave our institution's response to these new capabilities to chance, we can confine our planning to the IT organization, or we can engage our leadership in a discussion of near-term strategy. The strategic discussion about the evolution of virtualization, services orientation and delivery, open resources, web standards, and cloud computing is in fact a conversation about what constitutes the institution *as an enterprise* and about how the institution wishes to manifest its institutional presence in cyberspace. Embedded in this strategic conversation is the issue of the institution's predispositions as a provider or consumer of network-based services and whether these predispositions are outward facing or inward facing. For example, the institution may choose—for this time—to be dominantly a consumer of services externally and to not "cloudify" its external services. At the same time, the central IT organization may opt to virtualize elements of the institutional IT environment on behalf of local campus units. Strategic alternatives range from doing nothing, to becoming an aggressive integrator of infrastructure and services from the cloud, to rationalizing IT resources internally, to enabling the institution to become a supplier of services in this evolving fashion. Each option, of course, suggests a different infrastructure and bears distinct investment and operating costs.

Focus on IT Governance

Every IT leader understands the importance of governance in higher education. The emergence of cloud computing and of the issues raised in this essay suggests the need to redouble our efforts in this arena. If the wellspring of higher education's creative success and our organizational inefficiency is the empowerment of students and faculty in the academic enterprise, then the emergence of the cloud will amplify this empowerment. Just as PCs unleashed end-user creativity while proliferating copies and versions of the institutional record, and just as the emergence of the web and HTML have produced both a cornucopia of content and a multiplicity of front doors to our institutions, the next turn of the IT crank will make it possible for every member of our community to become her own IT provider. The potential both for unlocking human potential and for further fragmentation is profound. This potential will affect the institution's presence and reputation in cyberspace, our social compact with our community, our business controls, costs, and risks, our ability to manage risk and to comply with regulatory requirements, our competitive posture, and other major issues.

These issues may first become visible to the IT leader, but they are not IT issues. Therefore, it is essential that institutions begin to allocate concerted and ongoing leadership attention to the questions and challenges raised by IT in the years to come. IT governance will continue to focus on the institution's IT investment strategy and priorities but will increasingly focus on how the institution wishes to manifest itself online. Failure to govern will lead to accidental governance and to the future need to "rope in those clouds." As one imagines, clouds are hard to rope!

Focus on Information Management, Practices, and Policy

This topic is pressing. It is deceptively labeled, since everything in the Internet is information! How an institution manages its virtual presence has become as important as how it manages its campus and physical presence. Increasingly, these issues are merging as laboratory access, library access, building access, and so forth become mediated by IT. The institution's information system is increasingly the means by which the institution regulates the boundaries and conditions of its community, the rules of community engagement, and the boundaries, scope, and nature of that community's access to scholarly resources. These are issues that are instantiated in and enforced by IT but, again, they are not IT issues. Who are the citizens of our institution? Do all citizens have full rights of citizenship? What authorities do different citizens have? Who determines these authorities? Do citizens of allied institutions have rights at our institution (and vice versa)? These are profound questions that are shaped in part by the regulatory environment but even more by decades or centuries of campus experience and policy making.

Ubiquitous access to people and resources through the network makes the institution's information system the nexus of enforcement of these policies and practices. In many cases, this means that formal and informal practices must be made explicit. As new technologies make it possible to virtualize storage or to federate data, it will also become more critical for institutions to craft information management policies and strategies. Institutional information is increasingly subject to regulatory requirements related to access, privacy, confidentiality, discoverability, redactability, retention, disclosure, and so forth.

At the heart of the information policy issue is Professor Yochai Benkler's concept of *network permeability*. Benkler argues that the way information and knowledge are made available can either limit or enlarge the ways people can create and express themselves.[40] As well, institutions need to devise policies and practices to ensure the authenticity of official information and to preserve a record of the institution and its citizens for cultural and historical purposes.

Finally, the need to reshape information management, policies, and practices carries with it the need for institutions across higher education to rethink their revenue models. The revolution in open source computing is being fueled in part by competitive investments by some companies against the entrenched monopolies of others. Or it is motivated by a shift from product delivery to solutions. Open content strategies of search engineering organizations or social network operators also have an underlying revenue model—becoming the "library of the world" means attracting visits and therefore advertising; that is, attracting crowds attracts advertising revenues.

Higher education's impulses toward openness are essential to diffuse knowledge, build community, and stimulate innovation. Openness, however, is not free, and therefore colleges and universities, like others, will need to develop, evaluate, and eventually deploy new strategies for recovering the costs of their investments in openness.

Focus on Key Technologies and Enterprise IT Architecture

While the technologies themselves may be the least complex of the issues associated with this transformation, they are not at all simple. The enterprise IT leader will be charged with organizing the infrastructure and human capabilities that will enforce the leadership's views about the nature and privileges of the community. While it may be axiomatic that the IT leader must track and test virtualization technologies, web standards, cloud service offerings, and the like, the IT leader must also rethink enterprise IT architecture.

It is increasingly understood that validating identity and administering basic citizenship authorities can best be accomplished through middleware that spans institutional academic and business applications. It is also increasingly apparent that cross-cutting activities such as workflow management can also be rendered in middleware. Ongoing attention should be allocated to IT architecture and in particular to the tightness of how software functions are integrated and to which software operations can be abstracted from applications and embedded in middleware. IT leaders will have to become adept at identifying risk in systems and services they do not operate and will have to query cloud service providers deeply about policy choices that may be embedded in their service offerings. For example, some software capabilities may be enabled through information practices— such as mining and profiling student information—that are incompatible with laws such as FERPA.

Focus on Enterprise Compliance and Controls

The drive toward consumerization and unbundling is motivated by service. TripAdvisor, for example, has unbundled the hotel industry by aggregating room information and disconnecting this information from the hotels themselves. For the consumer, it is more pleasant to shop price and quality on one site than to call or surf dozens of hotel chains. Enterprise systems exist to facilitate service but also to mitigate risks, minimize costs, comply with regulations, safeguard privacy, protect reputations, and so forth. The drives toward unbundling and consumerization pose a real challenge to the enterprise, particularly to colleges and universities whose leaders are loath to impose strict limitations on a highly creative (and possibly tenured!) workforce.

Be warned: even the very idea of audit trail becomes difficult to understand in the context of software-as-a-service and cloud computing. The general counsel, auditor, business officer, and CIO, along with academic leaders, must work together to determine how much authority individuals and subunits have in the cloud. Just as institutions in the past have regulated purchasing activity, prequalified vendors, or injected CIO review into large-scale IT procurements, controls of some sort will be needed to make sure that what people can do in the cloud is consistent with what the institution wants them to do. This is very tricky. Colleges and universities have been embarrassed by data spills resulting from the theft of unauthorized copies of digital student or patient records. Imagine the fallout from news of institutional data loss, misuse, or leaks from third-party custodians *whose very existence was unknown to institutional officials.* Cloud services will not be limited to infrastructure and in time it will be relatively easy for well intended campus citizens to configure financial transactions and so forth.

The need for compliance and control is often misunderstood in the academy. Achieving control requires oversight, and in the context of networked information oversight is often achieved by filtering, monitoring, alerts, restrictions, and sanctions—activities that are unpopular in the academic enterprise. Nevertheless, strategic choices will need to be made regarding the institution's approach to compliance and control. In general, colleges and universities will have to choose control systems that constrain employee action automatically (dollar limitations, preauthorizations, vendor lists, and so forth) or control systems that maximize employee freedoms but accomplish control through dollar limits (campus cards) or through monitoring and posttransaction sanctions.

Taking increased advantage of cloud services will be neither easy nor without risk. While cloud computing promises to eliminate software upgrade cycles, free us from vendor lock-in, and so forth, this style of organizing IT, too, will be very hard. Invoking services from the cloud is unlikely to ever be analogous to plugging into the wall for electricity.

On February 15, 2008, Amazon's Simple Storage System suffered a massive outage. In a separate incident, thousands of early users of Apple's

MobileMe mail synchronization and backup utility were left unable to access their mail, and some witnessed the permanent loss of substantial amounts of mail. In a third contemporaneous incident, an online storage service called The Linkup shut down on August 8, 2008, after losing unspecified amounts of customer data. Company responses to all of these failures were reported in the press as being "substandard."[41]

It will be wise to remember that any service will always have points of failure and that institutions that depend on hosted services must take care with language about risk levels in their contracts. Agreements will also need to ensure that third parties implement reasonable safeguards when they process, store, use, or transmit institutional assets. Vendor agreements will need to ensure vendor compliance with Sarbanes-Oxley, FERPA, HIPAA, and other key regulations, as well as with institutional policy on confidentiality and security in electronic communications. Colleges and universities will want to ensure that third parties do not monitor the contents of electronic communications except to ensure the proper functioning and security of electronic communications. Security incidents, losses of data, and other issues must be handled in ways that meet the institution's policy and regulatory requirements, and contracting institutions should review the cloud suppliers' professional guidance (SAS 70 Audit Report) that documents and attests to the adequacy of the internal controls for the service being contracted. And, of course, issues related to indemnification and insurance need to be specified. This is not just like electricity.[42]

Manage the Institution's Online Presence

Since the early days of personal computing and the early days of the web, college and university leaders have realized that the willy-nilly proliferation of PCs and of institutional web pages was suboptimal from an investment viewpoint and presented the world with a fragmented and perhaps wrong-headed impression of the institution. The realization of the networked information economy suggests that over time, an organization's presence online will assume greater and greater *gravitas* with consumers, regulators, accreditors, and others. This rising *gravitas* in concert with the unbundling tendencies inherent in the evolution of the networked information economy suggests the need to redouble efforts and investments to nurture the institution's reputation in cyberspace. Creating and enforcing standards and guidelines for subunits regarding the use of the college or university name, its trademarks, message, and so forth will be essential, as will inventorying and monitoring the presence of institutional subunits and that of their partners in cyberspace. The reputations of enterprises in general will rise and fall increasingly as a result of actions, images, and impressions made in cyberspace. Colleges and universities and their faculty—like public officials, corporate executives, and movie stars—will need to monitor blog sites, wikis, social networks, faculty rating sites, newsgroups, and other social sites to inform efforts to maintain and elevate the institution's reputation. This will become even more the case as colleges and universities move to immersive environments. As these environments become compelling and popular, their impact on institutional reputation will become inseparable from that of the physical campus.

Manage Digital Spaces, Environments, and Tools

As just mentioned, virtual and immersive college and university environments such as Second Life will deeply influence the image and reputation of the institution. They will also become places of serious academic work and commerce and therefore will demand the same quality attention that is devoted to physical campus master planning, design, architecture, and construction. Already a great many students and faculty interact in online collaborative environments. Major research collaborations take place in academic teams whose members may never have met face to face. Such environments must be designed thoughtfully to both stimulate sound academic practices and safeguard research results, as well as to reinforce the presence of the institution in positive ways. The unbundling capacity of new cloud capabilities will make it possible for academics to assemble just-in-time collaborative environments and to assemble an infrastructure and open source tools that might be needed to facilitate a learning encounter or research effort. College and university leaders should understand that to the extent that assembling such environments is easy and effective, others will assemble them and use them to potentially draw away increasingly talented faculty. Increasingly, unaffiliated research institutes are attracting away political scientists and other social scientists. Indeed, improved network capacity is now making it possible for scientists in unaffiliated organizations such as the Space Science Institute to conduct world-class research from home or otherwise away from colleges and universities. This trend represents another form of unbundling and can be countered in part by methodical and serious institutional investment in digital learning and research environments and tools.

Focus on Scholarly Literacy

Ubiquitous access has disrupted the social landscape of higher education in unexpected ways. Persistent networked access to countless people and to mountains of digital resources, according to Professor Yochai

Benkler, go "to the very foundations of how liberal markets and liberal democracies have co-evolved for almost two centuries."[43] In this new environment, knowledge production has become an increasingly social activity. Ideas about authorship, provenance, plagiarism, collaboration, and ownership are all under experimentation in the wake of information technologies that make it possible to rip, mix, and burn. Unlike information in print, online digital information can be manipulated, extrapolated, extended, connected, hyperlinked, and mashed up. This new freedom "holds great practical promise: as a dimension of individual freedom; as a platform for better democratic participation; as a medium to foster a more critical and self-reflective culture; and, in an increasingly information-dependent global economy, as a mechanism to achieve improvements in human development everywhere."[44]

This new freedom also challenges many of our traditional ideas about scholarly quality, method, and literacy. Debates simmer about the usability of Wikipedia as a scholarly resource because of its ephemeral nature and because the academic *bona fides* of its contributors cannot easily be vetted. Mashups obscure our understanding of authorship, and so forth. Seasoned academics will need to debate and ultimately shape a new understanding of scholarly method in light of these evolving practices, and students will need to be taught how to sift and evaluate evidence in the context of networked information.

Focus on the Institution's Performance Management System and Analytics

Colleges and universities operate today in an overall period of educational ferment. Students and their parents describe feeling trapped between pressures to gain higher education *bona fides* for the workplace and the declining affordability of postsecondary education. This squeeze plays out in a number of ways. As the cost of collegiate education rises and as governments break with their long-standing commitments to underwriting this cost as a public good, students and parents have increasingly come to view the college or university offering as a consumer good. The enlightened consumer is less likely to accept academic offerings because such offerings are purported to be "for their own good." Today's students and their parents will pressure colleges and universities to create safe and fulfilling environments for study and personal growth, to foster their admission prospects with graduate schools, and to offer curricula that contribute to students' long-term earning prospects. The continually rising costs of collegiate education are also conspiring to focus parents' and regulators' attention on perceived value, rankings, and other methods of assessing the comparative performance of colleges and universities.

This political ferment and a host of structural factors—such as demographic change—are conspiring to make the management and reporting of institutional performance a matter of substantive and political concern. The development of meaningful metrics, and the careful mining, analysis, presentation, and reporting of performance information in ways that both guide the institution and convey intentions and achievements to stakeholders, is hard in the context of *any* set of information systems. Accomplishing these objectives when information may reside in the cloud or on infrastructures hosted by others will be even harder. In the years ahead, the institution's performance management system may become one of the defining elements of the enterprise. Thinking through what a distributed performance management system might look like should be a part of the action agenda for today's leaders in higher education.

Focus on Managing Talent and Intellectual Property

Colleges and universities, as mentioned earlier, are purposeful communities designed chiefly to develop and disseminate new knowledge. We accomplish these purposes in complex but largely social ways. Former Harvard University President James Bryant Conant perhaps said best how this is done: "pick men (sic) of genius, back them heavily, and leave them to direct themselves."[45] Three background forces are evident: (1) within the next decade, more than half the professoriate and staff in higher education will retire; (2) emerging nations will meet an increasing amount of their citizens' educational needs locally; and (3) all nations will seek to keep talented people within their homelands, and many will engage in a global hunt for talented people.

Colleges and universities in the West have long operated in an environment of abundant talent. In many areas of academic endeavor—particularly the humanities—the supply of talented instructors has far exceeded our ability to employ them. This is, of course, not true across the academic board. It seems clear that in an environment of extreme competition for talent, colleges and universities will be well advised to consider how the emergence of the cloud may make it possible to compete and win talented students and faculty. Many of our institutions are systematic, if antiquated, regarding the competition for students of talent, but nearly all are ad hoc and antiquated when it comes to developing the institutional workforce of the future. Commercial firms understand the prospects of a looming *talent war* and are organizing their federations, partnerships, relationships, databases, alert systems, and relationship management infrastructures to discover, uncover, source, evaluate, cultivate, develop, and retain people of talent—across the globe. If President Conant is right, higher education's stakes in talent management are very high, and the current informal and cottage industry approaches must likely give way. Talent development is an inherently "cloudy" activity since much of the activity and information lies outside the perimeter of the institution's borders. It is perhaps an enticing area for institutions to engage in early experimentation.

Consistent with President Conant's exhortation, colleges and universities must focus concerted effort on managing their intellectual property. The postscript to his advice, of course, is: and we do this so these bright people will produce great stuff! How institutions manage the great stuff they collect and create will become increasingly complex and consequential in the future. Today, the motion picture industry and the recording industry are asserting unprecedented hegemony over film and musical content. In the near future, the publishing industry will assert the same hegemony over text and still images. Higher education's historic rights of fair use will come under increased scrutiny and challenge as it becomes technically easier to monitor digital content flows at the level of the snippet or the individual image. How an institution manages these issues—as both a producer and consumer of digital information—will deeply influence that institution's implicit compact with students and faculty, its costs, its capacity to innovate, and the nature and depth of its external relationships.

Summary

During the past thousand years, Western colleges and universities have pursued a mission of instruction, research, and services. The process of research has changed dramatically while instruction continues to rely on personalized interactions among students, journeymen, and masters. In higher education, increasing demand for access abuts a delivery system that depends on personalized instruction, making it difficult to contain costs.

In the past 60 years, a revolution in computing and communications has occurred. Computers have become faster, smaller, and cheaper and intelligence is now embedded widely in things of all kinds. Computers have become connected and today more than 1 billion people regularly access the Internet. New technologies and standards are making it possible to virtualize computing power, network bandwidth, data storage, IT security, and a host of services and processes.

The revolution in IT is making possible the emergence of a networked information economy, one that is simultaneously centered on information and on the existence of cheap computation and persistent connection to a global network. Ubiquitous access to people and between people and information resources and services is profoundly disrupting institutions of all sorts. These disruptions include the massive empowerment of the individual consumer to do things and the ability of large-scale service and infrastructure providers to sell interoperable personal and enterprise capabilities over the network. These disruptions in turn are leading to the evolution of new creative relationships among people, new and beneficial cost structures for businesses, the unbundling of services, and the globalization of talent and economic prosperity. They are also contributing to increased fragmentation, balkanization, and politicization of discourse and to the rise of new industries and approaches that will threaten traditional ones. It is a fluid and uncertain environment.

Colleges and universities are institutions with long-standing reputations. In the United States and in much of the West, colleges and universities are intimately associated with the campuses. They bundle their academic programs, selling degree programs and certificates in preference to selling individual courses. This preference reflects both long-standing beliefs about education and a desire to insulate themselves from the full effects of economic markets. Bundling courses makes it possible for popular courses to subsidize less popular programs. Society in general and students in particular benefit from this academic diversity.

The emerging networked information economy creates unprecedented opportunities for colleges and universities to rationalize their highly distributed IT resources and to extend their institutional footprint. This economy also creates these opportunities for new producers, including providers of related services such as newspapers, media conglomerates, publishers, and others. For IT, the twin trends of consumerization and industrialization of IT raise concerns about the "end of the middle," that is, the disappearance of the enterprise role in managing and mediating information technology, resources, and services. Such concerns are articulated in a literature with titles such as *Does IT Matter?, The End of Corporate Computing,* and *The Big Switch.* It is important to note that the college and university enterprise itself is a "middleman" interposed between the teacher and learner. Consumerization and the industrialization of IT—*in extremis*—could undermine some institutions as well.

The twin forces of consumerization and industrialization of IT represent neither the end of enterprise IT nor the end of the enterprise in higher education, but an opportunity for colleges and universities to consider new ways of increasing access *while* remaining personal and affordable. These forces are making it possible to realize MIT President Emeritus Charles Vest's vision of the metauniversity, a "transcendent, accessible, empowering, dynamic, communally constructed framework of open materials and platforms on which much of higher education worldwide can be constructed or enhanced."[46] Virtualizing IT infrastructure and services—over time—will benefit from economies of scale and of standardization, enhanced power consumption, improved security, and so forth. Improved resource sharing techniques will also optimize the use of these resources, reducing again their cost. The ability to increase computing, storage, and network bandwidth on demand will make it possible for institutions to contemplate new growth options by substituting large, fixed capital costs in land acquisition and development with smaller variable costs in digital delivery of services.

The tower's place among the clouds will be a complex one. Rather than disappearing, the role of enterprise IT will expand. IT will become increasingly an activity that is strategic to the institution, and its conduct will depend on the effective inclusion of key leaders of the institution.

- An institution's effectiveness in the networked information economy in general and on the cloud in particular will depend on IT governance and on institutional strategy. It will depend, too, on a fabric of rules that will shape how people flow in and out of the campus community and how access to the institution's information, tools, services, and other resources is mediated. Most important in this matrix of decisions, institutions will need to develop points of view about the openness of their research processes, course content, publications, software, instruments, and information resources.
- Colleges and universities will need to understand what data and information are the responsibility of the enterprise. We will also need to grapple with how information can be stored and protected—perhaps in perpetuity—either on enterprise storage devices or "in the cloud." We will need to understand how an institution's digital holdings influence its reputation in the way that print library collections have.
- We will also need to develop shared views about the nature of the evolving epistemology and how concepts such as crowd sharing, mashups, and wikis interact with traditional scholarly methods and beliefs. Our disciplinary leaders will need to begin to articulate a new scholarly literacy to enable students to understand the authorship, credibility, valence, and

provenance of the digital evidence they use. Academic leaders will need to spread changing norms and values among their campus colleagues.

▪ Maintaining and enhancing the institution's identity in cyberspace will demand more attention than ever. As new technologies promote unbundling, there is a risk that many institutional reputations will be leveled. Thoughtful attention to an institution's presence in cyberspace will be important as well as attention to the use of its brand and trademarks.

▪ Increasingly, issues of institutional compliance and control will be mediated through the information system and, by some, through partners in the cloud. New skills in contract administration will be critical, and issues such as indemnification for service interruptions and data losses will be very problematic.

▪ Colleges and universities will need to manage the look, feel, and overall characteristics of virtual and online environments with as much deliberation and care as we manage physical space. This will become particularly true as immersive environments such as Second Life become platforms for the delivery of key institutional offerings and for academic collaboration.

▪ If and as enterprise activities move to the cloud, advance thought needs to be given to the institution's performance management systems and to how it wishes to use data and information to support decision making, student success, financial performance, and accountability.

▪ Colleges and universities are organizations that depend on attracting, developing, and organizing human talent for the purposes of creating and disseminating intellectual capital. In the environment described we will need to pay close attention to how IT extends the reach of the institution through the cloud and how institutional property is to be developed, disseminated, commercialized, and put to use.

Higher education will likely operate in a continually fluid and uncertain environment. Amidst this fluidity it seems clear that being digital is indeed a lifestyle and that all members of the academic community will engage the networked information economy. It is also clear that computers and networks will continue to become cheaper, better, and faster. Digital information will become cheaper to store, more plentiful, and easier to find. It is not clear whether information will become more openly accessible or if rights owners will demand economic rents on smaller and smaller snippets for longer periods of time.

What is certain is that the trend toward consumerization will continue. Colleges and universities loath to take a stand may discover that they have arrived at *accidental cloudiness*. Inaction may not be an option if institutions wish to regulate their IT, service, control, and information environments at all. What is also certain is that the shift to cloud computing will be hard—a "brutal slog" as one reporter calls it.[47] For some colleges and universities, engagement in the evolving networked information economy will—at the enterprise level—remain a choice. Well endowed and highly selective institutions will be able to choose whether, how, when, and for what reason they become cloudy suppliers or consumers. Large and highly decentralized universities will likely adopt cloud strategies internally to rationalize IT resources and will likely become selective suppliers and consumers of cloud services. Institutions that are more resource constrained will, as always, need to be more strategic about alternatives.

The end of the middle? Not likely. Exploiting the opportunity of so-called industrial computing will demand care, time, thought, and resources. The move to bring the tower to the cloud before the cloud grows to envelop the tower will engage nearly every institutional leader and challenge every institutional policy. The gathering cloud creates an unprecedented opportunity for the prepared. We are talking no longer about managing IT; we are managing the enterprise.

Endnotes

1. Plato, "Phaedrus," 67–71, Socrates to Phaedrus, *The Dialogues of Plato*.

2. At the same time (830 AD), the House of Wisdom in Baghdad was the first institution of higher learning in the Islamic world. This institution functioned as an academy and was a center for translation and an important library and observatory. By the 8th century BC, Chinese higher education was already mature and institutionalized and more than 3,000 students prepared for careers in the Chinese imperial bureaucracy at the Great Academy. Unlike their medieval or Renaissance counterparts, which encouraged disputation in the learning process, Chinese education focused on students' familiarity with "a general ethical outlook, and body of knowledge, not with [the] growth of knowledge ..." See John Merson, *The Genius That Was China: East and West in the Making of the Modern World* (New York: Overlook Press, 1990), 86.

3. See W. Warren Wagar, *H. G. Wells: Traversing Time* (Middletown, CT: Wesleyan University Press, 2004), 162.

4. John Seely Brown and Paul Duguid, *The Social Life of Information* (Cambridge, MA: Harvard University Press, 2000), 11.

5. Ibid.

6. Diana Chapman Walsh, *Envisioning the Future: Reflections from the 2015 Commission. Final Report* (Wellesley, MA: Wellesley College, 2007), http://www.wellesley.edu/PublicAffairs/President/DCW/Announcements/2015synopsis.pdf.

7. Thomas Jefferson, letter to Tench Coxe, 1795. In Jeffersonian fashion, Supreme Court Justice Potter Stewart argued that "in the absence of governmental checks and balances present in other areas of our national life, the only effective restraint upon executive policy and power ... may lie in an enlightened citizenry," in *New York Times v. United States*, 403 U.S. 713.

8. Rudolf Stichweh argues that "in its ultimate realization, higher education at a research university takes place as participation of the student in the research process," in Thomas Pfeffer, *Virtualization of Research Universities: Raising the Right Questions to Address Key Functions of the Institution,* Paper CSHE6-03. Berkeley, CA: Center for Studies in Higher Education, 2003, http://repositories.cdlib.org/cshe/CSHE6-03.

9. Thomas Jefferson, Autobiography, MW 1:54.

10. H. C. King, *Education and the National Character* (Chicago: The Religious Education Association, 1908).

11. U.S. Department of Education, Institute of Education Sciences, *Enrollment in Postsecondary Institutions, Fall 2004; Graduation Rates, 1998 & 2001 Cohorts; and Financial Statistics, Fiscal Year 2004* (Washington, DC: U.S. Government Printing Office, 2006), http://nces.ed.gov//pubs2006/2006155.pdf.

12. Jeffrey Thomas, "First-Time International Student U.S. Enrollments Up 10.2 Percent," America.gov, http://www.america.gov/st/washfile-english/2007/November/200711131634391CJsamohT0.5697748.html (November 13, 2007).

13. See *Education at a Glance, 2007, OECD Indicators* (Organisation for Economic Co-operation and Development, 2007), 57, http://www.sourceoecd.org/upload/9607051e.pdf (data are from 2005). Across 24 OECD countries, 36% of students have completed baccalaureate-level education. This is an increase of 12 percentage points over the last decade. Graduation rates have doubled or more during the past 10 years in Austria, Finland, Portugal, the Slovak Republic, and Switzerland but have been stable in the United States, which, along with New Zealand, had the highest rate in 1995.

14. Thomas L. Friedman, *The World Is Flat: A Brief History of the Twenty-First Century* (New York: Farrar, Straus, and Giroux, 2005).

15. Richard Monastersky, "The Number That Is Devouring Science," *Chronicle of Higher Education* (October 14, 2005): A12, http://chronicle.com/free/v52/i08/08a01201.htm.

16. Elsa Wenzel, "Number of PC's in Use to Hit 2 Billion by 2014," SmartPlanet, posted June 24, 2008, http://www.smartplanet.com/news/tech/10001448/number-of-pcs-in-use-to-hit-2-billion-by-2014.htm.

17. Robert H. Zakon, "Hobbes' Internet Timeline V8.2," http://www.zakon.org/robert/internet/timeline. See also the Wikipedia description of "Wi-Fi" at http://en.wikipedia.org/wiki/Wi-Fi.

18. Martin Trow argues that "IT is embedded in, and used by, institutions that have a history … . IT will cut its own channels, leading to the creation of institutions that differ from those of today; institutions where the weight of history does not condition and constrain IT's use," in "The Development of Information Technology in American Higher Education," *Daedalus* 126, no. 4 (Fall 1997): 294. Stanley Katz, on the other hand, exhorts us not to mistake IT as a goal, rather than a tool. See Stanley N. Katz, "In Information Technology, Don't Mistake a Tool for a Goal," *Chronicle of Higher Education* (June 15, 2001), http://chronicle.com/free/v47/i40/40b00701.htm.

19. R. D. Laing, *The Politics of Experience* (New York: Pantheon Books, 1967).

20. Grant McCracken, "The Cloudy Self: Or What Has Technology Done to Us," posted to his blog, January 30, 2007, http://www.cultureby.com/trilogy/2007/01/the_cloudy_self.html.

21. Brown and Duguid, 9.

22. On the democratization of IT, see Bruce Malloy, "'Digital Natives' Take Charge; Get Ready for the Democratization of IT," *New Jersey Tech News* (June 2008): 12, http://www.connotate.com/news/NJTech_080601_Democ_of_IT.pdf. On the industrialization of IT, see Nicholas Carr, *The Big Switch: Rewiring the World from Edison to Google* (New York: W. W. Norton & Co., 2008).

23. See the work of Nicholas Carr, such as his *Harvard Business Review* article "IT Doesn't Matter," *The Digital Enterprise* (Cambridge, MA: Harvard Business Press, 2001), *The Big Switch,* and others. Carr argues that as in the Industrial Revolution, when we moved from factory generation of power to power grids, so will we move from enterprise-based IT infrastructure to cloud-based IT services and infrastructure.

24. James Hilton, "The Future for Higher Education: Sunrise or Perfect Storm?," *EDUCAUSE Review* (March/April 2006): 60, http://net.educause.edu/ir/library/pdf/ERM0623.pdf.

25. Brown and Duguid, 15.

26. Farhad Manjoo, *True Enough: Learning to Live in a Post-Fact Society* (Hoboken, NJ: John Wiley & Sons, 2008), 16.

27. Ibid., 17–8.

28. Chris Dede, "A Seismic Shift in Epistemology," *EDUCAUSE Review* (May/June 2008): 80, http://net.educause.edu/ir/library/pdf/ERM0837.pdf.

29. Chris Anderson, *The Long Tail* (New York: Hyperion, 2006).

30. See B. G. Verghese, "Reflections on Gandhi," Writings and Commentaries, http://www.bgverghese.com/YouthCadres.htm.

31. Hilton, 64.

32. James Neal, quoted on Google Library Project website, http://books .google.com/googlebooks/partners.html.

33. Hilton, 64.

34. Ibid., 66.

35. Thomas Jefferson, letter to Isaac McPherson, August 13, 1813.

36. John Gerstner, "Cyber Cowboy: Interview with John Perry Barlow," *Communication World*, November 2005, http://findarticles.com/p/articles/ mi_m4422/is_n10_v12/ai_17772838/pg_2?tag=artBody;col1.

37. Walsh, 31.

38. Ibid., 44.

39. John Henry Newman, *The Idea of a University Defined and Illustrated* (London: Longman's, Green & Co., 1893). Derek Bok more recently proposed eight purposes of college in *Our Underachieving Colleges* (Princeton, NJ: Princeton University Press, 2006), 113–6.

40. Yochai Benkler, *The Wealth of Networks* (Cambridge, MA: Harvard University Press, 2006).

41. See Nicholas Carr, "Crash: Amazon's S3 Utility Goes Down," *Rough Type*, February 15, 2008, http://www.roughtype.com/archives/2008/02/amazons_ s3_util.php. See also Jon Brodkin, "Loss of Customer Data Spurs Closure of Online Storage Service 'The Linkup,'" The Industry Standard, August 11, 2008, http://www.thestandard.com/news/2008/08/11/loss-customer-data-spurs-closure-linkup, and Peter Bright, "Storms in the Clouds Leave Users Up Creek Without a Paddle," Ars Technica, August 13, 2008, http:// arstechnica.com/news.ars/post/20080813-storms-in-the-clouds-leave-users-up-creek-without-a-paddle.html.

42. Margaret P. Eisenhauer, "Protecting Personal Information in Third Party Hands: An Overview of Legal Requirements," PrivacyStudio.com, January 6, 2006.

43. Benkler, 1.

44. Benkler, 2.

45. James Bryant Conant, Letter to the *New York Times,* August 13, 1945.

46. Charles Vest, "Open Content and the Emerging Global Meta-University," *EDUCAUSE Review* (May/June 2006): 30, http://net.educause.edu/ir/library/pdf/ERM0630.pdf.

47. Sarah Lacy, "On-Demand Computing: A Brutal Slog," *Business Week,* July 18, 2008, http://www.businessweek.com/technology/content/jul2008/tc20080717_362776.htm.

Bibliography

Anderson, Chris. *The Long Tail*. New York: Hyperion, 2006.

Benkler, Yochai. *The Wealth of Networks*. Cambridge, MA: Harvard University Press, 2006.

Bok, Derek. *Our Underachieving Colleges*. Princeton, NJ: Princeton University Press, 2006.

Bright, Peter. "Storms in the Clouds Leave Users Up Creek Without a Paddle." Ars Technica, August 13, 2008. http://arstechnica.com/news.ars/post/20080813-storms-in-the-clouds-leave-users-up-creek-without-a-paddle.html.

Brodkin, Jon. "Loss of Customer Data Spurs Closure of Online Storage Service 'The Linkup.'" The Industry Standard, August 11, 2008. http://www.thestandard.com/news/2008/08/11/loss-customer-data-spurs-closure-linkup

Brown, John Seely, and Paul Duguid. *The Social Life of Information*. Cambridge, MA: Harvard University Press, 2000.

Bryant, James Conant. Letter to the *New York Times*, August 13, 1945.

Carr, Nicholas G. "Crash: Amazon's S3 Utility Goes Down." Rough Type, February 15, 2008. http://www.roughtype.com/archives/2008/02/amazons_s3_util.php.

Carr, Nicholas G. *Does IT Matter? Information Technology and the Corrosion of Competitive Advantage*. Cambridge, MA: Harvard Business Press, 2004.

Carr, Nicholas G. "IT Doesn't Matter." *Harvard Business Review* (May 2003).

Carr, Nicholas G. *The Big Switch: Rewiring the World, from Edison to Google.* New York: W. W. Norton & Company, 2008.

Carr, Nicholas G. *The Digital Enterprise: How to Reshape Your Business for a Connected World.* Cambridge, MA: Harvard Business Press, 2001.

Dede, Chris. "A Seismic Shift in Epistemology." *EDUCAUSE Review* (May/June 2008): 80–1. http://net.educause.edu/ir/library/pdf/ERM0837.pdf.

Education at a Glance, 2007, OECD Indicators. Organisation for Economic Co-operation and Development, 2007. http://www.sourceoecd.org/upload/9607051e.pdf.

Eisenhauer, Margaret P. "Protecting Personal Information in Third Party Hands: An Overview of Legal Requirements." PrivacyStudio.com, January 6, 2006.

Friedman, Thomas L. *The World Is Flat: A Brief History of the Twenty-First Century.* New York: Farrar, Straus, and Giroux, 2005.

Gerstner, John. "Cyber Cowboy: Interview with John Perry Barlow." *Communication World*, November 2005. http://findarticles.com/p/articles/mi_m4422/is_n10_v12/ai_17772838/pg_2?tag=artBody;col1

Hilton, James. "The Future for Higher Education: Sunrise or Perfect Storm?" *EDUCAUSE Review* (March/April 2006): 59–71. http://net.educause.edu/ir/library/pdf/ERM0623.pdf.

Jefferson, Thomas. Autobiography, MW 1:54.

Jefferson, Thomas. Letter to Isaac McPherson, August 13, 1813.

Jefferson, Thomas. Letter to Tench Coxe, 1795.

Katz, Stanley N. "In Information Technology, Don't Mistake a Tool for a Goal." *Chronicle of Higher Education* (June 15, 2001): B7. http://chronicle.com/free/v47/i40/40b00701.htm.

King, H. C. *Education and the National Character.* Chicago: The Religious Education Association, 1908.

Lacy, Sarah. "On-Demand Computing: A Brutal Slog." *Business Week,* July 18, 2008. http://www.businessweek.com/technology/content/jul2008/tc20080717_362776.htm.

Laing, R. D. *The Politics of Experience.* New York: Pantheon Books, 1967.

Malloy, Bruce. "'Digital Natives' Take Charge; Get Ready for the Democratization of IT." *New Jersey Tech News* (June 2008): 12–3. http://www.connotate.com/news/NJTech_080601_Democ_of_IT.pdf.

Manjoo, Farhad. *True Enough: Learning to Live in a Post-Fact Society*. Hoboken, NJ: John Wiley & Sons, 2008.

McCracken, Grant. "The Cloudy Self: Or What Has Technology Done to Us." Posted to his blog, January 30, 2007. http://www.cultureby.com/trilogy/2007/01/the_cloudy_self.html.

Merson, John. *The Genius That Was China: East and West in the Making of the Modern World*. New York: Overlook Press, 1990.

Monastersky, Richard. "The Number That Is Devouring Science." *Chronicle of Higher Education* (October 14, 2005). http://chronicle.com/free/v52/i08/08a01201.htm

Newman, John Henry. *The Idea of a University Defined and Illustrated*. London: Longman's, Green & Co., 1893.

Pfeffer, Thomas. *Virtualization of Research Universities: Raising the Right Questions to Address Key Functions of the Institution*. Paper CSHE6-03. Berkeley, CA: Center for Studies in Higher Education, 2003. http://repositories.cdlib.org/cshe/CSHE6-03.

Plato. "Phaedrus." *The Dialogues of Plato*.

Thomas, Jeffrey. "First-Time International Student U.S. Enrollments Up 10.2 Percent." America.gov, http://www.america.gov/st/washfile-english/2007/November/200711131634391CJsamohT0.5697748.html (November 13, 2007).

Trow, Martin "The Development of Information Technology in American Higher Education," *Daedalus* 126, no. 4 (Fall 1997).

U.S. Department of Education, Institute of Education Sciences. *Enrollment in Postsecondary Institutions, Fall 2004; Graduation Rates, 1998 & 2001 Cohorts; and Financial Statistics, Fiscal Year 2004*. Washington, DC: U.S. Government Printing Office, 2006. http://nces.ed.gov//pubs2006/2006155.pdf.

Verghese, B. G. "Reflections on Gandhi." Writings and Commentaries. http://www.bgverghese.com/YouthCadres.htm.

Vest, Charles. "Open Content and the Emerging Global Meta-University." *EDUCAUSE Review* (May/June 2006): 19–25. http://net.educause.edu/ir/library/pdf/ERM0630.pdf.

Wagar, W. Warren. *H. G. Wells: Traversing Time*. Middletown, CT: Wesleyan University Press, 2004.

Walsh, Diana Chapman. *Envisioning the Future: Reflections from the 2015 Commission. Final Report*. Wellesley, MA: Wellesley College, 2007. http://www.wellesley.edu/PublicAffairs/President/DCW/Announcements/2015synopsis.pdf.

Wenzel, Elsa. "Number of PC's in Use to Hit 2 Billion by 2014." SmartPlanet, posted June 24, 2008. http://www.smartplanet.com/news/tech/10001448/number-of-pcs-in-use-to-hit-2-billion-by-2014.htm.

Wikipedia, "Wi-Fi," http://en.wikipedia.org/wiki/Wi-Fi.

Zakon, Robert H. "Hobbes' Internet Timeline V8.2." http://www.zakon.org/robert/internet/timeline.

A Matter of Mission: Information Technology and the Future of Higher Education

Clifford A. Lynch

In late July 2007, Ithaka, a not-for-profit consulting organization, issued a report titled *University Publishing in a Digital Age,*[1] which received a good deal of discussion in higher education circles.[2] The primary focus of the report was the failure of university presses in the United States to adapt to the opportunities and needs involved in the steady move of scholarly work to the digital environment. Notable in the report was the depiction of the powerful disconnect developing between university presses on one side and faculty and university leadership on the other—the sense that the press was becoming increasingly tangential to the university's work and mission, perhaps even bordering on irrelevance. A consequence of this erosion of support was a growing unwillingness to continue to subsidize the budget shortfalls generated by almost all university presses, and certainly a strong unwillingness to very substantially increase these subsidies, or to inject large amounts of institutional "venture capital" into the presses. Finally, the report also described a number of experimental new scholarly publishing ventures being carried out by university libraries, often using various open-access economic models. Intriguingly, the Ithaka report says little about the systemic level of real intellectual and policy support these experiments are receiving from university leadership.

What I found most interesting upon reading the Ithaka report is that it failed to start from, or return to, first principles and fundamental questions. In particular: What is—and what should be—the university's commitment to the widespread dissemination of scholarship, particularly that created by its own faculty? Note that I've chosen my words carefully, and neutrally, in framing this question; I have not asked whether universities ought to be hosting, operating, and/or subsidizing presses, with all of the tacit assumptions that burden this much more narrow query.

There is no question that information technology, networks, and the onslaught of digital data are changing the way we can do teaching, learning, and research in absolutely fundamental ways. This is well documented in a long series of excellent reports,[3] though I am perhaps more persuaded that a persuasive and systematic case has been made concerning research as opposed to teaching and learning. However, when I read many of these reports and think about their implications for colleges and universities, I'm struck by how often the discussion is about what these technological developments are going to do to higher education, rather than about how educational institutions might choose to employ the technologies to advance their missions in previously unimaginable ways. And making these choices at a policy level means some fresh and uninhibited consideration of mission possibilities, alternatives, and expectations in the context of all of the social, societal, economic, technological, and ethical or philosophical forces that form the environment in which higher education functions.

The future of university presses is a classic case study; these were developed a very long time ago, under radically different economic and technical constraints. Presumably, they were established because their founding universities felt the need to advance the dissemination (and perhaps, albeit indirectly, preservation) of the scholarship that their faculty created.[4] Talking about the future relevance of university presses without really being clear about the mission objectives that they are supposed to address today leads to a sort of incremental organizational tinkering that seems to me to be incommensurate with the magnitude of the opportunities that are now visible.

In the remainder of this very short essay, which is intended to be provocative rather than comprehensive, I will look briefly at several dimensions of organizational mission that I believe are in question today within U.S. higher education (and indeed globally, though I will focus on the American situation). These are high-stakes decisions, both at the institutional level and at the collective level of the academy as a whole; they will help determine the role of universities in society in the coming decades, and indeed perhaps shape the nature of our society itself.

The Rhetoric of Knowledge and Scholarship

There's a strange rhetoric one encounters from time to time that speaks of the academy and of research universities in particular as having a mission to "create new knowledge"; from there we move to speaking about ways in which they "own" this knowledge, how they may have responsibilities to "disseminate" it, but also how they may have a mandate to "monetize" it. This is the language of technology transfer offices; it is primarily relevant to advances in science and technology, and perhaps in schools of professional practice.

No one university "owns" or "creates" the body of knowledge that comprises any significant field of intellectual inquiry for any length of time; these are built up out of the contributions of multiple scholars, at multiple universities (and sometimes at institutions beyond the academy). Further, the body of knowledge in any discipline is constantly being reinterpreted, reintegrated, reorganized, and reexpressed by the continuing efforts of scholars, and thus it lives, evolves, and grows. Collectively, the faculty of our colleges and universities represent very deep reservoirs of knowledge and scholarship across a tremendous range of disciplines and fields of inquiry. It is this full body of knowledge and scholarship, as expressed in the scholarly work of these faculty and their students, that I am concerned with here, not simply the "new knowledge" being created at a given time. And I want to stress that no single university or university system, even one as large and prestigious as Harvard or the University of California system, controls a critical mass within this body of scholarship, but that collectively the (international) academy does control such a critical mass in many—perhaps most—disciplines, at least prospectively. (The vast majority of the literature documenting the last century of scholarly work is controlled outside the academy, due to past practices of assigning copyright to publishers and the unprecedented retrospective extensions of the term of copyright.)

This situation, where the body of scholarship is held by many institutional participants, none of them enjoying dominant scale, helps to explain the difficulties involved in changing the scholarly communications system and the pragmatic difficulties of navigating such changes at the institutional level. But it also underscores the need for each institution to behave responsibly within the context of its mission and values and to recognize that its contributions are vital, its responsibilities are real, and its choices will matter.

University Roles in the Dissemination of Scholarship

Is the dissemination of scholarship, then, a fundamental part of the mission of the university? To answer this question, or to understand how institutions are currently answering it, we need to carefully examine what is meant by "disseminate."

In some parts of Europe, universities and even national university systems are taking an aggressive, unambiguous, and expansive position that says the dissemination of knowledge and scholarship is a central part of the university mission. By this they mean that faculty works—in the broad sense of scholarly and instructional materials—should be made public as soon and as widely as possible, with as few barriers (technical, economic, and legal) as possible; extensive use of information technology and the Internet make this economically feasible. This path leads toward mandates for the support of various forms of open-access strategies for faculty publications, for example, and systematic investments in institutional or national repository systems.[5]

If you asked the leadership at various universities in the United States, I believe that the responses to the question would be more variable, and perhaps often more equivocal. Some—perhaps particularly (but certainly not exclusively!), some of the public institutions of higher education—might argue for a broad dissemination mission and are beginning to move into such a role through the development and deployment of extensive public-access digital collections and learning materials, the deployment of institutional repository services, library- and/or university-press-based digital publishing efforts, and other initiatives. A particularly interesting development is the movement to make available large-scale collections of audio and video materials—mainly courses and lectures—through mechanisms such as local hosting, collectives like the Research Channel, or commercial media dissemination systems like Apple's iTunes or Google's YouTube; only rarely is the library currently involved in these efforts, and I do not know of any case of university press involvement. These programs represent substantial investments, and while extramural funding has helped with some of the early efforts, there's great concern about "sustainability" of these efforts—they either have to move, most likely, to some kind of recharge basis, which will add a great deal of overhead, impede access, and consequently reduce the contribution of the programs to the university's mission goals, or they simply have to be funded out of core institutional budgets as part of the essential, mission-critical activities of the institution. The choice of an aggressive interpretation of institutional mission to disseminate scholarship will not be without substantial ongoing cost.

It is worth noting that what seems to be a growing number of faculty are beginning to push for greater openness and dissemination of scholarship and of the underlying evidence that supports scholarship. This can be seen in the various movements toward open data, open-source software, open-access publishing, open-notebook science, and similar activities. Also of importance is a growing push from funding organizations—both governmental and private—for greater access to both published results and underlying data.

The way in which this question about institutional mission plays out will have a large effect on how accessible scholarly work will be in our society broadly. I think it will make a difference in the rate at which science and engineering, in particular, advance. It will influence the ability of a larger number of universities to participate meaningfully in the research enterprise. It will have implications for the future roles and, indeed, even the continued viability of various players in the scholarly communications system, including university presses, libraries, commercial scholarly publishers, and scholarly societies.

It is important to keep the two potential mission questions separate, while understanding that they are not entirely unrelated.

University Roles in the Stewardship of Scholarship

Some institution, or collection of institutions, needs to maintain the record of scholarship as well as the collection of evidence that underpins and supports scholarship past, present, and future. To what extent does this fall within the mission of the university?

Historically, the stewardship of the scholarly record has fallen to the research library system; while most research libraries in the United States are part of major universities, the systems are not coterminous, as institutions such as the Library of Congress, the National Libraries of Medicine and Agriculture, and the New York and Boston Public Libraries (to name only a few key players) are not part of universities. Responsibility for the broader base of underpinning evidence is more widely scattered; while research libraries play a major role, so do other cultural memory organizations such as archives and museums; some of these are also part of universities, but many exist outside the university system. Notable is the relatively recent emergence of very large and very important data archives that are part of various government agencies; in some cases the long-term stability of these archives seems precarious. And there has always been a certain amount of tension about the extent to which libraries, archives, and museums within universities should focus narrowly on the needs of their parent institutions as opposed to the extent to which they should serve the academy, or even society more broadly, as a whole.

In the print era, primary stewardship of the record of scholarship and shared stewardship of its underlying base of evidence wasn't cheap, and it was very closely tied operationally and economically to the dissemination system (publishing).

The growth of new kinds of scholarly communication today, the move to e-research, and the reliance of scholarly work on a tremendous proliferation of data sets (some of them enormous) and of accompanying software systems threaten to greatly increase the cost and complexity of the stewardship process and to at least partially decouple it from (traditional) publishing. Libraries need to reexamine and redefine their roles appropriately to address these new scholarly works and this new body of evidence for scholarship. Commitments to activities like data curation and management of faculty collections will increasingly characterize research libraries as much as the comprehensive collection and preservation policies for published literature and personal papers. The cost of stewardship is, I believe, going to rise substantially.

There are only about 100 university-based research libraries in the United States. Many additional colleges and universities will need to draw upon the collections that are held by these research libraries. How will the economic burden be shared? How can the many other institutions that rely upon the good and responsible stewardship of the research libraries help to underwrite this work? What expectations here will be built into institutional funding commitments that support such stewardship among the leading research universities?

And, at the same time, there are certainly faculty at more than those 100 universities with research libraries who are producing digital materials that will require stewardship by their institutional library; mission questions about stewardship responsibility may extend much more broadly than the top 100 research universities. We do not yet understand the distribution of interdependence, of distributed responsibility, or of needs and how these fit into the context of stewardship as institutional mission. Nor do we understand at what point the most effective *tactics,* after accepting instructional mission responsibility, may be to outsource implementation to other peer institutions with more cost-effective economies of scale and concentrations of expertise.

Conclusions

I have raised two simple questions about the mission of institutions of higher education: the institutional responsibility for dissemination of scholarship, and the institutional responsibility for the stewardship of scholarship (and supporting evidence). I believe that it's time for institutional leadership within the academy to explicitly consider both of these questions, particularly in light of the changing practices of scholarship and scholarly communication, and then to consider institutional responses to the opportunities offered by the digital dissemination environment in the context of such mission mandates. My personal view is that these are not missions that the leadership of higher education institutions of the 21st century can abrogate, but I think that matters become much more challenging when we consider the overall *system* of higher education in relation to these missions, and when we think about which institutions must engage the missions and about how the broader higher education community might be expected to support those institutions.

Endnotes

1. Laura Brown, Rebecca Griffiths, and Matthew Rascoff, *University Publishing in a Digital Age* (New York: Ithaka, July 2007), http://www.ithaka.org/publications/UniversityPublishingInADigitalAge.

2. See, for example, *The Chronicle of Higher Education* coverage at http://chronicle.com/weekly/v53/i48/48a01401.htm and *Inside Higher Ed* coverage at http://www.insidehighered.com/news/2007/07/26/ithaka and http://www.insidehighered.com/views/2007/08/01/mclemee.

3. See, for example, *Cyberinfrastructure Vision for 21st Century Discovery* (Washington, DC: National Science Foundation, March 2007), http://www.nsf.gov/od/oci/CI_Vision_March07.pdf; *Our Cultural Commonwealth: The Report of the American Council of Learned Societies Commission on Cyberinfrastructure for the Humanities and Social Sciences* (New York: American Council of Learned Societies, December 2006), http://www.acls.org/uploadedfiles/publications/programs/our_cultural_commonwealth.pdf; *Preparing for the Revolution: Information Technology and the Future of the University* (Washington, DC: National Research Council, 2002); James J. Duderstadt, Daniel E. Atkins, and Douglas Van Houweling, *Higher Education in the Digital Age: Technology Issues and Strategies for American Colleges and Universities* (Washington, DC: American Council on Education, 2002).

4. An interesting case study of the complex and shifting motivations at Harvard for the establishment and subsequent support of a university press can be found in Max Hall, *Harvard University Press: A History* (Cambridge, MA: Harvard University Press, 1986).

5. The specifics of the situations in the various European universities and national university systems are complex and fluid. An excellent source for tracking developments is Peter Suber's Open Access News blog at http://www.earlham.edu/~peters/fos/fosblog.html. For a general introduction to open-access issues, see John Willinsky, *The Access Principle: The Case for Open Access to Research and Scholarship* (Cambridge, MA: MIT Press, 2005), and also Neil Jacobs, ed., *Open Access: Key Strategic, Technical and Economic Aspects* (Oxford, UK: Chandos Publishing, 2006).

6. For some further discussion of this, see Clifford A. Lynch, "Digital Libraries, Learning Communities and Open Education," in *Opening Up Education: The Collective Advancement of Education through Open Technology, Open Content and Open Knowledge,* ed. Toru Iiyoshi and M. S. Vijay Kumar (Cambridge, MA: MIT Press, 2008).

Bibliography

American Council of Learned Societies. *Our Cultural Commonwealth, The Report of the American Council of Learned Societies Commission on Cyberinfrastructure for the Humanities and Social Sciences.* New York: ACLS, December 2006. http://www.acls.org/uploadedfiles/publications/programs/our_cultural_commonwealth.pdf.

Brown, Laura, Rebecca Griffiths, and Matthew Rascoff. *University Publishing in a Digital Age.* New York: Ithaka, July 2007. http://www.ithaka.org/publications/UniversityPublishingInADigitalAge.

Duderstadt, James J., Daniel E. Atkins, and Douglas Van Houweling. *Higher Education in the Digital Age: Technology Issues and Strategies for American Colleges and Universities.* Washington, DC: American Council on Education, 2002.

Hall, Max. *Harvard University Press: A History.* Cambridge, MA: Harvard University Press, 1986.

Jacobs, Neil, ed. *Open Access: Key Strategic, Technical and Economic Aspects.* Oxford, UK: Chandos Publishing, 2006.

Lynch, Clifford A. "Digital Libraries, Learning Communities and Open Education." In *Opening Up Education: The Collective Advancement of Education through Open Technology, Open Content and Open Knowledge,* edited by Toru Iiyoshi and M. S. Vijay Kumar. Cambridge, MA: MIT Press, 2008.

National Research Council. *Preparing for the Revolution: Information Technology and the Future of the University.* Washington, DC: National Research Council, 2002.

National Science Foundation Cyberinfrastructure Council. *Cyberinfrastructure Vision for 21st Century Discovery.* Washington, DC: National Science Foundation, March 2007, http://www.nsf.gov/od/oci/CI_Vision_March07.pdf.

Open Access News Blog. http://www.earlham.edu/~peters/fos/fosblog.html.

Willinsky, John. *The Access Principle: The Case for Open Access to Research and Scholarship.* Cambridge, MA: MIT Press, 2005.

The University in the Networked Economy and Society: Challenges and Opportunities

Yochai Benkler

T he networked information economy and society present a new social, technical, and economic environment within which the university functions. To understand the new challenges and opportunities this environment presents, we need a usable characterization of the core new characteristics of both the environment and the university as a system and how those characteristics interact to define today's challenges.

The Networked Information Economy

The critical characteristic of the networked economy is a radical decentralization of physical capital necessary for the production, storage, distribution, and processing of information, knowledge, and culture. This decentralization has caused a radical distribution of the practical capability to act in these areas, creating new levels of efficacy for individuals, who increasingly shift from being consumers to being users and producers. Individuals have now become capable of doing much more for themselves and for others, both alone and in vastly more effective loose collaborations with others.

In the industrial economy, hobbyists, no matter how committed, could not come together on the weekend and compete with General Motors. The degree of required concentrated physical capital made their decentralized, social practices ineffective as an economic production activity of any significant scale. Like GM, the industrial information economy required models that were able to finance large-grained capital investment: government, through taxes; business, through market transactions; or organized nonprofits, through large-scale and aggregated giving. News production bifurcated between government ownership in many countries and advertising-based mass media (with the exception of the BBC, hybrid model). Film and music also split among these three, and, for purposes of higher education, the role of the large, organized nonprofit was central, as was the role of government funding.

Decentralized Ownership and Excess Capacity

The networked information economy has not decreased the total capital intensity of information production, storage, processing, and communication, but it has decentralized its ownership. About a billion people on the planet today own the core physical means of producing information, knowledge, and culture: they own machines that sense, capture, store, process, and communicate their thoughts, observations, manipulations, and expressions. These machines are, in turn, "shareable," by which I mean that, given their production technology and the distribution of wealth in the populations that own the majority of them, they are placed into operation by individuals and families for whom they have excess capacity.

No one can, practically, buy only as much computation power as needed at any given moment. No one buys storage or bandwidth purely to fulfill that day's needs. These goods are "lumpy" and, for most owners, have significant downtime and excess capacity. In front of these machines sit people who themselves have a wide diversity of experience, wisdom, insight, and creativity and who have a wide diversity of motivations and availability at different stages of life and different moments of the day, week, or year.

The combination of distribution of physical capital and human capital creates a new situation. For the first time since the industrial revolution, the most important inputs into the core economic activities of the most advanced economies are widely distributed in the population. Moreover, there is a significant amount of excess capacity, both physical and human, that is being poured relentlessly into new forms of information, knowledge, and cultural production, as well as into provisioning of networking, storage, and processing capabilities.

If hobbyists could never have competed with General Motors, the same cannot be said for Microsoft or IBM. The rise of free and open source software has created real challenges for mainstream software publishers. Apache, in fact, has captured and held much of the market in web server software, despite 13 years of efforts by Microsoft to take that market. IBM has, on its software services side, adapted and adopted open source software development as a core component of its development ecology. But on the hardware side, IBM has a new primary competitor for "fastest supercomputer in the world"—the distributed computation projects, such as SETI@home or Einstein@Home.

Wikipedians compete with the commercial encyclopedias, citizen journalists with mainstream media. P2P networks offer real alternatives to proprietary networks as storage and distribution alternatives, as we see in the case of the "domesticated" uses such as Skype and, increasingly, BitTorrent. Mesh networks are beginning, more slowly than necessary because of the legal constraints on wireless equipment deployment and bloated security concerns, to develop a path toward user-owned, last-100-meter networks. In all these cases we see what I have called *peer production* (large-scale collaboration among individuals without price signals or hierarchical commands), together with large-scale material sharing of shareable goods, creating social alternatives to the traditional models thought necessary in the industrial information economy.

Decentralized Capability and Authority to Act

The creativity and innovation that we see on the Internet today are directly tied to the radical decentralization of the practical capability to act, on the one hand, and of the authority to act, on the other. This is where a combination of sensible social norms that diverge from the formal law—self-conscious, commons-based practices—and simple disdain for the law coalesce with the decentralization of capital. The technical/economic shift that networks have created is the location of physical and human capability to act in the hands of users. This technical capability to act, however, requires authority to act in order to be effective.

A variety of laws, some concerned with morality and security but mostly concerned with protecting incumbent business models (such as the intellectual property industries), separate authority to act on information and culture from the newly created capability to act. These have had partial success in slowing down adoption of social production of information and knowledge, but at the broad, macro level of social practices they have failed. Millions of users are creating videos on YouTube, sharing music and mixing it in ways that are sensible but arguably illegal.

The critical policy questions of the networked environment revolve around the battles between the progression of technology, which at the moment (this is not a deterministic trend, it is merely a happenstance of the fabrication technology of computers) is leading to decentralization on the one hand and on the other to the push of policy to moderate that decentralization by limiting the distribution of authority to act.

At one level, the effort to retain organization through assertion of authority is happening through copyrights and paracopyrights as well as patents. At another level, it is asserted through security concerns and the idea of trusted computing. At yet a third level, it occurs around social acceptance of new forms of authority: How do I know that a Wikipedia entry is correct? How do I trust a blog story? Our old forms of assigning credibility and authority to a claim were closely aligned with the institutional origins of the claim. As information production becomes radically decentralized, new models of authority are seeking similar recognition.

The University

The university predates the industrial information economy and has retained much of its preindustrial guild model (not least visible on graduation days). Industrialization entered more heavily in the material sciences and biomedical sciences, where large-scale capital investment was necessary to perform the basic science. At first, this was more purely based on the government-funding model of industrialization, and later it shifted to include market funding, both around patents and more loosely around research support and university–industry relations. Still, research is done by relatively autonomous and small-scale units, and explicit reliance on market signals is not the norm.

The humanities, in turn, are much lower cost and remain heavily oriented toward a teaching-based, subsidy-for-research model, with long apprenticeship periods for graduate students and junior faculty until they are inducted to master status. Research in these areas often continues to depend heavily on individuals working alone, subsidized by their teaching, with fierce claims of autonomy and narrow claims of unassailable authority.

As a subsystem within the knowledge production system of modern society, the university has several characteristics that give it a distinct role. The town–gown tension has long typified the relationship of the university to the market and society as one of partial remove, that is, removed from the pressures and enticements of the market and a dedication to internal system values, usually embodied in the ideas of academic freedom, intellectual discipline, and peer review. As many have shown, the history of science has not, in fact, been quite as insulated as the self-conception sometimes suggests. Nonetheless, the values, practices, and structures of the university have allowed it as an institution to engage as a system that pulls the knowledge production system away from the pursuits driven by market signals, political signals, or popular cultural fad and toward directions characterized by the relatively high intensity of communication within the academic community, among people engaged in the practice of conversation, writing, mutual commentary, and critique. These practices have, in turn, fed into and been sustained by spatial removal.

The university campus has been a place for students to be immersed in learning and find others like themselves. This is, of course, heavily mixed in with late-teen/early-adult socialization, but it does offer a framework and basis that orients this socialization, with wide-ranging degrees of seriousness, around learning. Scholars do come together and exchange views, read, and mutually reinforce their commitment, through repeat performance of discourse, to the academic enterprise standing distinct from market, polity, and society at large. Again, I do not want to sound starry-eyed; I hear there is occasional backbiting, too. But that is not the point. It is, rather, that the remove of the university—its relative coherence as a distinct subsystem— tends to be based on repeat practices of structured conversation that represent a certain set of values and commitments and, therefore, orient its participants to a particular kind of conversation, inquiry, and output. These practices make the university a discrete subsystem for knowledge production, quite different from, say, industrial research and development.

As we shift to the networked information economy, the ability of some parts of the university to skip over industrialization entirely, and the potential for others to transition more gracefully than could some of the actors in industry, creates new opportunities. For purposes of technical architectural design of the university networks and information system, the shift presents three core challenges:

1. how to manage increasingly permeable boundaries between the university and the world, to enable the higher degree of effective participation in the world that students and faculty can have, while avoiding a fragmentation of the coherent university system;

2. how to preserve the practical capability and authority to act in the hands of students and faculty, in the face of pressures to centrally control use in order to avoid "bad" uses, both external (such as copyright violations or security threats) and internal (such as destabilization of the traditional lines of authority in the classroom); and

3. how to build platforms for cooperation that enhance the central experience of the university—intense structured discourse around a set of shared values and practices oriented toward knowledge and education.

Permeable Boundaries

Many contributors to free and open source software projects, to Wikipedia, or to the blogosphere are students and faculty. The relative freedom of both groups from structuring constraints of job performance, and the internal system values regarding their role as knowledge producers and young people exploring the limits of their knowledge and creativity, have made universities an important platform for the system of commons-based social production. Like the university, this system stands apart from market and state. Unlike the university, it is not based on formal accreditation, hierarchy, and membership but on more fluid practices of contribution and loose association. The university can offer its systems to support social production of both its own internal workings and its members in those of the outer world.

Examples of the kinds of contributions university systems can make to the social production system beyond their boundaries include ibiblio, the MIT OpenCourseWare initiative, COSL, and Connexions.

- ibiblio represents a contribution of resources and expertise. It is an Internet library, archive, or depository of materials that are freely available for reuse, which can be contributed to by anyone and is usable by anyone. ibiblio is a collaboration of the University of North Carolina–Chapel Hill with the Center for the Public Domain, itself a nonprofit created by and heavily anchored in the Duke University faculty.
- The OpenCourseWare initiative is an effort to format course materials created by faculty and make them available on the Internet to anyone who wants to use them—self-learners or educators outside MIT—as inputs into their own learning. Here, the university platform both serves a physical role in distributing the materials and builds expertise in preparation and conversion from the idiosyncratic forms used by individual teachers— the vestige of the guildlike freedom individual teachers have—and the needs of a platform of university-level teaching materials available for universal use.
- COSL, the Center for Open and Sustainable Learning at the Utah State University, and Connexions, a collaborative platform for the creation and sharing of educational materials founded at Rice University, offer yet another step up in the level of contribution to capacity to act. Here, the university-based organizations are building tools and

platforms and hosting them to pool contributions, not only from within universities but also, more generally, from the social production system, into a project central to the role of the university—the creation and sharing of educational materials.

A different kind of permeability comes from the increasing capability of researchers to collaborate in networks that ignore institutional boundaries. The Human Genome Project is one such example; the International Haplotype Mapping (HapMap) project is even more so. Science today, in many cases, requires thousands of collaborators and simply cannot be managed within the old silo model. Here, the permeability required is across distinct institutional boundaries.

Permeability allows faculty and students to engage with and in the world. As such, it is an important new dimension of town–gown relations at a time when the kinds of nonmarket, nonstate action that students and faculty are so oriented toward by institutional habit and practice have become so much more important a component of the information production system generally. Yet, as we have noted, the geographic separation, the distinctness of the campus, has also been central to defining the university. There is a certain safety or trust, possible in the classroom, to experiment with ideas, questions, and inquiry that performance on a more public stage makes difficult. Identity is important to trust, and yet anonymity is important to free engagement in the world outside. Managing the tension between engaging the university in the world and preserving the internal trust and structure of university discourse is important and not always easy.

Proprietary systems such as Blackboard seem optimized for allowing teachers to control the discussion and the materials, replicating in many senses the security of the traditional classroom while erecting barriers to student contribution to the syllabus and to external participation in a class. Open blogs and wikis, on the other hand, provide little or no safety other than through obscurity, which at the moment seems enough for those courses that use them. One goal of university platforms should be to develop free platforms that would integrate the benefits of both, most likely building on the increasing use of private wikis as a platform.

End-to-End Versus Centralization

The end-to-end principle, originally characterized by Saltzer, Clark, and Reed as an Internet design principle, has now developed into a broader architectural principle, for some even a political commitment. At core, its argument is that functions should, to the extent possible, be pushed to the edges of a network while keeping the core of the network as simple as it can be. This, in turn, allows for innovation to come from anywhere and to go anywhere, without requiring large systemic modification in the network itself. As a broader architectural principle, it is tied to building as little as possible of the functionality into the hard-to-change elements of a system.

The end-to-end principle has come under significant pressure for several years now, for a variety of good reasons. Usability, security, standardization within an organization, pricing, and quality of service have all been interjected as reasons to implement more significant elements of services into the network itself, rather than leaving everything to the edges. Universities have the opportunity to control their own networks and have various reasons to do so. Be it managing P2P file sharing because of fear of lawsuits, system burden, or malicious software, or the will to separate out what is available to registered students and others, universities have strong motivations to control their systems.

This is, I think, a mistake.

Most, if not all, of the best examples of collaboration online where universities have played a role started with demonstration projects and beyond, done by individual faculty members or students. Innovation in institutional engagement, just like innovation in voice over Internet protocol or instant messaging, comes from the edges, not the core. Furthermore, precisely because the individual members of university communities can play such an important role in the social production system in general, university systems should resist the urge to centralize. Instead, the emphasis should be on implementing solutions to whatever concerns there are through (1) identifying or developing solutions that can be implemented at the ends of the network, preserving the autonomy of users, and (2) where the practices are unacceptable to the university, solving them through the university's disciplinary system in a formal, transparent way, rather than architecturally in ways that have negative spillover effects on other, desirable uses.

It is important in this context to remember that people exist in multiple systems of constraint and affordance. Technical systems are only one kind of system, and different affordances and constraints for any given individual or community can be implemented in one or more of these systems. In the case of technical constraints on usage, the costs, in terms of incapacitation, imposed by technical solutions seem larger than the costs, in terms of imperfect enforcement, of using an institutional disciplinary system.

The basic commitment of university system architecture needs to ensure that each member of the community has the systems capability to be an active contributor and participant in communication—both internal to the university and external, to the networked world at large. Authority and capacity to act on all things digital should be located at the edges, rather than centralized in the university system. Solutions to what are perceived as threats to that system should be designed not purely with the technical system in mind but with the range of interlocking systems—technical, organizational, cultural, and institutional—that the university is made up of. These solutions should be implemented through the system that will have the least negative impact on the capacity of the university to function as a learning and research community and platform.

Building Platforms for Cooperation

The observable emergence of online cooperation coincides with several academic trends in thinking about human cooperation. These go beyond a selfish rational actor model, emphasizing a diverse set of motivational profiles, not all selfish, and the centrality of communication and human interaction to forming preferences for cooperation and the commitment to ongoing cooperative processes. Where implemented, cooperation-based systems seem primarily aimed to construct human systems capable of observing a complex and rapidly changing environment, learning about new conditions and practices within it, and pursuing them in flexible, adaptive ways.

One anchor of these trends is the large literature in several disciplines on the prevalence of observations of human cooperation inconsistent with the predictions of the selfish, rational actor model. In experimental economics, we see a line of work on human proclivity to cooperate in patterns that are rational but inconsistent with uniformly selfish preferences. This work is distinct from the mainstream concern of experimental economics—behavioral deviations from rationality. From this literature we learn that somewhat more than half the population predictably behaves as cooperators or reciprocators in social dilemma and altruism-adducing games, while about one-third act as selfish actors. Various manipulations are associated with decay of cooperation, while others are associated with increasing cooperation. These findings suggest that, under appropriate designs, cooperators cooperate, reciprocators cooperate and invest in punishing defections by selfish agents, and selfish agents increase cooperation over time to avoid that punishment. While the literature itself is not oriented toward characterizing design levers for systems of cooperation, it is possible to synthesize these out of it.

Parallel work in experiments and field studies has been done in political science, in particular around governance of commons. There is also crossover work in neuroeconomics to support some of the observations of the experimental work. As to ultimate causes of cooperation, evolutionary biology has seen a trajectory leading it from selfish gene theory of the 1970s to increasing emphasis on cooperation, both through indirect reciprocity and through multilevel selection. In anthropology, we see uses of evolutionary dynamics to explain cultural practices of cooperation, on much shorter timescales and with greater sensitivity to cultural variation, destabilizing the gene–culture binary.

A second, distinct line is seen within organizational sociology. Growing from the work on post-Fordism, trust, and increasing knowledge intensity in firms, sociologists had observed increasing adoption of networked organization models emerging within firms, and in some cases across firms, in supply relationships. Globalization and rapid technological change put organizations under increasing pressure to innovate in their processes, adapt to changes, learn about a rapidly changing environment and increasingly complex processes, and implement learning continuously. Under a variety of monikers, such as *team production, quality circles,* and so forth, a variety of business processes have emerged that depend heavily on communication, on relatively higher responsibility in the hands of employees, or on the emergence of trust-based collaboration, replacing the traditional models of market and hierarchies to govern internal relations within and between firms. The two critical points, from the perspective of designing information platforms, are that the turn to cooperative models and decentralization of action is seen as driven by a need to improve the learning and adaptation capabilities of organizations and interorganizational networks, and that many of the characteristics of successful collaborations fit those that one sees coming out of the experimental work.

A third line of work is the emergence, within software systems design, of an effort to characterize "social software" as its design objective, that is, designing software that is intended to be run for and by a group of people, fostering their interaction, including its social dynamics. This literature at the moment is in a heuristic stage and tends to characterize successful and unsuccessful practices. Nonetheless, it offers a good basis for observing cooperation in practice, running on a designed system with, therefore, relatively easily characterizable design features.

These lines of work do not speak to each other, yet they all point to the increasing importance of human cooperation across multiple domains, arrived at from a wide-ranging and diverse set of approaches and methods.

They allow us to begin to characterize what design elements would be necessary to foster cooperation and therefore allow us to design systems for cooperation more systematically.

Going into the details of such systems here would be beyond the goal of this discussion. To presage future work, I will simply note that these design levers will include communication, as a central necessary facility, as well as humanization, trust, clear norms, fairness, discipline and punishment, transparency, self-selection, group identity, crowding out, cost, and leadership. A major challenge of the next few years will be to refine this literature into testable design levers, translate these into working designs, and learn from experience about how best to build systems for the diverse beings we in fact are.

Conclusion

Throughout the period of the industrial information economy, the university maintained a stance apart from much of the rest of that economy. As we move to a networked information economy, the distinct values of the university—its relative freedom from the pressures of the market, polity, and popular fashion—are a major source of strength. Universities can become an even more significant force in the knowledge production system, one that distinctly pulls in the direction of professional values. Universities can provide an anchor "against" commercial incentives and build a strong complementary system with the amateur commons–based peer production system, as we have indeed seen in areas such as free and open source software.

University networks and technical platforms will have to focus on managing the increasingly permeable boundaries among universities, and between universities and the world outside them. University platform design should be focused on ensuring that faculty and students have the greatest degree possible of authority and capacity to act freely, innovate internally, and participate externally. And university systems should be attuned to the need to build platforms for cooperation, as the new practices of cooperation and sharing become more prevalent and more based in a broader shift from an image of hierarchical or market-oriented systems to systems based on individuals collaborating with each other in loose networks.

Cairo University

The Globalization of Higher Education

Growing in Esteem: Positioning the University of Melbourne in the Global Knowledge Economy

Glyn Davis, Linda O'Brien, and Pat McLean

The emerging global higher education market, facilitated by advances in information and communication technologies, challenges all universities to reconsider their mission and direction. The University of Melbourne, one of Australia's leading research universities,[1] has undergone a fundamental reshaping to ensure its place in an evolving global knowledge economy.

The result is a strategy called "Growing Esteem,"[2] developed after extensive consultation. Growing Esteem signals the university's intention to remain a leading education provider in the 21st century. The metaphor of a triple helix defines the strategy's character and purpose. Setting three priorities for the university—research and research training, learning and teaching, and knowledge transfer—the helix captures the complex and shifting relations between three disparate spheres of activity that are tightly bound, each reinforcing the other.

Central to the Growing Esteem strategy is the "Melbourne model" (a term coined by Australian media), the most significant curriculum reform in the university's 154-year history. The Melbourne model is premised on creation of a small number of broad undergraduate programs, followed by intense professional training at a postgraduate level.

Integral to the achievement of the university's vision will be the way in which the university's information services, systems, and technologies come together to support the vision: to bind the strands of the helix to achieve strategic outcomes, to underpin the educational model, to enhance the quality of the student experience, and to provide the foundation for strategic agility in a changing global environment.

This essay outlines the university's 2015 vision, the steps taken to "dream large,"[3] and the way information services and technologies are working toward the realization of the 2015 vision.

The Context: A Rapidly Changing Higher Education Sector

The higher education sector worldwide is responding to a raft of global influences—an international market, the influence of the knowledge economy on education, the influence of technology on learning and teaching. Key drivers include the evolving needs of graduates and employers, the increasing importance of international rankings, a continued decline in public funding, and rapid technological change. When he visited the University of Melbourne late in 2006, Professor James Wilkinson, director of the Derek Bok Center for Teaching and Learning at Harvard University, advised: "I don't think Australian higher education has any choice but to diversify and innovate now. There's a long lead time in education. It is not smart just to think that what worked well in the past might work well in the future."[4]

Expectations of University Graduates Are Changing

Australian students, like their international peers, are globally mobile. The career trajectories of graduates in the 21st century will likely include time spent overseas, working for international companies, or managing multicultural environments. Graduates expect to be global citizens, carefully attuned to cultural diversity and able to communicate across cultures.

In a global knowledge economy, what students learn today may be outdated before they complete their degrees. Career pathways can be expected to shift direction several times. Students expect transferable skills such as learning how to learn, problem solve, analyze, and communicate effectively across cultural and discipline boundaries. Discipline boundaries are shifting to accommodate new academic alliances in an effort to comprehend complex systems, such as global warming.

Universities Must Compete in a Global Education Market

Universities now compete for students—and quality staff—in a global market. International research rankings, especially those based on research indices, have become important. Just as good students prefer to study with other good students, the best researchers want to work with the most able and stimulating colleagues. Increasingly, international rankings are an important factor as students and faculty alike make choices about which university to select.

Melbourne has long been a leader in Australian indices of research performance but performs less well by international measures. In the *Times Higher Education* world rankings, Melbourne sits at 22 in the world, but in the more rigorous, research performance–based *Shanghai Jiao Tong* index, the university is number 79, one of only two Australian universities among the top 100. North American universities count for 8 of the top 10 universities in the *Shanghai Jiao Tong* index.

While global competition has yet to impose a single model of higher education, there are signs of convergence around the familiar North American model of broadly based undergraduate degrees followed by graduate entry professional degrees. While four-year undergraduate degrees tend to be distinctly North American, the Bologna approach adopted across Europe accepts the same architecture of foundation studies, followed by professional training, in an undergraduate–masters sequence. The Bologna model incorporates easily readable and comparable degrees, uniform degree structures, and increased student and staff mobility. Adoption of the Bologna model across Europe is influencing higher education worldwide as countries that follow neither North American nor European degree programs ponder how to compete globally.

A global market means not just some measure of standardization; it also means competition from institutions that set up campuses outside their home territory. In Australia, changes in the government protocols and loans scheme have fueled the growth of private higher education providers. In 2006, a campus of an American research university, Carnegie Mellon University, opened in Adelaide, supported by funding from the South Australian government. It may only be a matter of time until one of the big and successful universities from the United States employing online delivery with local tutorials—such as the University of Phoenix or Kaplan University—begins to operate in this nation. In addition, Australia can expect to experience increased competition for students, as English program delivery at European Union and Asian institutions makes these more attractive to students from the broader region.

Shifts in the Way Universities Are Funded

Pressure on national public funding for higher education in the United Kingdom, Australia, and New Zealand has encouraged or forced most institutions in these countries to seek additional income from other sources. In Australia, universities have increased their revenue from full-fee-paying international students from 5.8 percent of university income in 1995 to 14.5 percent in 2004[5]; federal funding as a proportion of total higher education revenue dropped from 57 percent in 1996 to 41 percent in 2005.[6]

Recent trends in international student markets have highlighted the unsustainability of continued dependence on revenue from international students. While Australia has been a preferred destination for those in the region seeking higher education, rapid growth in the overseas student numbers has stalled—a situation that leaves chronically underfunded Australian universities particularly vulnerable to global competition. In addition, these trends raise questions about the traditional responsibilities and roles of national governments in higher education. Simon Marginson and Marijk van der Wende suggest that terms such as "public" education and related notions of priority and accountability take on new meanings as universities go beyond national borders.[7]

In a Global Knowledge Economy, Universities Are Experiencing a Digital Revolution

Underlying these changes to the higher education sector has been a fundamental transformation in the process of creating, synthesizing, and disseminating knowledge through the advent of advanced information and communication technologies. Initially, the digital revolution began with dissemination of scholarly information and stand-alone e-learning tools. With the advent of the Internet and growth in digital multimedia capabilities, access to full-text scholarly information and more sophisticated e-learning opportunities, which rely on communication and collaboration tools, became a reality.

As the tools that generate research data increasingly provide digital output, the Internet has provided the catalyst for distributing access to research data and instruments, furthering research collaboration. No longer must a scientist be located with the instrument to access, analyze, manipulate, and interpret data. The capabilities for accessing research data and collections and collaborative capabilities are also being exploited by the social sciences and humanities.

A threshold was crossed some time recently into a world in which all academic pursuits now include at least some digital component. Indeed, many research and teaching and learning activities use predominantly digital information management and communication technologies. Hence, information and communication technologies are not simply "utilities," like electricity or water, but a "rapidly evolving, mission critical resource."[8] This makes digital communication the backbone of a university's knowledge management capability.

A Strategic Imperative: The Interface between Technology and Teaching and Learning

In the higher education sector, three key trends in the management and use of information and technologies are transforming the academic enterprise—the blurring of research, learning, and teaching boundaries; the proliferation of technologically fueled new ways of communicating; and recognition of an important trend toward standardization.

The Blurring of Research, Learning, and Teaching Boundaries

Chris Dede has written: "Our ways of thinking and knowing, teaching and learning are undergoing a sea change, and [that] what is emerging seems both rich and strange."[9] The ease with which people can now publish to the Internet allows anyone to contribute to the world's store of knowledge—and others to build on the foundation using collaboration and social networking tools. Students can become creators of content in new ways, changing the relationship between teacher and student. And as research increasingly becomes a digital endeavor, everyone has the potential to become part of this research. Amateur astronomers now easily contribute to the world's astronomical research. Students can become active participants in the research process in ways never thought possible, changing the boundaries between research, learning, and teaching.

New Ways of Communicating

Today's "new-generation" undergraduate students have grown up with the Internet and use information and technology in ways quite different from previous generations. *The ECAR Study of Undergraduate Students and Information Technology, 2006* in the United States provides an excellent insight into students' use of technology and their expectations. This study showed PC ownership among undergraduate students to be 97.8 percent, with three-quarters owning laptops and almost one in five owning a PDA. While the students were clearly enthusiastic users of technology, only just over half wanted information technology (IT) used in their courses. By far they saw convenience as the single most important benefit of IT in their university experience, but most also agreed that IT in courses improved their learning.[10]

Of course, such changes also have the potential to create a digital divide, significantly disadvantaging those students with limited access to, or experience of, the new technologies. Ways of defining and measuring educational disadvantage must now also take into account IT disadvantage.

In many cases, university administrations are making (incorrect) assumptions about how the new technologies influence communication using the outdated frameworks of "old-generation" teachers and administrators.

A Trend toward Standardization

Within the university sector, digital leaders realize that business agility relies on standardization and integration of information systems and technologies. The corporate sector for some time has focused on automation of transactional processes, IT consolidation, shared-service initiatives, and process standards such as Information Technology Infrastructure Library (ITIL) to drive their IT effectiveness and efficiency. Research by authors such as Peter Weill, Jeanne W. Ross, and David C. Robertson clearly demonstrates that increased business success, greater agility, and innovation paradoxically require more standardized, automated core processes.[11] The foundations for business success are the IT infrastructure and digitized business processes, which automate an organization's core capabilities. By standardizing and integrating these routine processes so that they are reliable and predictable, the organization's human capability can be directed toward those activities that most add value.

Peter Weill and other colleagues found that "IT savvy" firms can convert investment in IT infrastructure into business value within the same year. IT savvy firms are those with committed senior management who champion IT initiatives, higher firm-wide skills in effective use of IT, more use of IT for internal and external communication, higher Internet use, and more digitized transactions.[12] Universities, given their propensity to localize and distribute organizational authority, have been slower to consider how to apply these concepts within their organizations. It seems likely that increasing student expectations for IT-enabled convenience, coupled with emerging opportunities for global collaborative research, will impel universities to embed IT standards and automate core processes.

New Directions in Learning and Teaching

So what does global transformation mean for research-intensive universities such as Melbourne?

Reforming the Curriculum, Reshaping Student Service Delivery

Lord Broers, an alumnus of Melbourne, vice-chancellor of Cambridge 1996–2003, and now president of the Royal British Academy of Engineering, observed in a 2006 lecture to the Higher Education Policy Institute:

> What we need first and foremost from our universities
> is the provision for young people of an adequately broad
> knowledge base, together with modern analytical and
> communication skills ... many of our undergraduate
> courses have become too narrow and overspecialized and
> do not equip the young with flexible intellects that will
> be able to adapt to changing circumstances.[13]

Under the direction of a 2006 Curriculum Commission chaired by the university's Deputy Vice Chancellor (Academic) Professor Peter McPhee, the University of Melbourne undertook the most significant reform since it was first established in 1853. The resulting Melbourne model reflects the global trend toward broader undergraduate programs followed by intense professional training at postgraduate level. In the Australian context this gives students more time to consider career choices. The new-generation degrees provide a multidisciplinary curriculum with a strong international focus. Students will experience discipline breadth as well as depth, with one-quarter of their study coming from outside their core discipline. Choices include a raft of new university breadth subjects such as Climate Change, The Internet: A Society Transformed, and Critical Thinking with Statistics and Data.

The "Melbourne Experience" (discussed in more detail later) aims to provide students with a cohort experience, building strong peer networks and encouraging close links with academic units. Students will have opportunities to build interdisciplinary, cross-cultural, and technological awareness and skills, with direct exposure to leading research and knowledge transfer projects on campus, along with opportunities for off-campus experience such as industry and community work placements and international study.

In parallel with curriculum reform, the university undertook a major review of its administrative and student services. The quality of the Melbourne student experience was a key focus of the reforms and has involved a significant reshaping of the university's services and administrative effort from a student-centric perspective. Under the Melbourne model, the individual needs of students come first, from their first contact with the university as prospective students to an ongoing relationship as alumni. The student hubs, which will be developed under the Melbourne model, will provide students with close links to their discipline areas. A "one-stop-shop" approach to administration and academic support should end students being sent from one corner of the university to another for student cards, course information, language support, or career advice. There are plans for the student centers to colocate with new learning hubs—state-of-the-art information access located where students learn—within their faculty or graduate school. The design allows for 24×7 access to places where students want to congregate to learn with their peers.

A New Role for Information Services

A university is uniquely positioned to realize the emerging opportunities offered through information and communication technologies. Within one division at Melbourne, Information Services, the university brings together information professionals, librarians, archivists, multimedia specialists, specialist academics, and information and communication technologists. The different expertise of these professional groups can be combined and applied in ways that ensure that the university realizes the potential of information and technologies. As the Growing Esteem strategy notes: "Information technology is the backbone of the university's knowledge management capability, critical to developing closer links between research and research training, learning and teaching, and knowledge transfer."[14]

The three trends outlined above—the blurring of research, learning, and teaching boundaries, changing student expectations, and standardization and integration of processes—are evident in the University of Melbourne's reshaping. The following section illustrates the tightly integrated way in which the university's strategic aims shape, and are shaped by, its information and technology strategies.

A Triple Helix Strategy: Binding the Strands Together

The Melbourne vision of a fine university can be represented as a triple helix in which sharply focused, well-supported research, teaching, and knowledge transfer remain tightly bound, each shaping and reinforcing the other. The academic mission of the university "sets priorities, structures programs, designs enterprise systems, and deploys institutional resources" to realize the talents and contributions of staff, students, sponsors, and partners.[15]

To bind the strands of the helix through information services, the concept of "e-scholarship" has been used to frame the approach. While most universities have embraced e-learning and more recently many are engaged in discussion around e-research, Melbourne's unique concept of the triple helix provides a framework for differentiation. By leveraging the capacity of information and communication technologies to provide access to scholarly data and research instruments, regardless of location, and to the necessary know-how, collaborative tools, and infrastructure, we provide the opportunity for our students and staff to be engaged in learning, research, and knowledge transfer in an integrated way. Perhaps this is best illustrated by an example.

Currently, the university's Information Services division, through its newly formed E-scholarship Research Centre, in partnership with the Faculty of Arts, is imaging and generating XML transcripts of the convict records of the Archives Office of Tasmania. It is one of the world's most comprehensive sets of records of people placed under confinement. It is a collection of great complexity, comprising more than 30,000 records that relate to 75,000 men, women, and children transported to Australia during the first half of the 19th century. The vigilance invested in controlling the penal colony was collected on paper records covering all aspects of convict lives: behavior, character, work, health, family life, and death. It is a collection requiring a high level of historical skill to use without expert assistance, so the challenge for the electronic archivist is to make this complex collection accessible so that students, researchers, or genealogists can focus on an individual convict in a wide range of collectivities (birthplace, crime, religion, personality type, work, punishment, and so forth). This information needs to be not only connected internally but also connected to other data: genealogies, family, and criminal data in place of origin, and family and public records data in the place of refuge after sentence. The faculty will be using this collection as a rich research tool, often working in partnership with other disciplines, such as population health, to mine the data. The collection will serve as a teaching tool, which provides potential opportunities for students to undertake their own research. At the same time it creates a rich knowledge transfer tool of international value.

Such a case exemplifies the opportunities to link the triple helix of research, teaching and learning, and knowledge transfer through information services, systems, and technologies. They bind the three core activities of the university in ways that enrich each of these activities.

The Role of E-Learning in the Melbourne Experience

The Melbourne model fits well with the emergence of lifelong learning and multiple careers in the changing workplaces of the 21st century. Enhanced e-learning opportunities have a significant role to play in the distinctive Melbourne Experience envisaged under the Melbourne model, given the principles underpinning the use of technologies in the new-generation curriculum. Thus, students will

- have a coordinated e-learning experience that increases in sophistication and complexity based on year level across the life of their program of study;
- develop an online portfolio to support personal and academic development;
- use e-learning environments to link to and be engaged in current research activities and programs;
- participate in e-learning experiences with diverse cohorts of students in online communities of practice, social, and learning networks; and
- use e-learning mechanisms to strategically complement, enhance, and extend their opportunities for internationalizing their learning experiences.

Enhancing the Cohort Experience

The cohort experience of students is strengthened through programs such as AIRport (Academic Interactive Resources Portal) and Postgraduate Essentials. Designed for undergraduate students, AIRport provides a plethora of interactive quizzes and activities. Importantly, though, it includes online language tutorials, designed either for specific groups within particular courses or for students whose second language is English. For many international students, online tutorial participation is much valued, for it allows time to formulate a response. As one second-year student commented, "In class, by the time I've worked out what to say and how to say it the tutor has moved on … in online tutes I find I have much more to say." In Postgraduate Essentials, research higher-degree students are able to ask questions of the online tutor and their peers in ways not always possible for students who spend long hours in labs or who may be based many kilometers from campus. The first-year online journal or blog also provides a forum for discussion for students new to university life.[16]

Managing Career Pathways

One key pedagogical driver of the Melbourne model was an under-standing that for many students, direct entry from school to a professional degree may be problematic. Advice from well-meaning teachers, friends, and parents "not to waste a high ENTER"[17] has meant many bright students follow safe and prestigious, but personally unfulfilling, career choices. Under the Melbourne model, career choices can be delayed until the end of undergraduate education. On completing a new-generation bachelor degree, a student will have the maturity and self-knowledge to make an informed career choice. Some may go immediately to employment. Others will choose to enroll in one of Melbourne's new graduate schools and pursue a professional qualification or undertake a research master's or PhD.

Under the Melbourne model, course advice takes on a much greater significance as students navigate pathways through to careers. Students will be supported to build e-portfolios recording their skills development and experience. A student may enroll in a bachelor of commerce degree program with the intention of following a career in international business. An internship with a human rights organization and success with breadth subjects in law (and the online global opportunities subject, which links students in classrooms across the world) may lead them to follow their new-generation BComm, either immediately or some years later, with a juris doctor, facilitating a pathway to a career as a lawyer specializing in human rights law.

The Melbourne model facilitates a career pathway many with old-generation degrees will recognize. Few graduates work in the jobs they anticipated when choosing subjects in year 10 with an eye to their chosen career. Under the Melbourne model, career pathways are managed and negotiated as students undertake a range of breadth studies and knowledge transfer experiences. The Melbourne model framework and its e-campus experience are made possible through the new information technologies.

The Need for Caution

Many undergraduate students have spent their entire lives surrounded by information technologies, including the Internet. This has shaped what students expect from universities, but it has also shaped assumptions we make about how our students wish to use technologies. In 2006, a study of more than 2,000 first-year students—students born after 1980—was undertaken at the University of Melbourne. Referred to as the *Kennedy study,* it examined students' access to, use of, and proficiency with a wide range of information and communication technologies and tools.[18] (It in part mirrored ECAR studies undertaken in the United States.) The Kennedy study found that students were overwhelmingly positive about the use of information and communication technologies to support their studies. More than 90 percent use computers for general study and to search for information, and more than 80 percent use the learning management system and use technology for general course administration activities. Ninety percent of students had unrestricted access to a desktop computer and more than 70 percent had broadband Internet access.

Yet the Kennedy study also demonstrated distinct patterns of access based on gender, background (for example, international students used technologies more frequently), and discipline area. There was sufficient evidence to negate the argument of a one-size-fits-all approach. Kennedy notes that "we need to think carefully about how we can use particular 'core' and 'emerging' technologies to support learning in higher education, given the known diversity of experiences, attitudes, and expectations of students."[19]

Information and communication technologies are already used extensively to enrich the on-campus student teaching and learning experience. The study undertaken by Kennedy underlines the need to consider carefully how best to enrich the teaching and learning experience through technologies.

These findings confirm those of the 2006 ECAR study that students overwhelmingly wish to use technology to increase convenience. Nearly 84 percent want to use the web for student services such as to enroll, sign up for classes, and pay fees, yet 80.9 percent also want to use the web to access a learning portal. Given the desire of students to use technology to increase convenience, the University of Melbourne, as part of its strategy to enhance the quality of the student experience, plans to automate all student transactional processes. Achieved over the next few years, such automation will ensure consistent, integrated, convenient, and cost-effective service delivery. The university will also seek to increase the use of information and technologies in student enrichment. This approach not only enriches the quality of the student experience but leads to standardization and automation of core business processes, thus increasing the university's ability to innovate and be agile.

Ensuring We Have the IT Infrastructure to Support the Melbourne Model

Enhancing the expectations of the Melbourne Experience is a noble goal, but it also carries risks. To succeed, the Melbourne model requires an agile and responsive system. Standards and consistency in core processes are an imperative, not an option. As Craig Barrett, CEO of Intel, notes: "When you have common interfaces, common protocols, everyone can innovate and everyone can interoperate. Companies can build their businesses, consumers can expand their choices, the technology moves forward faster, and users get more benefit."[20]

Like many Australian higher education institutions, a long-established distribution of decision-making authority at the University of Melbourne reflects presumptions of academic autonomy and is reinforced by budget practices. As a result, faculties and departments have adopted different and sometimes incompatible systems and technologies for their research and teaching. Such devolution of decision making and expenditure contributes to inconsistency in quality and offerings of IT services to students and staff, duplication and increased risk, poor value for the money invested, and an inability to prioritize investment in IT to achieve the best outcomes. Despite some significant local investment, the objective quality of user support remains low. There had been a growing recognition of the importance of investing in university core systems and infrastructure. Over the last five years the university has replaced all of its core enterprise systems, with the final system, the student management system project, due to be completed in mid-2008.

In recognition of benefits to be gained from a common IT infra-structure and digitized business processes, the university embarked on an IT shared-services project in 2006. This initiative acknowledged the importance of taking a university-wide view of IT in order to balance quality, cost, and risk for the university as a whole and balance the trade-off between local agility and the consistency required for high-quality, reasonable-cost services and to facilitate collaboration. Figure 1 illustrates the thinking underpinning this approach.

Some progress has been made toward implementing common systems and processes, largely through investment in common enterprise systems on a project-by-project basis, coupled with implementation of appropriate methodologies such as the ITIL and Prince2. However, only limited progress has been made on business process integration and standardization. In a highly devolved organization, technologies that imply organizational change are particularly challenging.

As Indiana University CIO Brad Wheeler notes: "For many institu-

Figure 1. Toward a Strategically Unified Information Future

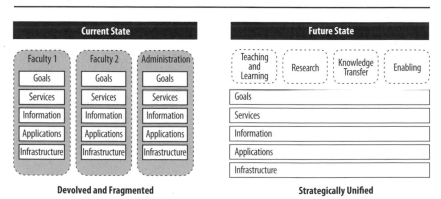

Current State			Future State

Devolved and Fragmented   **Strategically Unified**

tions, this [shared services] is a chicken-and-egg situation where the money to provide shared services is in the research projects and schools who may prefer the use of university infrastructure, but can't trust it until it exists. It can't exist if the money isn't aggregated to fund it."[21]

Over the coming years, the University of Melbourne will use the concepts developed around the new student services model to continue its journey toward being an IT savvy organization. By focusing on enhancing the quality of the student experience, automating core processes, and enhancing enrichment services through targeted use of information technologies, the university will build critical IT foundations and business capability. Over time, this approach will be applied to all university core processes, with the aim of being an exemplar in interlocking its business and IT practices and competencies.

Summary

In many ways, the history of higher education in Australia has been shaped by isolation from the rest of the world. Australia's first universities were staffed by academics wooed from the mother country with promises of opportunity—fueled by the discovery of gold. In architecture (the "sandstones" of Australia's Group of Eight) and curricula, the first Australian universities followed the models of Oxford and Cambridge.

Thanks to IT, Australia is isolated no longer, and U.K. universities no longer dominate world higher education rankings. If Melbourne is to fulfill its aim to be one of the world's finest universities, it must respond to global educational challenges. Through its Growing Esteem strategy, the University of Melbourne signals an intention to remain a leading education provider in the 21st century. The Melbourne model brings closer alignment to global changes in the sector while establishing a pioneering higher education model for Australia. The strategy has received bipartisan political support, with government and opposition alike recognizing the need for domestic diversity if the sector is to compete globally.

Growing Esteem posits a university understood as three intertwined activities—research and research training, teaching and learning, and knowledge transfer. Each relies on IT, and the overall strategy requires enterprise systems to bind together the strands. Like other universities, Melbourne is part of an academic world with blurred boundaries around the development of new knowledge, proliferation of technologically fueled, new ways of communicating, and recognition that an agile institution paradoxically needs standardized systems to enable collaboration. The vision presented in Growing Esteem embraces information technologies as the essential platform for a successful contemporary university.

Endnotes

1. The University of Melbourne is ranked number 1 in Australia for research income (Australian Department of Education, Science and Training 2007) and is one of only two Australian universities ranked in the top 100 in the international *Shanghai Jiao Tong* index: University of Melbourne is ranked 79th, Australian National University is ranked 57th. (The Department of Education, Science and Training is now the Department of Education, Employment and Workplace Relations.)

2. The name *Growing Esteem* comes from the University's motto, *postera crescam laude*, from Horace's famous ode. A common translation is "I shall grow in the esteem of future generations."

3. "Dreamlarge" is the campaign theme chosen to promote the university's vision.

4. "HEd diversity offers choice—Harvard expert," *UniNews* 15, no. 13 (2007), http://uninews.unimelb.edu.au/articleid_3536.html.

5. Simon Marginson and Marijk van der Wende, *Globalization and Higher Education* (Paris: Organisation for Economic Co-operation and Development, 2007), http://www.cshe.unimelb.edu.au/people/staff_pages/Marginson/OECD-Globalisation&HigherEd.pdf.

6. Simon Marginson, "Global Setting, National Policy and Higher Education in 2007" (paper presented at Education, Science and the Future of Australia, a CSHE seminar series on policy, at the University of Melbourne, July 9, 2007).

7. Marginson and van der Wende, op. cit.

8. Brian L. Hawkins and Diana Oblinger, "IT Myths: The Myth about IT as a Utility," *EDUCAUSE Review* (July/August 2007): 11.

9. Chris Dede, "Introduction: A Sea Change in Thinking, Knowing, Learning, and Teaching," in *The ECAR Study of Undergraduate Students and Information Technology, 2007* (Research Study, Vol. 6), Gail Salaway and Judith Borreson Caruso, with Mark R. Nelson (Boulder, CO: EDUCAUSE Center for Applied Research, 2007), 25, available from http://www.educause.edu/ir/library/pdf/ers0706/rs/ers07062.pdf.

10. Gail Salaway, Richard N. Katz, and Judith Borreson Caruso, with Robert B. Kvavik and Mark R. Nelson, *The ECAR Study of Undergraduate Students and Information Technology, 2006* (Research Study, Vol. 7) (Boulder, CO: EDUCAUSE Center for Applied Research, 2006), available from http://connect.educause.edu/Library/ECAR/TheECARStudyofUndergradua/41172.

11. Jeanne W. Ross, Peter Weill, and David C. Robertson, *Enterprise Architecture as Strategy* (Cambridge: Harvard Business School Press, 2006).

12. Peter Weill, Stephanie Woerner, Sinan Aral, and Anne Johnson, *Becoming More IT Savvy and Why It Matters* (Research Briefing, No. VII–1D)

(Cambridge, MA: Center for Information Systems Research, MIT Sloan School of Management, 2007).

13. Quoted in *Growing Esteem: The 2007 University Plan* (Victoria, Australia: The University of Melbourne, 2007), 15, http://growingesteem.unimelb.edu .au/2007universityplan/index.html.

14. Ibid, 23.

15. University of Melbourne, *The University of Melbourne Plan: A Strategic Overview* (Victoria, Australia: The University of Melbourne, 2007), http:// www.unimelb.edu.au/publications/docs/2007UniPlan_StrategicOverview.pdf.

16. For more information about these programs, see https://airport.unimelb .edu.au/ for AIRport; http://www.sgs.unimelb.edu.au/prog_services/ programs/pge/ for Postgraduate Essentials; and http://www.services.unimelb .edu.au/transition/starting/blog.html for the first-year online journal or blog.

17. The Equivalent National Tertiary (Higher) Education Entrance Rank, or ENTER, is the percentage score out of 100 awarded to students completing high school study.

18. Gregor Kennedy, "Digital Natives + Others = First Year Student Experience" (paper presented at EDUCAUSE Australasia 2007, Melbourne, Australia, April 29–May 2, 2007), http://www.caudit.edu.au/ educauseaustralasia07/authors_papers/Kennedy.ppt.

19. Ibid., slide 24.

20. Quoted in *An E-Research Strategic Framework: Interim Report of the e-Research Coordinating Committee* (Canberra, Australia: Australian Government, 2005), 20. For the original interview, see http://www.intel.com/standards/execqa/qa0904.htm.

21. Brad Wheeler, "Leading Beyond the ICT Conundrums for Scholarship 2.0" (paper presented at EDUCAUSE Australasia 2007, Melbourne, Australia, April 29–May 2, 2007), 4, http://www.caudit.edu.au/educasueaustralasia07/ authors_papers/Wheeler.ppt.

Bibliography

Dede, Chris. "Introduction: A Sea Change in Thinking, Knowing, Learning, and Teaching." In Gail Salaway and Judith Borreson Caruso, with Mark R. Nelson, *The ECAR Study of Undergraduate Students and Information Technology, 2007* (Research Study, Vol. 6). Boulder, CO: EDUCAUSE Center for Applied Research, 2007, available from http://www.educause.edu/ir/library/pdf/ ers0706/rs/ers07062.pdf.

E-Research Coordinating Committee. *An E-Research Strategic Framework: Interim Report of the E-Research Coordinating Committee.* Canberra: Australian Government, 2005.

Hawkins, Brian L., and Diana G. Oblinger. "IT Myths: The Myth about IT as a Utility." *EDUCAUSE Review* (July/August 2007): 11–12.

"HEd Diversity Offers Choice—Harvard Expert." *UniNews* 15, no. 13 (July 24–August 7, 2007). http://uninews.unimelb.edu.au/articleid_3536.html.

Kennedy, Gregor. "Digital Natives + Others = First Year Student Experience." Paper presented at EDUCAUSE Australasia 2007, Melbourne, Australia, April 29–May 2, 2007. http://www.caudit.edu.au/educasueaustralasia07/authors_papers/Kennedy.ppt.

Marginson, Simon. "Global Setting, National Policy and Higher Education in 2007." Paper presented at Education, Science and the Future of Australia, a CSHE seminar series on policy, at the University of Melbourne, July 9, 2007.

Marginson, Simon, and Marijk van der Wende. *Globalization and Higher Education.* Paris: Organisation for Economic Co-operation and Development, 2007. http://www.cshe.unimelb.edu.au/people/staff_pages/Marginson/OECD-Globalisation&HigherEd.pdf

Ross, Jeanne W., Peter Weill, and David C. Robertson. *Enterprise Architecture as Strategy.* Cambridge: Harvard Business School Press, 2006.

Salaway, Gail, Richard N. Katz, and Judith Borreson Caruso, with Robert B. Kvavik and Mark R. Nelson. *The ECAR Study of Undergraduate Students and Information Technology, 2006* (Research Study, Vol. 7). Boulder, CO: EDUCAUSE Center for Applied Research, 2006. http://connect.educause.edu/Library/ECAR/TheECARStudyofUndergradua/41172.

University of Melbourne. *Growing Esteem: The 2007 University Plan.* Victoria, Australia: The University of Melbourne, 2007. http://growingesteem.unimelb.edu.au/2007universityplan/index.html.

University of Melbourne. *The University of Melbourne Plan: A Strategic Overview.* Victoria, Australia: The University of Melbourne, 2007. http://www.unimelb.edu.au/publications/docs/2007UniPlan_StrategicOverview.pdf.

Weill, Peter, Stephanie Woerner, Sinan Aral, and Anne Johnson. *Becoming More IT Savvy and Why It Matters* (Research Briefing, No. VII–1D). Cambridge, MA: Center for Information Systems Research, MIT Sloan School of Management, 2007.

Wheeler, Brad. "Leading Beyond the ICT Conundrums for Scholarship 2.0." Paper presented at EDUCAUSE Australasia 2007, Melbourne, Australia, April 29–May 2, 2007. http://www.caudit.edu.au/educasueaustralasia07/authors_papers/Wheeler.ppt.

Higher Education and the Future of U.S. Competitiveness[1]

David Attis

C ompetitiveness has become a buzzword recently. Nearly every day in the press we read accounts of "America's competitiveness crisis," our "innovation shortfall," or how the United States is "losing its edge." A growing number of Americans from all walks of life and all political persuasions worry that the rise of emerging economies threatens our continuing prosperity. These concerns have led to a flood of reports during the past few years charting America's putative decline and proposing a range of solutions.

The need for action—and the recent sense of urgency—was neatly crystallized by Thomas Friedman's 2005 book *The World Is Flat.* As incomes have stagnated, many have pointed the finger at offshoring, seeing in the rapid rise of India and China the explanation for the struggles of working Americans.

The Changing Competitive Environment

The global competitiveness environment has indeed changed dramatically during the past decade. As the smoke from the Internet boom cleared, Americans began to notice that other countries had made tremendous gains in science and technology, dramatically narrowing America's historic lead. China has pulled ahead of the United States in high-technology exports, and U.S. trade in advanced technology has fallen into deficit. The European Union now generates more scientific publications and graduates more PhDs in science than the United States. China graduates nearly three times as many four-year degrees in engineering, computer science, and IT and is projected to graduate more PhDs in science and engineering by 2010.[2]

In many ways, this is simply the consequence of our own success. Throughout the 1990s, other countries recognized and began to imitate the U.S. model of economic growth—improving access to higher education, increasing government investment in R&D, and lowering barriers to trade and investment. At the same time, multinational corporations (often led by American companies) accelerated their globalization, both to gain access to the enormous and rapidly growing consumer markets in emerging economies and to tap into overseas talent pools. Not only have call centers, accounting departments, and other back-office functions been reorganized globally, but even R&D can now be performed all over the world. America's unique advantages are no longer so unique.

In an effort to address these concerns, political leaders in both parties have taken up the banner of competitiveness. And these days, competitiveness means science, technology, and innovation. In his 2006 State of the Union address, President Bush launched his American Competitiveness Initiative, explaining, "By investing in research and development, unleashing the innovative spirit of America's entrepreneurs, and making sure that our economy has workers highly skilled in math and science, we will lay the foundation for lasting economic prosperity."[3] Legislation with these goals passed both houses of Congress with bipartisan support in 2007.[4]

The Council on Competitiveness released *Innovate America*, the report of our National Innovation Initiative, in December 2004. Our report contained more than 80 recommendations, not just for the federal government but also for companies, universities, and state and local governments. It was designed to address the entire innovation ecosystem. Recent legislative proposals, however, have focused on five main areas: increased federal funding for basic research (especially in the physical sciences), more support for K–12 science education (especially teacher training), better incentives for graduate education in the sciences, increased high-skills immigration, and making permanent the tax credit for corporate investment in R&D.

While there is a pretty broad consensus that these are all good things to do, on their own they are by no means sufficient to achieve the results that policy makers desire. They are all based on the assumption that increasing the inputs to innovation (R&D spending, scientists, and engineers) will generate a corresponding increase in outputs. Higher education—the performer of the vast majority of basic research and the source of new scientists and engineers—plays a central but rarely explicit role in the discussion. It is the black box that magically transforms federal research dollars and high school seniors into U.S. prosperity. For this reason, the next phase of the competitiveness debate must look inside the black box and attempt to understand how our colleges and universities can better promote innovation.

Enabling Innovation

While most people accept (and econometric evidence supports) the contention that federal R&D funding contributes to U.S. economic growth, in a global innovation environment it is no longer true that basic research performed in the United States will necessarily benefit American firms or American workers. Rather, the economic benefits depend on the degree to which universities (together with entrepreneurs, venture capitalists, and corporations) can translate the results of basic research into marketable innovations. The benefits now also depend on how corporations choose to commercialize and produce those innovations through global networks. Doing the research here no longer necessarily means that the technologies, the factories, or the jobs will be created here.

This is not to say that federal R&D spending is a waste of money, but it does force us to think about the mechanisms by which such funding promotes innovation in the United States. If knowledge is universal, why should it matter where it is produced? Geographical origin may not matter from the perspective of a peer review panel, but a large amount of scholarship has shown that from the perspective of someone trying to commercialize knowledge, place does matter. Venture capital, for example, is highly localized, and innovative activity tends to "spill over" from universities to the regions that surround them.

The main reason is that tacit knowledge—the kind of knowledge that cannot be captured explicitly in publications or patents—is often the most valuable kind of knowledge. Cutting-edge scientific and technical knowledge is embodied in people more than in machines or equations. And it flows through informal networks that tend to be highly concentrated in specific locations. As regional economic development expert Randall Kempner likes to say, "Innovation is a contact sport." And the lesson from economic geographers and regional economic developers is that it is the personal connections between academics, corporate researchers, entrepreneurs, and venture capitalists that enable innovation. These networks are very difficult to copy and can take decades to evolve.

What does this mean for higher education? It means that the degree to which higher education contributes to innovation depends not just on the level of inputs but perhaps even more strongly on how the people at educational institutions engage with the outside world, particularly within their region. This is an area in which government policies play very little role and where individual institutions are struggling to find better ways to encourage new forms of behavior. It requires a rethinking of how faculty are rewarded and how students are educated.

More Than a Numbers Game

It has become an article of faith among CEOs that America currently has a shortage of scientists and engineers. And many of the recent policy proposals include mechanisms to encourage more Americans to go into science and engineering. Proponents of this view point to difficulties in filling technical positions (particularly those that require American citizenship due to security restrictions), declining enrollment in science and engineering programs, looming waves of retirement among baby boomer scientists, and the fact that the entire annual supply of H1-B visas (for highly skilled immigrants) is used on the first day they become available.

The underlying assumption is that companies are desperate for people with the type of clearly defined scientific knowledge and technical skills indicated by a PhD, but at the same time, companies say that the skills they find most valuable—collaboration, communication, creative problem solving—are not typically found in science and engineering graduates. While the public debate has focused on the need for technical skills, it is the nontechnical skills that are often the hardest to find. (Increasingly so, as the number of technical graduates around the world increases exponentially.) Innovation, these companies realize, depends on more than science and technology. It requires a hard-to-define, and perhaps even harder-to-teach, ability to transform science and technology into products and services that customers can use.

As countries around the world have improved science education, increased their investment in R&D, and encouraged global corporations to invest in high-technology manufacturing or research, an ever broader range of science and technology capabilities have essentially become commodities. High-tech manufacturing, qualified engineers, PhD researchers, and advanced laboratory facilities are now widely available around the world. On their own these factors no longer provide the competitive advantage they once conferred. As a result, national governments now obsessively pursue innovation and creativity in an attempt to define a new niche.

Yet the debate in the United States continues to focus on graduating ever greater numbers of scientists and engineers as the key to increasing U.S. competitiveness. While we must continue to improve standards and encourage more students to study science and engineering, we need to acknowledge that we will never win the race to produce the highest test scores or the most engineers. Simple demographics dictates that we will never outproduce China in engineers. But that does not mean that America's innovation capacity is doomed. The best test-takers do not always make the best innovators, and a range of countries with high test scores—such as Japan, Singapore, Korea, and China—are increasingly worried that their educational systems stress conformity at the expense of creativity. The challenge is not to train the most scientists and engineers but to train the scientists and engineers (and artists and anthropologists and managers) who are best able to work within the global innovation system to create valuable new products and services.

Two examples illustrate the types of higher education challenges that go beyond simply increasing funding or graduation rates for scientists and engineers.

Like most institutions, Georgia Tech was facing declining enrollment in computer science and its graduates were facing increasing competition from highly skilled and significantly cheaper graduates in emerging economies. They were struggling to redefine the relevance of a computer science degree. One employer remarked, "Don't send me engineers who can be duplicated by a computer. I am sending that work to India. Send me engineers who are adaptable, who can think across disciplines." Georgia Tech remade their computer science curriculum using the concept of "threads" (http://www.cc.gatech.edu/education/undergrad/bscs/the-8-threads). A computer science major now consists of two threads out of eight possible options—Foundations, Embodiment, Intelligence, Computational Modeling, Platforms, Information Internetworking, People, and Media. Each thread defines a problem—how can people interact with machines, how can computers simulate natural phenomena—that provides a context and a meaning for individual computer science courses as well as courses from other departments such as anthropology or design. The goal is both to keep students engaged and to help them develop the skills that will enable them to solve real-world problems.

Another example is the Professional Science Master's degree, a two-year master's degree that combines graduate-level courses in science or mathematics with skills-based coursework in management, policy, law, or other subjects (http://www.sciencemasters.com). Rather than training academic researchers, the program is intended to cultivate practitioners with advanced technical skills but also with communication, collaboration, and leadership skills. Each degree program is focused on a specific niche—such as applied genomics, computational chemistry, or food safety and toxicology—developed with input from industry and typically tailored closely to the needs of a local industry. The goal is to identify the skills demanded by innovative companies rather than to simply turn out more PhDs.

The same forces that demand a rethinking of science and engineering education are also reshaping the demand for skills from the broader population. The global proliferation of information technology has enabled a "trade in tasks" that opens more and more American workers to potential foreign competition. But those pundits who focus exclusively on offshoring often fail to recognize that its effects are often dwarfed by the impact of automation. The American call center worker is more likely to lose his or her job to IVR (interactive voice response) technology than to an offshore call center. Both offshoring and automation enable routine tasks to be performed at a lower cost, reducing the value of jobs structured around routine tasks but increasing the value of jobs that require more complex tasks that cannot easily be automated or offshored. The salient distinction is not necessarily between those with more or less education but between those whose work can be replaced by a computer or someone far away using a computer versus those whose productivity is enhanced by a computer.[5]

The irony is that our education policy emphasizes standardized testing at precisely the moment when anything that can be standardized can be done more efficiently by a computer or outside the United States. The 2006 Spellings Commission on the Future of Higher Education extended this mass production metaphor to the world of colleges and universities. Expanding access, increasing quality, and improving accountability are all important—even essential—goals for higher education, but turning out a larger number of graduates according to some minimum specification will not address the most important challenges that we face as a nation.

Conclusion

If innovation were simply a numbers game, our future would indeed be bleak, but the strength of U.S. higher education has always been more than sheer numbers of graduates. America's phenomenal economic success has rested in large part on the dynamism of our economy, driven by the creativity, innovativeness, and entrepreneurialism of our students and faculty. That is our competitive advantage and it is our greatest hope in a world of more nearly equal competitors.

Recent debates about America's competitiveness have resulted in some very insightful analysis and many useful proposals, but they tend to rest on the mistaken assumption that we can spend ourselves out of this problem. Asking how much the federal government should spend on basic R&D or how many scientists and engineers we need are the wrong questions. We should instead be asking how research can drive regional and national competitiveness, what skills students need to contribute to innovation and, ultimately, how higher education can support American competitiveness.

Endnotes

1. This essay was developed as part of the Innovation Universities initiative of the Council on Competitiveness. I would like to thank Deborah Wince-Smith, Deborah Van Opstal, and Sam Leiken for their guidance and Maura Mondelli for research support.

2. Council on Competitiveness, *Competitiveness Index: Where America Stands* (February 2007), http://www.compete.org/publications/detail/357/competitiveness-index-where-america-stands.

3. Domestic Policy Council, Office of Science and Technology Policy, "American Competitiveness Initiative: Leading the World in Innovation," February 2006, http://www.whitehouse.gov/stateoftheunion/2006/aci.

4. The America Creating Opportunities to Meaningfully Promote Excellence in Technology, Education, and Science Act (COMPETES), H.R. 2272, was signed into law by President Bush on August 9, 2007.

5. See Frank Levy and Richard J. Murnane, *The New Division of Labor: How Computers Are Creating the Next Job Market* (Princeton, NJ: Princeton University Press, 2005).

Bibliography

Council on Competitiveness. *Competitiveness Index: Where America Stands.* February 2007. http://www.compete.org/publications/detail/357/competitiveness-index-where-america-stands.

Domestic Policy Council, Office of Science and Technology Policy. "American Competitiveness Initiative: Leading the World in Innovation." February 2006. http://www.whitehouse.gov/stateoftheunion/2006/aci.

Levy, Frank, and Richard J. Murnane. *The New Division of Labor: How Computers Are Creating the Next Job Market.* Princeton, NJ: Princeton University Press, 2005.

Trinity College, Dublin

Accountability

The Social Compact of Higher Education and Its Public[1]

Larry Faulkner

Acompact is such a civilized idea. It evokes an atmosphere of amicability and trust—the community interest placed foremost, everyone honorable, no accountability needed. The idea of a compact creates a far different image from a treaty, or even a contract. Indeed, most of us like to think of the time when there was a social compact concerning higher education. The real questions for today are whether one ever existed, whether "compact" is just a label for our wistfulness for a simpler era, whether anything like a compact can be fashioned in our time.

There is not much doubt that wishful nostalgia is involved. The turbulence of our times makes it natural for us to desire escape from the daily pressures of striving to deliver on higher education's promise in a contentious, ever questioning world. It is also easy to imagine that a compact existed during simpler, better times—probably in the 1960s, before things got too complicated. And there is not much doubt that we are being poetic when we speak of a compact. In given local settings, there might have been brief, fairly formal understandings about how higher education would conduct its business and how it would be supported, but we are not really speaking of a relationship in which the responsibilities were delineated in a specific way.

But recognizing all of these limits, something does seem to have been lost. Somewhere in our recent past, there was an atmosphere of amicability and trust. The community interest was generally placed foremost. The players were mostly honorable. And by today's standards, elaborate accountability was not needed. What was the "something"? It was a broadly shared frame for doing business, a persistent cultural environment in which advances could be made. Let's call it a social compact, for short.

The roots of this social compact are easily found in American history.

Origins of the Compact

Clark Kerr argued that two forces molded the modern American university system and made it distinctive: the land grant movement and federal support of scientific research during World War II and afterward.[2] I would add a third: the GI Bill.

The Morrill Act of 1862 does merit placement as the centerpiece, because it changed the stage on which American universities, both public and private, would develop over the next hundred years. Central to the impact of this law were its immense scale and its inherently egalitarian, populist nature. Over time, these qualities drove American society to redefine the goal of higher education, which became, in Kerr's words, "to serve less the perpetuation of an elite class and more the creation of a relatively classless society, with the doors of opportunity open to all through education."[3]

The Morrill Act also made universities responsible for the creation of new knowledge in service to the larger society and established a basis for a new habit of extending knowledge-based support into the daily work and life of the society. Through the Morrill Act, research became a mission of public universities—and, essentially simultaneously, a mission of private institutions, as well. Thus, 1862 dates the partnership between universities and the federal government to establish the platform for fundamental and applied research in the United States. The act also defined a role for universities in public service. As Kerr notes, the act "created a new social force in world history. Nowhere before had universities been so closely linked with the daily life of so much of their societies."[4]

The Second World War modified the social contract and sowed the seeds for its eventual failure. The urgency and technological nature of the war created a need for tremendous expansion of the national research capacity, setting the stage for research to play a much larger part in the higher education mission. Research would become linked in the public mind with national and local economic viability. In addition, the GI Bill aggressively encouraged a generation of young people to build a future through college education. They took up the opportunity in droves and became the well-educated, pragmatic, innovative workforce that powered America to global leadership in so many spheres during their working years. The GI Bill changed the nation's view of what a college education could mean and dramatically increased the share of families who defined a collegiate experience as essential for their children.

Out of these roots grew a uniquely American concept of how higher education should operate and how it should be financed:

- Essentially, all high school graduates should have broad access to local and flagship public institutions, as well as to private institutions of varying character. Elite, selective private institutions could be exceptions.
- Tuition and fees for undergraduate education at local and flagship public institutions should be so low that a student working a half-time job could pay them while also handling living costs.
- The states would finance the institutions' educational programs sufficiently to generate needed capacity and to keep tuition and fees to negligible levels.
- Private donors would help independent institutions keep their tuition and fees within an affordable range.
- The national universities would recruit faculties capable of forming the core research base for the nation.
- Research would be financed by the federal government, private foundations, and interested corporations, while state government would provide infrastructure, particularly physical facilities.
- Graduate programs would be sustained by using students as apprentices in research and in the teaching of undergraduates.
- Outreach would be financed in ways particular to the nature of the endeavor: cooperative extension in a federal–state partnership; off-campus instruction by the states or through tuition and fees; other efforts piggybacked on mainstream teaching and research programs.

The Demise of the Compact

What has become of the compact? Our very success has upset it. Nowadays, higher education is perceived by nearly everyone to be essential for individual economic viability, and its institutions are centerpieces for the national research effort and for national and local economic and social renewal. Our universities have become taproots of vitality, and the public knows it. Just as war is too important to be left to the generals, the work of universities has become far too important to be left to those who make the universities work daily. And the stakes have made us rougher players, too. The loss of amicability is not just a phenomenon of the outside. The compact failed because it could not be sustained in changed times. Here are some of the reasons:

- Under the press of eligible students, many institutions had to restrict admissions, so they were no longer broadly accessible to high school graduates. As public institutions become more selective, the public sees them as less relevant to their family interests.
- State government, faced with demands to address crime, health care, and other immediate social needs, began to recognize the private benefit of a collegiate education and began to back away from full subsidy.
- The demands of the research enterprise began to raise the cost of faculty talent and alter the economics of teaching. In addition, the rapid expansion of research as a fraction of overall effort taxed the capital capacity of institutions and states.
- The old funding patterns gave way as the federal government took a role in financing undergraduate education, as the state governments became more aggressive about research, and as private support began to be sought and received by public institutions. As responsibilities have blurred, distinctions have become less compelling.
- Regulatory requirements became enormous.
- The general erosion of public confidence in institutions, beginning in the 1960s, finally reached higher education with full impact.

The symptoms of an unsustainable public environment for higher education lie before us. They are obvious and fearsome:

- For two decades or more, we have experienced a steady, global erosion of appropriated state support. In the 1970s, state general revenue appropriations covered 85% of the core academic costs (faculty salaries, operating costs of academic units, core administration). Today, they cover about a third, and the share falls every year.
- There have been huge rises in tuition and fees, with no moderation in sight.
- Mean-spirited remarks by officeholders, once rare, have become common.
- There seems also to be a loss of trust cutting two ways. Many public officials and segments of the general public doubt that university leaders and university faculty really are interested in students, parents, and the health of their society. Folks close to educational institutions, including their large body of close supporters, question whether legislators and other state leaders have any commitment to educational quality or to the future beyond the next election.

Establishing a New Compact

Can we revive the compact? No, we can't. Not the old one. It was rooted in a simpler, less plural America, one with fewer voices, fewer challengers, fewer urgencies, fewer hopes. It was also based on the fact that higher education, while important, was not too important.

So the old compact is gone, just as are other things from a bygone era. Does it matter, really? Is it worthwhile to spend time talking more about this? I think it is, precisely because the universities and their work are so important to the health of our nation. We need rules that create a healthier environment for the public business of higher education. We need a new compact.

Establishing one is much easier said than done, not least because there is no one to define the public side of the compact. And because that is true, the responsibility for changing the environment rests with the leadership of American higher education. A new compact depends, I think, on an ambitious five-point agenda.

First, we must work to rebuild a broad understanding in the larger society and its leadership of what our institutions do and how they establish—through their several missions—public benefits for a healthier present and future. To a remarkable extent, folks see only one mission when they look at us. To a very great fraction of the public, we are strictly about undergraduate education. To other stakeholders, we are about research and occasionally about graduate education. To others, our mission may be athletics, the arts, agricultural extension, regional economic development, libraries, or cultural preservation. The power of America's institutions of higher education lies in the total of what we do and how our parts fit together. Because the public and public leadership are not grasping that reality, they become frustrated by our segmented financial picture—about "why resources over there can't be used for my concern"—and they see us as afflicted by a foolish lack of focus. Related is the loss of recognition for higher education's contribution to the common good. Over the past three decades, our work has been largely redefined in the public mind as yielding mainly private benefits, in the form of undergraduate and professional degrees having personal economic value. This one misconception is central to the erosion of support from state legislatures across the nation.

Second, we must work to restore trust that we are genuinely committed to serving our students and our larger society and that we work daily with competence and quality. With public leaders and elected officials, we have to do a better job of establishing regular contacts, engaging in honest, mutual development of long-term and short-term goals, frankly discussing financial trade-offs, and reinforcing the balance of missions that we must undertake. Greater texture is needed in the relationships, especially with key leaders. We must at the same time recognize that public leaders have many mouths to feed. To build trust with the public at large, we need to *sponsor* accountability, not just accept it grudgingly. We ought to help to define indices of performance that make sense, and we should help to found a credible reporting center. We need to be forthright about shortcomings, and we ought to embrace a culture of continuous improvement.

Third, we must work with public leaders and among ourselves to establish sound, credible mechanisms for continuing the national tradition of ready financial access to higher education by middle-class students. This is a serious problem, and it needs attention now. I believe that a solution can be achieved. That solution could also become the central point on which a new social compact is founded. The key is to strive for a consensus among public leaders and the leaders of higher education concerning a target for the out-of-pocket academic cost of attendance at public institutions of various kinds as a fraction of median family income. This is what matters to people, and this is what will determine the evolution of public policy concerning higher education. Note the focus here. The conversation should be about what people actually have to pay to go to school. It should not be conflated with the student's living costs, which can be addressed in various ways and may not be limiting to opportunity. If there are scholarship or grant programs, or if tax benefits exist, or if there are habits of discounting, these factors should be reflected in the out-of-pocket academic cost. If consensus on the target can be achieved, the annual discussion with all participants— administrations, students, parents, governing boards, and government officials—can be consistently pointed toward realizing it through actions that are much more thoughtful and concerted than today's. In the United States, the states will continue to have the definitive role in this regard. A stable, healthy pattern can be achieved only if legislatures and governors make a sustained commitment to affordability with quality.

The fourth imperative is to find a way to make a college education seem essential and more reachable to the parents of the most talented students from lower-income families. Too many of our students leave high school prematurely, do not grasp the value of a college education to their future, and do not believe us when we say that we can make college financially possible. We in higher education must develop a more coordinated, more effective strategy to reach talented students from lower-income families. Here are two critical points:

1. Families have to be recruited as well as students. The attitude of impossibility runs deeper than the student. In particular, we need to help families understand how the financial demands of a higher education can be addressed. We need to simplify the packaging of the finances. They are typically much too complex now to inspire confidence from these families, who are mistrustful of promises and debt.

2. Educators need to identify strong talent earlier in the education process. Research shows that decisions about going to college are generally made before high school or early in high school.

Finally, we must address costs. More specifically, we must mount serious, effective efforts to limit the rate of growth in the educational cost per student. It is in the range of 4.5 percent per year, a substantially inflationary figure, but more important, a figure significantly larger than the long-term growth rate of the economy. It is very likely that a growth rate of 4.5 percent cannot be sustained indefinitely. While we can reduce the growth rate of costs by degrading quality, that is not the answer. We need to look for ways to take that growth rate down while sustaining quality so that whatever advances are made along that line can become broadly shared among us. This is a hard task, but it is important for stability of our mission and our work. It merits serious initiative, both collaborative and local.

Conclusion

At the establishment of the Republic of Texas, Mirabeau B. Lamar, the Republic's second president, proposed the creation of two universities. He declared these institutions to be foundations for the future. And people followed him. The Congress dedicated public land for the vision. Lawmakers of that time were looking far beyond the unrelieved crudeness of their immediate world, not just to a more pleasant, more prosperous home, but literally to the vision of a fresh, vigorous civilization. And that required the resources of universities. They believed that a university would become a social engine of great common value. That view took root and grew strongly for another 150 years. They were asking, "How can we create institutions of higher learning that will educate and transform our state?" and not "How can I get my niece on the short list for admission?" Sometime in the past two or three decades, the emphasis has shifted from the common good to individual benefit. There is nothing inherently wrong with self-interest, of course, but it cannot be the foundation of what higher education is about.

Is anyone looking out for the common good? Those of us in the academy are, and we need to tell that story. Our continuing obligation is to give this and future generations the discipline to take a longer, fuller view. Surely such a wish is not quixotic, because we know from our own history that such discipline existed and was sustained in public life in America and is increasingly being sustained throughout the world.

Endnotes

1. Adapted from Larry R. Faulkner, "The Changing Relationship between Higher Education and the States" (The 2005 Robert H. Atwell Distinguished Lecture, delivered at the 87th Annual Meeting of the American Council on Education, Washington, DC, 2005), http://www.utexas.edu/president/past/faulkner/speeches/ace_021305.html.

2. Clark Kerr, *The Uses of the University* (Cambridge, MA: Harvard University Press, 1963).

3. Clark Kerr, *The Uses of the University,* 3rd ed. (Cambridge, MA: Harvard University Press, 1982), 47.

4. Ibid., 47.

Bibliography

Faulkner, Larry R. "The Changing Relationship between Higher Education and the States." The 2005 Robert H. Atwell Distinguished Lecture, delivered at the 87th Annual Meeting of the American Council on Education, Washington, DC, 2005. http://www.utexas.edu/president/past/faulkner/speeches/ace_021305.html.

Kerr, Clark. *The Uses of the University.* Cambridge, MA: Harvard University Press, 1963 and 1982.

Accountability, Demands for Information, and the Role of the Campus IT Organization

Brian L. Hawkins

Higher education is encountering unprecedented pressure for accountability from both internal and external constituencies. Frank Rhodes, the former president of Cornell University, has stated: "Accountability…is the newest buzzword for all institutions. It is an important—indeed, a vital—obligation, but it means very different things to different people."[1] These constituencies include legislators, the families of prospective students, accreditors, trustees, current students, faculty, and administrators—each wanting something quite different from the institution and each wanting the information for varying reasons and purposes. This pressure for accountability in higher education is actually nothing new; it has been a top concern for nearly 15 years. Today, however, the rising price of tuition is exacerbating the call for colleges and universities to demonstrate their effectiveness and to become more transparent about how resources are used.

Higher education, meanwhile, has been extremely reluctant to step up to the challenge of measuring the outcomes of its teaching, learning, and research. Ironically, researchers can measure the movement of subatomic particles and the radiation and other effects of unseen nebulae, but when it comes to measuring and assessing the impact and effectiveness of teaching, learning, and research on campus, we all too often hear that such an effort is too difficult. Whether the difficulty is because we have not yet learned how to do this effectively or because we have merely avoided the task is irrelevant. Society is becoming increasingly intolerant of such responses, and political pressures are mounting for campuses to deal with these issues or to have the government do it for—and undoubtedly to—higher education.

Demands for Information: The Spellings Commission

In 2005–2006, a national committee was established by Secretary of Education Margaret Spellings to carefully examine and make recommendations about higher education in the United States. The committee report, *A Test of Leadership: Charting the Future of U.S. Higher Education,* came with a wide variety of recommendations, largely focusing on accountability, affordability, and access. Many of these recommendations directly related to the information needs of higher education. The report stated:

> Our complex, decentralized postsecondary education system has no comprehensive strategy, particularly for undergraduate programs, to provide either adequate internal accountability systems or effective public information. Too many decisions about higher education—from those made by policy makers to those made by students and families—rely heavily on reputation and rankings derived to a large extent from inputs such as financial resources rather than outcomes....
> ... Parents and students have no solid evidence, comparable across institutions, of how much students learn in colleges or whether they learn more at one college than another. Similarly, policy makers need more comprehensive data to help them decide whether the national investment in higher education is paying off and how taxpayer dollars could be used more effectively.[2]

One of the foci of the Department of Education for the past several years has been on developing a unit record system that will track every student, at every higher education institution, for every quarter or semester—in order to develop a longitudinal data collection of students' progress over the years, at all institutions attended. The purpose of this extraordinarily complex (as well as expensive and intrusive) system is to provide information to policy makers and consumers alike about two primary variables: graduation rates and the net price of higher education.

Although the Spellings Commission report calls only for a pilot of this system, the intent is to create more information and to focus on accountability and also on transparency within higher education. Yet accountability and transparency are different concepts calling for different information elements: one is for policy makers and the other is for consumers. Viewing these two concepts as two sides of the same coin has led to the mistaken conclusion (by the Department of Education) that the unit record system will play a critical role in providing the data for transparency and hence the basis for accountability. While the rhetoric talks about accountability (in terms of the assignment of federal aid and funding of higher education), the focus narrows in on transparency, which is really about consumer information rather than the information that drives informed policy. The metrics of graduation rates and net price may have policy implications, but the clear focus of the proposed unit record system is on providing consumers with information that will allow them to compare and contrast colleges and universities, as if they were purchasing an automobile.

Higher education must avoid falling into this one-size-fits-all mentality. Although this approach is officially disclaimed by Secretary Spellings and her colleagues, there is a strong push to have "comparability across institutions." Higher education leaders all live, breathe, and believe the mantra that the greatness of U.S. higher education lies in its diversity and that it is up to them to provide a means of demonstrating account-ability so that this diversity can emerge and be seen. The notion of trans-parency highlights differences as well as what we have in common—a point that the Spellings report completely misses. All institutions desire and strive to be different in some way, segmenting themselves in a competitive environment. Education is not a commodity that can be bought like an automobile or a box of tissues. Across institutions, there are certainly common aspects that may be compared, but there are also factors that are intangible, hard to measure, or pertinent only to some segments of the community and to some institutional missions. Institutions must continue to focus on their uniqueness and their noncomparability. The higher education community could develop a list of data elements that are appro-priate and desirable for consumer information, but it must also consider ways to demonstrate and highlight institutions' unique aspects.

There is a substantial difference between the kinds of metrics and indicators that are meant to measure students' and consumers' information needs and those that are meant to measure institutional accountability and public policy needs. When we talk about net price and graduation rates, we are not focusing on the more deeply rooted issues of learning and outcomes and how they affect our society, communities, workforce, economy, and quality of life. We need to segment the discussion. Although some of the policy-related metrics might be of consumer interest, the inverse is not necessarily true—except to supply uninformed sound bites in what should be a serious discussion of higher education and its directions.

This distinction between information for consumers and information for policy makers is vitally important, because what we measure will shape behavior and define results. For example, focusing on "time to degree" suggests that it is a good thing to get a degree faster—perhaps at the expense of more important accomplishments such as learning, developing self-confidence, attaining knowledge, and finding what makes one tick. Asking for something like graduation rates by institution, as a measure of accountability, will reveal and drive behavior across the educational system in ways we cannot fully know or predict at this point. If higher graduation rates are the goal, then students—following an institution's counseling—might take more coursework to complete their associate degree to show degree attainment, and yet the transfer process won't recognize their additional credits, thus creating a greater total price for a student's degree. Alternatively, schools might simply change the type of students they admit, and this too could have significant social impact. Although our institutions wouldn't deliberately lead students down these paths, we should be concerned about the unintended consequences that might result from adopting arbitrarily defined metrics.

Another example of a deceptive measure is net price. As most higher education insiders know, the problem is that the net price an institution charges a student to enroll depends on the family income of the student, the number of siblings simultaneously enrolled in college, and other factors. Just as virtually all passengers on board an airplane pay different prices for the plane tickets, so do students at higher education institutions pay different prices for tuition. So how can we provide reasonably accurate price information to the public? The answer is not by simply calculating the sticker price less the various sources of aid, since that will not be the price for the most economically disadvantaged students or for the richest students. Such an average will only add more confusion.

Institutions need to work on a national basis to determine what data are really needed, to define the level of granularity for such data, and to provide a template for these variables. This effort could best be led by the key higher education associations in Washington, D.C. It requires coordination across all segments of higher education; it is not something that can be dealt with effectively on a campus-by-campus basis. However, that leads to the logical question: What role can and should the campus information technology leader play in this new world of accountability?

The Role of Information Technology and the Campus CIO

Clearly, the public demand for transparency of information, accountability, and outcomes has implications for the role of the CIO (chief information officer). In an *EDUCAUSE Review* article, Casey Green highlights a new role for information technologists—a role brought to the fore by the Spellings Commission report. He argues that information technology (IT) has a unique opportunity to help institutions address the increasing demand for more and better institutional data:

> Information technology now offers viable methodologies
> to address the mandates for outcomes assessment.
> The question here no longer concerns *if* information
> technology has a role to play in the campus conversations
> and public discussions about assessment and outcomes.
> Rather, the issue before us in the wake of the Spellings
> Commission report concerns *when* college and university
> IT leaders will assume an active role, a *leadership* role,
> in these discussions, bringing their IT resources and
> expertise—*bringing data, information, and insight*—to the
> critical planning and policy discussions about institutional
> assessment and outcomes that affect all sectors of U.S.
> higher education.[3]

Today, we have information of all kinds: student information, financial information, research data, transactional records, donor records, medical images, climatological data, and so on. And to manage information *technology* on our campuses, we have CIOs. Yet though the term "CIO" has been adopted to describe the head of a campus technology group, CIOs now wrestle with more than technology challenges. They increasingly wrestle with how to make the information that they have at their disposal useful to the campus in addressing these accountability issues. Even though this is a responsibility of all senior campus administrators, the CIO may lead the discussion, explaining the value of information technology, identifying useful data sources, and clarifying why it is important that IT be a partner with other units in addressing these needs.

The CIO has a great deal of data that can be combined and used to understand the accomplishments of the students at the college or university. Data from learning management systems and student record systems could be combined and mined to help the institution better understand the dynamics that lead to—or prevent—various learning outcomes. Using the powerful technological and statistical tools that are available and drawing on new sources of information are the elements of the emerging field of analytics in higher education. As stated by Mark Milliron in a recent article:

> Technology is neither good nor bad. It is our *use* of
> technology tools—within our contexts and toward
> specific ends—that can make a difference. This idea is the
> foundation on which today's *insight initiatives* are built.
> Insight initiatives are known by other names in other

sectors: *business intelligence,* in the corporate world; *evidence-based medicine,* in healthcare. These efforts, which combine explorations of information from the past (hindsight) with looks to the future (foresight), come together in a moment of insight to power decisions that make a positive difference. These initiatives leverage technology, planning, research, strategy, and a host of other key elements to truly realize the treasure of student and institutional data at our fingertips.[4]

We do not currently have meaningful outcome data with which to refute the various attacks on higher education. Analytics potentially provides a useful methodology for exploring available data and for developing significant models that could serve this purpose. What factors lead to greater time to complete a degree? How can the institution mitigate these factors? What costs can be reduced or eliminated by business process evaluation? These are the kinds of questions institutions must address in the years to come. To help institutions in this effort, the EDUCAUSE "Grand Challenges" initiatives—originally conceived in 2005—include a major focus on analytics.

Summary

The pressure for greater accountability has been coming from both Republicans and Democrats, from corporate America, from accreditors, from trustees, and from other stakeholders. This is not a partisan issue, and it will not be going away. Trying to identify learning outcomes and to measure whether a college or university is fulfilling its mission is not easy, but that difficulty is not an excuse to avoid the issue, as higher education has tended to do for all too long.

Higher education has never before encountered the current level of pressure to change and to modify its methods. The effective use of information within our systems is a change method that should be explored and capitalized on, but the impetus for change must come from the leadership of our institutions. Campuses cannot continue to use the slow, "bottom-up" change methods of the past. The pressures are too great. In addition, for the most part those at "the bottom"—the faculty and the participants within the institutions—are not directly feeling the pressures. And those who *are* aware have been resistant to change.

The times are different today. Bold leadership from our presidents and chancellors is called for. Higher education needs to act directly and quickly to prevent Draconian solutions from being imposed by legislators and others who are demanding greater accountability and transparency on campus.

Endnotes

1. Frank H. T. Rhodes, *The Creation of the Future: The Role of the American University* (Ithaca, NY: Cornell University Press, 2001), 242.

2. U.S. Department of Education, *A Test of Leadership: Charting the Future of U.S. Higher Education,* a Report of the Commission Appointed by Secretary of Education Margaret Spellings (Washington, D.C.: U.S. Department of Education, 2006), 14, http://www.ed.gov/about/bdscomm/list/hiedfuture/reports/final-report.pdf.

3. Kenneth C. Green, "Bring Data: A New Role for Information Technology after the Spellings Commission," *EDUCAUSE Review* (November/December 2006): 46, http://www.educause.edu/er/erm06/erm0661.asp.

4. Mark Milliron, "Insight Initiatives," *EDUCAUSE Review* (March/April 2007): 68, http://www.educause.edu/er/erm07/erm0727.asp.

Bibliography

Green, Kenneth C. "Bring Data: A New Role for Information Technology after the Spellings Commission." *EDUCAUSE Review* (November/December 2006): 30–47. http://www.educause.edu/er/erm06/erm0661.asp.

Milliron, Mark. "Insight Initiatives." *EDUCAUSE Review* (March/April 2007): 68–69. http://www.educause.edu/er/erm07/erm0727.asp.

Rhodes, Frank H. T. *The Creation of the Future: The Role of the American University.* Ithaca, NY: Cornell University Press, 2001.

U.S. Department of Education. *A Test of Leadership: Charting the Future of U.S. Higher Education,* a Report of the Commission Appointed by Secretary of Education Margaret Spellings, Washington, D.C., 2006. http://www.ed.gov/about/bdscomm/list/hiedfuture/reports/final-report.pdf.

Rajabai Clock Tower, University of Mumbai

IT Governance

E-Research Is a Fad: Scholarship 2.0, Cyberinfrastructure, and IT Governance

Brad Wheeler

I've seen this movie before, though it was cast in a different setting. When I was an assistant professor of information systems in the business school, the mid to late 1990s seemingly declared that all things that could be digital *would* be digital. "E-commerce" was the rage, and I taught my first MBA e-commerce course in 1995. It was soon supplanted by a more proper e-business moniker a few years later, and companies everywhere started e-business projects or "e" divisions. eBay, Amazon, and Yahoo were start-ups (as were flameouts WebVan, Boo.com, and eToys), and Bill Gates abruptly rechartered Microsoft's entire strategy to embrace this new Internet.

Astute observers of commerce at the time, however, had it right in seeing e-business more clearly. E-business was best understood and pronounced as "business," where the "e" is silent. While speculative equity money hastened the dizzying pace and the Internet provided instant access to the marketplace at scale, the phenomenon was nothing more than pedestrian Schumpeterian creative destruction at work. By 2007, efficient digital connections in the supply chain and with customers became a common and somewhat invisible element of effective commerce.

E-science, e-research, and e-scholarship can expect the same. They are best understood as "e-research," where the "e" will eventually be silent. Scholars in the sciences, humanities, and arts will identify those digital tools that advance their endeavors, that maintain and even enhance rigor and quality, and embed those tools and practices in their daily work. National funding agencies are providing the venture capital to hasten the pace of this evolution, and scholarly conferences and some leading projects already demonstrate efficacy in digital scholarship. "Data-driven science" is debated as a fourth paradigm alongside classic theory, experiment, and computational science.

What then is the role for college and university CIOs and their leadership teams as this e-research movie plays out? Is there a strategic agenda where attention, advocacy, and action can be effective? In this short essay, I contend that understanding Scholarship 2.0, developing scalable campus cyberinfrastructure, and seriously assessing governance of research IT are essential for great 21st century universities.

Twenty-First Century Scholarship

In 1945, James Bryant Conant, Harvard president, made three assertions regarding the elements for advancing pure and applied science:

> There is only one proved method of assisting the advancement of pure science—that of picking men of genius, backing them heavily, and leaving them to direct themselves. There is only one proved method of getting results in applied science—picking men of genius, backing them heavily, and keeping their aim on the target chosen.[1]

While Conant wrote of science, with some liberty, let me extend these assertions to the humanities, arts, and all areas of scholarly inquiry. The thesis is that real advancements in knowledge and human creativity come from exceptional minds that have all the tools and resources they need. In the 20th century, this was the great scientific lab working in some isolation at a single university or institute. The enormous expense of the best research tools, however, rationed their scarcity to elite labs with (presumably) the best minds to leverage the investment.

Now seems a prudent time, in this first decade of the 21st century, to question if and how Conant's assertions should steer research investments for this century. We already observe several important trends: First, we have many more faculty—both men and women of genius— at research-intensive institutions worldwide. Their scholarly work products are increasingly multiauthored, and often with scholars from two or more institutions and multiple disciplines. Second, the Internet has hastened the informal and formal communication of scholarly results, and the research process is increasingly a process of contributing to community data repositories and conducting further research from community data. The Human Genome Project, NEESGrid, and the National Virtual Observatory are early exemplars, and the new Large Hadron Collider ($8 billion) with more than 2,000 collaborating physicists from 34 countries shows community and leveraged investment at scale. Finally, these connectionist endeavors are not only with a research community, but many advances in human knowledge rely on deep interdependencies between disciplines (for example, metabolomics' use of biology and chemistry).

Who, then, is the 21st century "them" in Conant's "back them heavily"? Increasingly, we see that cross-institutional research communities, operating at scale and pace and making use of common and specialized facilities, are becoming an essential means of advancing modern scholarship. Numerous reports from the National Science Foundation, the American Council of Learned Societies, and others call for investments in cyberinfrastructure to support these communities.[2] Charles Vest uses the term *meta-university* to describe these connectionist trends among universities for research, teaching, and learning: " ... we are seeing the early emergence of a meta-university—a transcendent, accessible, empowering, dynamic, communally constructed framework of open materials and platforms on which much of higher education worldwide can be constructed or enhanced."[3]

Scholarship 2.0

In the business world, Tim O'Reilly coined the term *Web 2.0* as a revolution that argued for "harnessing collective intelligence" via the Internet as platform and for developing applications that harness network effects through communities, social networking sites, wikis, folksonomies, and other collectivist tools.[4] Arguably, we can apply the term *Scholarship 2.0* to label a similar adaptation of IT tools as a platform and distributed communities to harness collective intelligence of scholars: "Scholarship 2.0: The rise of IT, digital repositories, and electronic collaboration in achieving and improving the quality of the scholarly endeavors of research, teaching and learning, and service."[5]

The form of Scholarship 2.0 and its pace of adoption differ among disciplinary scholarly communities. For example, some scholarly communities have already transitioned the scholarly record to bypass traditional journal publishers and embrace open access and rapid publication. Other disciplines have not yet chosen or found a way to do so. At Indiana University (IU), research in ethnomusicology is leading the way with sophisticated video markup, annotation, and indexing as a form of digital scholarship in the humanities, but many other humanist fields have only modest experience with (or perceived need for) new digital tools. Many medical sciences are now moving rapidly from research paradigms of laboratory experimentation to extensive data modeling and simulation for understanding disease and potential treatment.

Institutional Cyberinfrastructure

It is tempting to look at national and international endeavors for cyberinfrastructure development as the province of national funding agencies. Not so. Each institution—especially the research university—is a microcosm of the cyberinfrastructure challenge, and there is a need for alignment of local cyberinfrastructure investments with national and disciplinary investments.

Figure 1, drawing on the notion of the software stack from computing, illustrates a conceptual relationship of disciplinary research stacks and institutional cyberinfrastructure. Each research discipline varies in its need for components of cyberinfrastructure (a nonexhaustive list). Some research disciplines may need dedicated lambdas of optical networking for moving massive quantities of data. Others need lots of high-performance computation cycles or massive storage. Others may need only trivial uses of networks and storage but have extensive needs for sophisticated metadata consultation or specialized visualization devices. The blend of these needs changes over time as a discipline evolves in its use of Scholarship 2.0 practices. For example, while simulation researchers have long been voracious consumers of computational cycles, they have now turned their appetites to storage and networks. One researcher recently told me

Figure 1. Scholarly Infrastructure

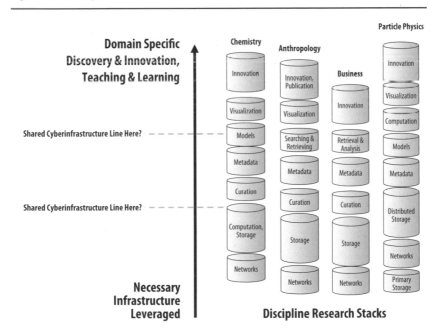

he had to dumb-down the data rate of his simulations as the network and storage were incapable of handling the volume.

Left to their own devices and with sufficient funding, researchers would rightly seek to solve their IT needs by purchasing and providing services for their projects or academic departments—Conant's "leave them to direct themselves." The proliferation of small (and growing) computing clusters is one example of this, and costs for electricity, cooling, and equipment life cycle funding are often overlooked until they become problematic. Likewise, the human staffing for system administration or metadata development often falls between the cracks. In many cases, these critical roles become filled by doctoral students, postdocs, or even faculty, and this is, at best, a misallocation of skills and time.

Figure 1 asserts that there are favorable economies of leverage—getting more for less—in the lower parts of the research stack (networks, computation, and so forth), where economies of scale, scope (serving multiple disciplines), and career path development can retain the best technical talent. The effort of scholars is best applied at the top of the stack—the edge—where their creativity and innovation are the very basis of research. Thus, using doctoral students for advanced server administration and security patching does not advance scholarship and may, in fact, leave a project's IT investments vulnerable to an ever-growing array of security threats.

The critical question for CIOs and research leaders is to begin thinking of disciplinary IT needs as shared cyberinfrastructure investments that can be leveraged across the scholarly endeavors of an institution.[6] Such thinking should go beyond the obvious boxes and wires of IT to include help and consulting for effective IT use, security and system administration, and other hidden but very real needs and costs. For example, IU has decided that extensive data storage is common cyberinfrastructure. IU's Massive Data Storage System, which provisions more than 4 petabytes of storage and is automatically replicated at two sites for continuous backup, is available to any graduate student or faculty member without chargeback. Thus, digital texts for the humanities sit alongside financial databases and genomics data as a leveraged service to all disciplines. The service has full help desk and consultant support.

Figure 1 also illustrates the institutional cyberinfrastructure question by asking where the line is drawn for common resources. Drawing the line lower, near networks, leaves the remainder of the research stacks to the individual scholars or their academic unit. Drawing the conceptual line higher means that more capabilities are provided in some shared-services model but at the risk of possibly impeding disciplinary creativity.

It is important to note that not all of the shared services should come from an IT organization. Cyberinfrastructure thinking enlightens many opportunities for partnerships with university libraries or academic units (a school or department), or even for leverage via interinstitutional consortia.

While Figure 1 presents some conceptual elegance to the notion of leverage (that is, that it costs considerably less to provide 2 petabytes of fully supported storage than to provide four 500-terabyte systems), there is often less elegance in funding models. For many institutions, this is a chicken-and-egg situation, where the money needed to provide quality, shared services is fragmented in the research projects and academic units. Even if the scholars actually would prefer to use common institutional infrastructure, they can't trust it until it exists and has proved itself. It can't exist until sufficient money is aggregated to fund it and competently manage it to demonstrate service quality.[7]

This may seem a typical university turf and funding battle, but that simplistic view fails to understand the opportunities and challenges of interconnected, 21st century scholarship. Even rich institutions with seemingly unlimited resources to support scholars and projects may find their efficacy in 21st century communities held back by 20th century thinking veiled by largesse of purse.

IT Governance for Institutional Cyberinfrastructure

For many institutions, progress on an institutional cyberinfrastructure strategy can be meaningfully advanced only as part of a holistic and rigorous discussion of IT governance. Though the term *governance* is often used loosely with many implied meanings, Peter Weill and Jeanne W. Ross define IT governance as "specifying the decision rights and accountability framework to encourage desirable behavior in using IT," and much of this section is adapted from their book, *IT Governance*.[8]

All institutions have IT governance, but some have much more effective IT governance than others—anarchy is also a form of IT governance. Five types of IT decisions are presented in sequence as part of establishing effective IT governance for research IT:

Decision 1: IT principles—clarifying the institutional role of IT

Decision 2: IT architecture—defining integration and standardization requirements (if any)

Decision 3: IT infrastructure—determining common, shared, and leveraged services

Decision 4: Disciplinary application needs—specifying the disciplinary need for IT applications (either purchased or internally developed)

Decision 5: IT investment and prioritization—choosing which initiatives to fund and how much to spend

In this brief essay, I'll address only decisions 1, 3, and 5, without reference to who makes these decisions, as that will vary greatly with local context. Ideally, IT principles should flow from institutional strategy, with a clear linkage between the two. Practically, one of the first explicit decisions should be a philosophy for research technologies. Examples of IT principles include the following:

Principle 1: Each research project should bear its own full costs.

Principle 2: Technology resources for research are efficiently matched to projects through user chargeback. (User fees fund research technologies.)

Principle 3: Research technologies are provided in abundance and with few limitations to encourage use in all forms of scholarship. (Research technologies are centrally funded or via broad-based tax.)

Principle 4: Academic units and projects are responsible for all specialized technology needs beyond basic networks, computation, and modest storage. (Research technologies have a blended funding model.)

IT principles, whether established through explicit process or tacit neglect, establish much of the domain for decision 3 of IT infrastructure (that is, the shared cyberinfrastructure line in Figure 1). Principle 1 above would effectively limit the creation of common infrastructure as rich projects and disciplines as they would likely do their own thing. Likewise, principle 2 would make it difficult for less well funded disciplines or graduate students to have access to advanced research technologies. Principle 3 overtly endorses cross subsidization for the breadth of the institution. Principle 4 invokes ongoing turf and service coordination challenges among units over what is common infrastructure or disciplinary applications.

Finally, the IT principles also substantially shape decision 5 regarding IT investment priorities and how much to spend. IT principle 3, a philosophy of abundance, necessitates substantial IT expenditures with coordination of timing, policy, and support.

CIO Engagement and Advocacy

University CIOs have an opportunity and responsibility to help university leaders frame cyberinfrastructure investment philosophies and decisions. For some, the opportunity arises through the pain of no space for fragmented research computing clusters or the tragedy of a research data security breech. Others may be able to frame the discussion as part of a strategic plan that looks to the essential elements of leading 21st century institutions.

Whatever the impetus for local action, there is no doubt that Scholarship 2.0 practices and needs for leveraged cyberinfrastructure will continue to advance for the foreseeable future. CIOs should engage in relationship building, educational efforts with administrative colleagues, and extensive data gathering to understand the current expenditures, value, and challenges that researchers have with IT. For many institutions, a comprehensive review of funding may reveal that the institution does not have a funding problem for research technologies; rather, there is a complex coordination problem of where funding goes and where it is needed for leveraged cyberinfrastructure.

There are also considerable time lags and path dependencies in developing leveraged shared services, effective partnerships with other administrative units (for example, libraries), and skilled staff with disciplinary expertise.

Conclusion

This essay argues that notions of e-research and e-science are transient ideas as scholars embrace and mainstream a range of digital tools for their work. The practice of digital scholarship may be labeled as Scholarship 2.0 to reinforce that it is first and foremost the classic and rigorous form of scholarship, but it now further harnesses distributed intelligence of global scholarly communities via new collaborative tools. Conant's wise advice to advance pure science by engaging scholars of genius and leaving them to direct themselves remains unchanged. The "back them heavily" admonition, however, has in part shifted to multi-institutional scholarly communities that make extensive use of local, national, and international cyberinfrastructure. A portion of that financial backing—especially to advance the whole of a university—must now be targeted at leveraged cyberinfrastructure investments. Effective and purposeful IT governance is an essential tool for framing discussions of institutional cyberinfrastructure.

Endnotes

1. James Bryant Conant, "Letter to the Editor," *New York Times*, August 13, 1945, 18.

2. Anthony J. G. Hey and A. E. Trefethen, "The Data Deluge: An e-Science Perspective," in *Grid Computing: Making the Global Infrastructure a Reality*, eds. Fran Berman, Geoffrey Fox, and Anthony J. G. Hey (New York: John Wiley and Sons, 2003), 809–24; *Revolutionizing Science and Engineering Through Cyberinfrastructure: Report of the National Science Foundation Blue-Ribbon Advisory Panel on Cyberinfrastructure* (Washington, DC: National Science Foundation, January 2003), http://www.nsf.gov/cise/sci/reports/atkins.pdf; *Our Cultural Commonwealth: The Report of the American Council of Learned Societies Commission on Cyberinfrastructure for the Humanities and Social Sciences* (New York: American Council of Learned Societies, December 2006), http://www.acls.org/uploadedfiles/publications/ programs/our_cultural_commonwealth.pdf; and *Cyberinfrastructure Vision for 21st Century Discovery* (Washington, DC: National Science Foundation, March 2007), http://www.nsf.gov/od/oci/CI_Vision_March07.pdf.

3. Charles Vest, "Content and the Emerging Global Meta-University," *EDUCAUSE Review* (May/June 2006): 30, http://www.educause.edu/ir/ library/pdf/ERM0630.pdf.

4. Tim O'Reilly, "Web 2.0 Compact Definition: Trying Again," *O'Reilly Radar* (December 10, 2006), http://radar.oreilly.com/archives/2006/12/web_20_ compact.html.

5. Brad Wheeler, "Open Source 2010: Reflections on 2007," *EDUCAUSE Review* (January/February 2007), 67, http://www.educause.edu/ir/library/pdf/ ERM0712.pdf.

6. Bradley C. Wheeler and Michael McRobbie, *Final Report of the Indiana University Cyberinfrastructure Research Taskforce* (Bloomington, IN: The Trustees of Indiana University, 2005), http://hdl.handle.net/2022/469; Thomas J. Hacker and Bradley C. Wheeler, "Making Research Cyberinfrastructure a Strategic Choice," *EDUCAUSE Quarterly* 31, no. 1 (2007): 21–29, http:// www.educause.edu/ir/library/pdf/EQM0713.pdf.

7. Brad Wheeler, "Research Technologies: Edge, Leverage, and Trust," in "The Organization of the Organization: CIOs' Views on the Role of Central IT," *EDUCAUSE Review* (November/December 2007): 44, http://net.educause .edu/ir/library/pdf/ERM0761.pdf.

8. Peter Weill and Jeanne W. Ross, *IT Governance: How Top Performers Manage IT Decision Rights for Superior Results* (Boston: Harvard Business School Press, 2005); see also Peter Weill and Jeanne Ross, "A Matrixed Approach to Designing IT Governance," *Sloan Management Review* 46, no. 2 (Winter 2005): 26–34.

Bibliography

Conant, James Bryant. "Letter to the Editor." *New York Times*, August 13, 1945, 18.

Cyberinfrastructure Vision for 21st Century Discovery. Washington, DC: National Science Foundation, March 2007. http://www.nsf.gov/od/oci/CI_Vision_March07.pdf.

Hacker, Thomas J., and Bradley C. Wheeler. "Making Research Cyberinfrastructure a Strategic Choice." *EDUCAUSE Quarterly* 31, no. 1 (2007): 21–29. http://www.educause.edu/ir/library/pdf/EQM0713.pdf.

Hey, Anthony J. G., and A. E. Trefethen. "The Data Deluge: An e-Science Perspective." In *Grid Computing: Making the Global Infrastructure a Reality*, edited by Fran Berman, Geoffrey Fox, and Anthony J. G. Hey, 809–24. New York: John Wiley and Sons, 2003.

O'Reilly, Tim. "Web 2.0 Compact Definition: Trying Again." *O'Reilly Radar*, December 10, 2006. http://radar.oreilly.com/archives/2006/12/web_20_compact.html.

Our Cultural Commonwealth: The Report of the American Council of Learned Societies Commission on Cyberinfrastructure for the Humanities and Social Sciences. New York: American Council of Learned Societies, December 2006. http://www.acls.org/uploadedfiles/publications/programs/our_cultural_commonwealth.pdf.

Revolutionizing Science and Engineering Through Cyberinfrastructure: Report of the National Science Foundation Blue-Ribbon Advisory Panel on Cyberinfrastructure. Washington, DC: National Science Foundation, January 2003. http://www.nsf.gov/cise/sci/reports/atkins.pdf.

Vest, Charles. "Open Content and the Emerging Global Meta-University." *EDUCAUSE Review* (May/June 2006): 18–30. http://www.educause.edu/ir/library/pdf/ERM0630.pdf.

Weill, Peter, and Jeanne Ross. "A Matrixed Approach to Designing IT Governance." *Sloan Management Review* 46, no. 2 (Winter 2005): 26–34.

Weill, Peter, and Jeanne W. Ross. *IT Governance: How Top Performers Manage IT Decision Rights for Superior Results*. Boston: Harvard Business School Press, 2005.

Wheeler, Brad. "Open Source 2010: Reflections on 2007." *EDUCAUSE Review* (January/February 2007): 48–67. http://www.educause.edu/ir/library/pdf/ERM0712.pdf.

Wheeler, Bradley, and Michael McRobbie. *Final Report of the Indiana University Cyberinfrastructure Research Taskforce*. Bloomington, IN: The Trustees of Indiana University, 2005. http://hdl.handle.net/2022/469.

Beyond the False Dichotomy of Centralized and Decentralized IT Deployment

Jim Davis

As we consider IT deployment in higher education, we must take into account factors that include growing expectations when it comes to access and functionality, the integrative effects of a "network economy," and the movement toward data as an institutional resource. IT is also playing an increasingly important role in research and education, compelling institutional IT to become more deeply involved with individual academic units. The university's teaching and research economies are becoming more interlinked while simultaneously regulatory and security requirements escalate rapidly and accountability broadens. It's true that one of the challenges to operating in this complicated environment has to do with the technology itself—the sheer complexity of technology deployment is increasing and technology requirements continue to change.

But our long-standing IT deployment practices are also breaking down. As universities struggle with how to piece together centralized and decentralized models in a way that will meet the needs of both the institution as a whole and the individual units it comprises, powerful forces are pushing these models toward failure. The centralized-versus-decentralized approach no longer aligns well with the programmatic objectives and regulatory requirements of the university. Hierarchical IT organizations and empowerment through budget and reporting lines are faltering and the organizational chart is failing to describe the real practice of IT. Institutional and departmental IT units can no longer compartmentalize their services and are forced to wrestle with their respective roles, turf, and accountability about services that are inherently integrated. Too often, we refer to IT services provided by a central organization *versus* those provided by individual units or departments. This has become a false dichotomy, creating an unproductive kind of competition among IT operations and preventing our common goal of a seamless, responsive, end-user IT environment.

In this essay, I argue that we need to actively move toward a new model, which I call *service layering,* and away from strictly centralized-versus-decentralized approaches. Even though the technology supports layering, such a move is not likely to happen naturally. It requires definition and practice with new accountability structures, significantly strengthened governance over shared environments, and forms of empowerment that go beyond reporting lines and budgets.

Embracing Local Autonomy and Institutional Involvement

Any consideration of what is needed from an IT deployment model must begin with two value propositions: (1) there is great value in IT deployment autonomy, especially at the school or department levels; and (2) there is equally great value in schools, departments, and individuals operating in a connected environment that supports sharing. In combination, these values become significant forces driving a need for IT deployment responsibility and accountability to be *jointly held* by institutional and local service units—a sea change in deployment context. Today's technology is not the problem; rather, the problem is that siloed, centralized, and decentralized IT service models fail to adequately address this changing landscape.

The solution lies in a hybrid model. To be sure, certain administrative and business systems must remain institutionally provisioned (centralized) to the end user without the involvement of local IT, while those that pertain solely to one unit require no institutional involvement and should remain decentralized. But many IT services, especially those needed at the "front lines" of research, education, and the academic environment, should be "horizontally layered" as locally managed service components on top of institutional service components to form complete services. Horizontal service layering creates the potential for a "sweet spot" that encompasses the advantages of both institutional and local service delivery.

To better understand the need for horizontal service layering to meet the goals of both the institution and its individual parts—the values outlined above of both autonomy and shared responsibility and account-ability for IT services—it is useful to think of the university as a global corporation. In this analogy, each frontline unit has its own unique interests, competing among state, national, and/or international peers much like a line of business (education and research) using human resources (faculty, students, and staff) to generate product (intellectual capital, students ready to enter a profession, successful faculty, social and economic impact, and a recognized institution). The competition is for students, funding, resources, rankings, visibility, and prestige. Line-of-business success contributes to overall school and university success, making improvements in the flexibility and autonomy of the line of business—where it contributes to these objectives—far more valuable than institutional operating economies.

At the same time, the academic structure is increasing in complexity. Academic disciplines continue to be the predominant front lines of the academic enterprise. While this organizational form has its advantages from the perspective of program quality assurance, other trends such as problem-based research, student educational expectations, and the fusion of research and education are demanding interdisciplinary and connectedness approaches. The marriage of these disciplinary and interdisciplinary forces produces an overlay structure on the more slowly changing disciplinary foundation. Academic competitiveness among institutions of higher education is played out along disciplinary lines; thus, the education and research "revenue side" of the university benefits when autonomy is combined with institutional involvement to accommodate interdisciplinary and interinstitutional demands.

Finally, the computational research and education enterprise is growing dramatically in scale and complexity such that high-performance computation, database management, visualization, data center, and backup, storage, and preservation of data demand institutional facilities and investment. If each research group is responsible for establishing its own facilities, research autonomy actually becomes more difficult and in some cases infeasible. And yet, the vastly different computational research and education taking place in the humanities from that of the physical sciences, for example, demands variability and autonomy. This is another argument for the layered approach—local management of services on shared, co-owned facilities.

In federating the research and education IT enterprise in support of autonomy, our job is to build a robust and responsive environment heavily defined by *each* line of business. This notion is reinforced in a December 2004 META Group article suggesting that the complexity of IT needs, the diversity of business drivers and risks, and the need for responsiveness and business-specific expertise among lines of business cannot be adequately served with only a centralized IT delivery model; local autonomy also must be embraced.[1] At the same time, it is understood that there is need for "corporate" IT structures to coordinate the relationships among the lines of business and leverage the benefits of being local within the shared economy of the whole.

The Layered Model in Practice

Moving to a layered IT deployment model requires a new accountability structure that embraces the marriage of autonomy and connectedness, enabling local and institutional IT to operate jointly in an environment of shared responsibility and coordinated accountability. Autonomy is valued within an institutional structure designed to facilitate interaction, integration, and harmonization. In establishing a vocabulary for this model, we use the terms *coordinated autonomy*[2] to refer to the deployment context; *layered services* to map the system of operations, support, and accountability; and *sweet spot* to describe the specific point where layered service delivery, responsibility, and accountability resonate between the local and institutional needs.

The layered model has proved beneficial in the service arena at UCLA even for something as commonly used as enterprise exchange services. For example, because of significant value placed on the ability to locally filter different file types and spam as well as on personalized responsiveness for more general purpose functions (such as managing guest accounts), the careful development of management tools that allow for local action and accountability has proved useful. Institutional accountability rests with high availability provisioning of the exchange services and the tools for local management. Local units are accountable to local variations in needs. Institutional and local units take joint responsibility for defining and maintaining the service portfolio sweet spot. Autonomy is embraced and institutional responsibility is preserved. The total service is neither decentralized nor centralized; it combines the advantages of each.

UCLA research faculty have become much more responsive to institutional cluster hosting, storage, and data center services as a result of "grid appliances" deployed as part of a layered services model. Simultaneously, the institution is benefiting from broader access to computational resources, greater standardization, and the avoidance of replicated facilities and operating costs. The grid appliance permits individual owners to locally manage the resource and retain direct authority over how the physical or virtual cluster, paid for by their grant, is used and who can use it. The quid pro quo is to participate in a shared, standardized resource that can provide the owners and others greater capability than the locally owned resource and can broaden secure access of unused cycles to others.

Institutionally, the appliance–resource combinations enable secure access to a range of computational resources, offer geographically distributed researchers ready access, and provide sophisticated tools to view resources, manipulate input files, and submit jobs. Institutional IT is accountable for network, data center hosting services, and the secure operation of the grid and the grid appliances. The Institute for Digital

Figure 1. Illustrating the Layered IT Service Deployment Model

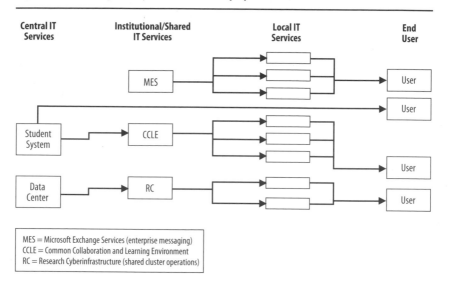

Research and Education (IDRE), representing the cohort of researchers and institutes that wish to take advantage of an institutional infrastructure, is accountable for the governance of the grid services and cluster hosting services (research cyberinfrastructure). The owner is accountable for the cost, management, and research production of the cluster. There is now high faculty demand for institutional IT hosting and shared services.

UCLA has also applied the layered model to a campus-wide desktop/server purchase contract, a software license for Microsoft products (Microsoft Exchange Services), and security policy. Most recently, the model has formed the deployment basis for UCLA's Common Collaboration and Learning Environment (CCLE) in Moodle. Figure 1 illustrates the layering approach.

Making It Work: Changes in Staffing, Governance, and OIT

Moving toward an IT deployment model that both embraces autonomy and extends accountability to increase institutional effectiveness is not easy. To engineer a successful transition, campus-wide and local IT units must construct a plan that identifies and takes into account critical elements of autonomy and accountability. Support staff must establish shared management structures and shared service agreements and put into place a process for resolving conflict. Moreover, strong campus IT governance, as opposed to "decisions by committee," is vital.

Peter Weill and Jeanne W. Ross are often referenced in the context of IT governance and decision making and indeed provide essential constructs.[3] I argue that the Weill and Ross approach in practice requires: (1) formal acceptance of the governance organization and processes by the campus administration and the academic senate; (2) executive sponsors with functional and funding authority to champion initiatives; (3) structures and processes ensuring that decisions are ultimately made on functional rather than technological grounds, but with significant technology input; (4) a strategic decision-making and policy body that combines the academic senate and executive administration; (5) integration of IT governance into the campus planning and budget processes; and (6) willingness to invest in the management and administration of a governance structure and process that is comparable to a board of trustees. The single most important campus agreement in the governance process is formal acceptance of a decision matrix that defines which body has responsibility for which decision and what kind of decision. The process of reaching a goal of decision acceptance is long and arduous, but without acceptance there is no governance and decision making, only committee input.

In coordinating this approach, the institutional office of information technology (OIT) must be more than a university services provider and cost center. Such an institutional OIT should manage the IT governance and institutional planning processes, have authoritative involvement in campus IT investment decisions, and have oversight of the campus IT portfolio, architecture, and services infrastructure. It is particularly important to conduct these processes from a position of credibility and neutrality rather than from the "authority" of organizational budget and number of reporting lines. If it is to help foster a layered services environment, the OIT needs to shift from client to board relationships, from budget competitor to co-investor, and from an operational to a balanced integrative focus that accounts for the full breadth of local and institutional objectives. In this way, empowerment stems more from the ability to engage the broadest expanse of line-of-business drivers, priorities, and needs.

The OIT can "see" IT on the campus in ways that no other organization can, and it can translate that view into operational impact. Impact comes first with the capacity for institutional planning and analysis, management oversight of the governance process, responsibility for IT policy, joint decision-making authority on campus IT investments (that is, the decision matrix), and campus "ownership" of architecture. Operational impact follows and depends on the operating deployment structure on campus. This form of empowerment is supported by the analysis of Joseph

Nye, who has observed that this form is likely to be more important than the command-and-control form when campus IT is dispersed (federated).[4] For this to occur, the institution must be receptive to this role—not an easy task.

Summary

I have argued in this essay that the deployment model is as important, if not more so, than the technology itself for a university seeking to maximize its IT potential. I have further argued that long-standing IT deployment models, which tend to cobble together centralized and decentralized approaches, are no longer working in higher education. I have suggested the need to move toward a hybrid deployment model that continues to provide only local or only institutional control where it makes sense to do so but that also incorporates the layered approach, in which autonomy is valued and responsibility and accountability are shared by institutional and local service units.

I believe that line-of-business autonomy as I have described it is a significant value worth pursuing in a time of powerful trends that also demand institutional solutions: interdisciplinary interactions, interlinking information, and powerful computation facilities for research and education. UCLA's experiences with layering services, building relevant governance, and working in different accountability structures have been very positive—more than sufficient to keep us pressing ahead with the layered deployment model. But we also understand that it is early in a long process of change. Discussion and consideration of the issues raised by this new IT deployment model will help us to move beyond long-standing practices that no longer serve our needs.

Endnotes

1. Brian Burke, *Federating the IT Organization: Enterprise Planning and Architecture Strategies*, META Group Practice 2301, December 31, 2004.

2. Jim Davis, "Coordinated Autonomy," *EDUCAUSE Review* (November/December 2001): 86–87, http://connect.educause.edu/Library/EDUCAUSE+Review/CoordinatedAutonomy/40298.

3. Peter Weill and Jeanne W. Ross, *IT Governance: How Top Performers Manage IT Decision Rights for Superior Results* (Boston: Harvard Business School Press, 2005).

4. Joseph S. Nye, Jr., "The Benefits of Soft Power," *Harvard Business School Working Knowledge* (August 2, 2004), http://hbswk.hbs.edu/archive/4290.html.

Bibliography

Burke, Brian. *Federating the IT Organization: Enterprise Planning and Architecture Strategies.* META Group Practice 2301. December 31, 2004.

Davis, Jim. "*Coordinated Autonomy.*" EDUCAUSE Review (November/ December 2001): 86–87, http://connect.educause.edu/Library/ EDUCAUSE+Review/CoordinatedAutonomy/40298.

Nye, Joseph S., Jr. "The Benefits of Soft Power." *Harvard Business School Working Knowledge* (August 2, 2004). http://hbswk.hbs.edu/archive/4290 .html.

Weill, Peter, and Jeanne W. Ross. *IT Governance: How Top Performers Manage IT Decision Rights for Superior Results.* Boston: Harvard Business School Press, 2005.

From Users to Choosers: The Cloud and the Changing Shape of Enterprise Authority

Ronald Yanosky

For a long time, people working in IT have been accustomed to describing those they serve as users. It's an unsentimental term that suggests a division between those who merely *use* computers and those who make the magic happen—the ones who are really in control. The term is a lingering reminder of the days when computers were rare, housed in glorious isolation, and tended by professional staffs whose main focus was keeping the machine running, preferably at a healthy distance from the users. And keeping it running was critical: The organization that owned the machine often owned the institution's whole computing environment.

Granted, it's been a long time since that state of affairs prevailed. But even though the central IT organization's monopoly on computing resources has dissolved into messy complexity, a potent legacy remains: what might be called central IT's "enterprise authority," that is, the responsibility (and often, at least, the power) to define computing norms that protect the interests of the enterprise, and thus the interests of the user community as a whole.

The origins of this authority lie in the era of technological scarcity. When higher education IT administrators controlled most or all of the cycles and programming skills available, they effectively had the power to allocate computing itself. Computing at higher education institutions might be divided between administrative and academic units, each with its own mainframe, but each of these served large and diverse communities that crossed departmental boundaries. Over time, IT administrators had to develop new skills beyond the care and feeding of the technology: understanding the requirements of users who often could not articulate their own technical needs; determining priorities, allocations, and funding models; and, critically, arbitrating among departments that competed for IT resources but rarely communicated with each other.

This king-of-the-hill position made IT units uniquely conscious of how different uses of computing were related. Their domination of programming skill also gave IT units growing influence over business and academic operations on campus. Business rules and enterprise controls were increasingly embedded in the applications that IT developers built, and because they had to make different applications work together, the developers often came to understand overarching enterprise issues better than the functional departments themselves. This, in turn, gave them a degree of ownership over enterprise controls. All this, of course, was deeply disturbing to users who were accustomed to a high degree of operational autonomy.

Minicomputers, PCs, and the Internet eroded IT's direct control over cycles and programming skills, yet at the same time they fed the need for an ever more refined and complex exercise of enterprise authority. Users exulting in their liberation from the cycle gatekeepers in IT soon discovered that they had inherited system administration tasks that either sent them back to the IT organization asking for support or forced them to develop their own IT skills and sensibilities. And as soon as they tried to connect their departmental and personal machines to resources outside their immediate domain, the newly empowered users found themselves dependent on a central IT connectivity monopoly and tangled up in interdepartmental politics in which central IT played the role of arbiter.

The Federal Model

By the time of the client-server era, this mix of new capabilities and new dependencies had shaped higher education's user–IT relations into a roughly "federal" model. Users had, in fact, broken free from many of the constraints of the data processing era. PCs put computing power on the desktop, and the new platforms and applications on them had helped create a popular user group culture in which participants could sharpen their skills and discover their common interests. Increasingly, even people who weren't technically adept began to identify themselves by their technologies of choice. The user group culture often had a libertarian ideology that prefigured later web-based cyberculture, yet its anti-institutional impulses were to some degree curbed by user reliance on departmental, school, and enterprise resources.

Above the "citizen" layer of individual users stood the "local" and "state" layers of the federal IT hierarchy. At large institutions, departments and schools began to develop their own IT organizations, ranging from small local-area networks (LANs) in offices or labs to big, ambitious data centers in computing intensive areas. Likewise, more and more of the functional work of administrative (and some academic) departments migrated from manual to automated systems. In contrast to the more freewheeling nature of the popular user groups, these users came together along organizational lines, some concerned with specialized or cross-cutting computing needs, such as research support, and others representing slices of enterprise functions, such as the line business units and the registrar's office. As these users became more numerous, savvy, and familiar with technology, their political influence grew correspondingly.

Yet central IT was not completely shut out from the big decisions affecting these constituents. A degree of technical dependence remained, increasingly focused on network and support issues, but central IT's enterprise authority was the really dynamic element in preserving its influence in user relations. Central IT's administrative applications development skills remained important, and with the advent of integrated enterprise resource planning (ERP) systems, IT shifted from being an automater of business systems to an integrator and process designer, accentuating its pan-institutional profile. After some painful lessons, central IT units learned to shun the perception that they "owned" ERP projects. Yet even as they shared power with user departments, they remained a sort of first among equals, and often the most energetic advocates of business process change, in the project and IT steering committees that oversaw these initiatives.

Furthermore, central IT remained in the driver's seat of the revolutionary new network technologies and other crucial aspects of the computing infrastructure. It controlled the increasingly essential network backbone and negotiated most of the wide-area network (WAN), telecommunications, and Internet connectivity contracts that governed the institutional network environment. It also operated the "big iron" servers that increasingly absorbed old mainframe workloads, and had backup and disaster recovery capabilities unmatched elsewhere on campus.

These powers reinforced central IT's role managing the growing interconnections that now typified campus computing. Executive leaders reflexively looked to their CIOs for solutions and policy recommendations for any problem remotely connected to technology, from implementing telecommuting programs to disciplining students who sent malicious e-mails, and this growing executive concern gave the CIO's office political weight. Central IT was far from a technology autocracy, but it had a set of carrots and sticks at hand that no other technology unit enjoyed, including the supreme sanctions of refusing support for shadow systems or (something like the IT death penalty of the early Internet era) cutting off network connectivity. All of these powers placed central IT at the top or "national" level of the federal pyramid of user relations.

If the first decade of mass Internet usage didn't quite break the federal model of user relations, it put tremendous and distorting stresses on it. At the root of the problem was the geometrically expanding complexity of both enterprise architectures and user demands. Users found new avenues to unmediated expression through technology, first in websites and later through blogs, wikis, and other emerging tools. Self-service via the web made enterprise systems far more visible, changing them from staff-facing systems used during working hours to constituent-facing systems with implied 24 × 7 availability. E-learning introduced major new enterprise applications that served new and increasingly self-aware faculty and student constituencies. Most painfully, the new Internet-based environment brought exotic new forms of malware, enhanced hacking opportunities, and a legal morass surrounding filesharing. Increasingly, the Internet became a vehicle for expressing lifestyles and a battleground for freedom of expression, and the boundary lines between personal, professional, and enterprise concerns became fuzzier still. Demands for support and for computing independence both grew explosively.

IT federalism got more complex but managed to stay functional through all this. At many institutions, the newly conceived role of chief information officer (CIO) put a leadership layer above stovepiped administrative and academic computing divisions. Central IT took on new responsibilities and got new powers, especially in the regulation of security and privacy, which built on its ownership of the network backbone and the major enterprise systems. At the same time, institutions began to formalize IT governance and open it up to a wider range of inputs, recognizing that IT had become a resource relied on by the entire community. Even so, highly autonomous and well-funded local IT units and research labs often found it desirable and feasible to circumvent central IT's systems and policies, while the technology itself—increasingly powerful, inexpensive, portable, networked, and ready to deliver sensitive information—conspired against effective control over the much-enlarged user community. CIOs began to complain that their jobs had become more political and more concerned with risk management than ever and that their practical ability to exercise enterprise authority was diminishing.

The Impact of Cloud Computing

Cloud computing can help address some of the problems that came with the early Internet era. The cloud's democratization of access to computing power is, as we've seen, nothing new; what is new is that cloud resources can at least potentially come with the professional system administration that personally administered PCs and servers often lack. A user who can fulfill his needs from the cloud will be less tempted to set up the unpatched, insecure, backup-free, under-the-desk rogue server that lies at the center of so many higher education IT tales of woe. Making it easier for users to acquire and maintain the technology they need will reduce certain of the functional/technical demands they place on IT units, and could mitigate at least some of the complexity and exposure that now characterize enterprise IT environments.

But it also seems likely that new complications will attend new simplifications. To a greater degree than ever before, the cloud will make users into choosers who are able to make technology choices without mediation from other parts of the institution. User liberation in the PC and Internet revolutions came with attached strings of dependence that led naturally upward to departmental, school, or central IT units, giving federal relationships some measure of hierarchical coherence. Central IT acted as an intermediary between users and enterprise vendors, which allowed the institution to conduct its relationship with each vendor on a one-to-one basis while extending one-to-many support services to users. This created some valuable symmetries in IT administration: manageability in vendor relationships balanced with scalability in user support and a service provider role balanced with the role of enterprise authority. Users who depended on central IT for connectivity, enterprise agreements, systems administration, and other services knew that their ability to get what they wanted depended (within bounds) on paying attention to what central IT told them to do.

Cloud computing creates new strings of user dependence that lead outward rather than upward, upsetting the balances in institutional and especially central IT authority. Where users directly employ a service from the cloud, they disintermediate institutional IT as a service provider. But that doesn't necessarily mean they eliminate IT as a support provider. Like Wall Street's financiers, users may well be attracted to the chance to privatize reward and socialize risk. There is a danger of cloud relationships that begin as a two-way user-to-vendor interaction turning "triangular" when unhappy cloud users draw IT in for support.

The nightmare scenario for central IT arises when multiple users who have independently drawn collections of cloud providers into institutional business plead *ex post facto* for help to sort out multiparty, multiproduct support issues. Central IT will be tempted to refuse, yet a long history of past efforts to do just that with "unsupported" platforms and applications suggests it will not be an option, at least above a certain threshold. Sooner or later cloud dependencies will create institutional exposures, and the institution's first reflex will be to turn to IT to address the problem.

This breakdown of symmetry between central IT's ability to shape product choices and its responsibility for user support is only one example of how the cloud can pull mutually reinforcing IT roles apart. Another is the looming disconnect between central IT's service provider role and its responsibilities as enterprise authority. In the early Internet era, CIOs could say to users, "You must use certain precautions and behave in certain ways because if you don't you'll compromise our network and we'll be forced to kick you off." In the cloudy environment, central IT no longer enjoys monopolies on connectivity or access to applications, nor does it have the same ability to define safe harbors and auditable systems. The concerns of enterprise authority—from system and data security to process efficiency and online behavior—will continue to be critically important, perhaps more than ever. Yet they will increasingly be disembodied from the "plumbing" that central IT has historically overseen. Who, then, will speak for the enterprise? And in what tone of voice?

Enterprise Authority in a Cloudy Academy

To some extent, the user community itself will fill the vacuums in support and enterprise authority. Cloud users freed from dependence on the IT bureaucracy may be more conscious of their mutual interests and their ability to self-organize, and the same grassroots self-help impulses that one now sees in open source and Web 2.0 communities could become generalized. Support blogs, wikis, and other collaborative forums will spring up around many cloud resources to supplement vendor support tools. Virtualization and commoditization could also reduce the technical idiosyncrasies users have to grapple with, making it easier for functional user communities to rely on internal support competencies. Nor should we dismiss the possibility that users may develop a more sophisticated and effective sense of enterprise responsibility as they venture into cloud environments. As critics of the idea that every commons ends in tragedy point out, local self-regulation among those most affected by the quality of common resources can be an effective way to protect them.[1]

Yet every shift in computing paradigms has brought its disap- . pointed utopian hopes, and the cloud will be no exception. Computing may, indeed, look simpler to users in a mature cloud environment than it does in today's messy world where desktop, departmental, enterprise, and Internet resources constantly clash; but this, at least, is the devil that institutions know. Besides exposing themselves (and the institution) to the unknown reliability and viability of cloud service providers, users are bound to discover more subtle limits on the integratability of cloud resources, especially as they begin to mix and match them to support complex processes. These issues will often arise from specific local needs whose unique and possibly confidential nature works against the open source premise that "given enough eyeballs, all bugs are shallow." More broadly, we need to consider the fact that decades of deploring and fighting institutional stovepiping has resulted in only modest progress toward true enterprise information systems. The centripetal forces that have made enterprise sensibility a constant struggle aren't going to go away.

How, then, should IT administrators handle a new profusion of outward-leading attachments that bypass the internal controls IT has historically provided? One logical option that will have its adherents is pure laissez-faire—neither regulating what users do nor providing institutional support if they get into trouble. But as we've already seen, institutional dynamics will likely make this option untenable. Too often in higher education, individual actions lead to institutional sanctions. Institutions can't simply relinquish due diligence on the grounds of individual choice, and users are certain to run into issues that they can't address on their own.

A Locked-Down Cloud

On the other end of the spectrum one might envision a locked-down enterprise environment carved out of the cloud. In this model, web traffic entering and leaving the institution would pass through an institutionally managed intermediary that dynamically applies rules about what users can and can't do. An aggressive implementation might not only block undesired sites in the manner of today's URL filters but set many terms of use: how long users can remain on a site, what they can download or upload, even what sort of language is allowed when posting to a blog or social networking site. It could also generate a highly detailed record of usage. Institutions would not necessarily have to set every parameter in granular detail; already emerging cloud security vendors such as ZScaler and Purewire promise heuristics-based technologies that assess websites and even personal reputations dynamically.

An environment like this could help institutions contain support demands, reduce assorted kinds of exposure, and keep an eye on process efficiency and staff productivity. Yet it's hard to imagine successfully implementing this regime in a higher education environment. Even putting aside nontrivial issues relating to user evasion and induced latency, a highly regulated enterprise cloud would be sure to arouse passionate objections on the grounds of academic freedom, personal privacy, organizational unit autonomy, and incompatibility with modern methods of teaching and research. To put it in the language of civil liberties, a locked-down cloud would constitute "prior restraint," perhaps justifiable in some settings but completely unacceptable to the sensibilities of an academic community.

Certification-Based Cloud Computing

A much more acceptable way to shape user activity would be to certify rather than dictate good behavior. To borrow a line from pedagogy, central IT might manage a cloudy environment as "the guide by the user's side," rather than "the sage on the IT stage." Web resources could be certified on the basis of good security and enterprise practices, such as use of open standards, robust identity management, encryption and other data management protections, auditability, and business continuity practices. Likewise, certification might address contractual issues such as indemnification, liability, and escrow arrangements in the event of vendor failure or takeover. Users would be encouraged to use certified resources (which would be easily identified as such), warned of the dangers of uncertified ones, and held accountable if they got into trouble straying into uncertified territory.

Certification-based institutional cloud computing would have many of the advantages of a locked-down cloud, such as rationalizing support needs and articulating enterprise requirements, but would be more open and politically sustainable and would better leverage the advantages of the cloud. Presumably, certification would be a collaborative process involving multiple concentric rings of participation. At the core, a basic set of enterprise certification guidelines could specify institution-wide practices, drawing on input from surrounding rings of school, departmental, and user-group entities and deferring to them on matters of local scope. Surrounding these would be additional rings representing external communities of practice, standards bodies, product user groups, and other entities with relevant expertise.

While it's likely to be a better fit both with the spirit of cloud computing and with the culture of higher education, a certification approach has its problems. It obviously places a great deal of hope on the slender reed of standards and certification assessments. Standards processes are notoriously slow and prone to the disproportionate influence of interested parties; they are subject to interpretation; and they can be either too general to be meaningful or so detailed as to be impossible to implement. Even when standards are clear and up to date, deciding whether a particular resource meets a given standard requires investigation and judgment. Nor is it entirely clear what kinds of standards cloud computing might call for. Moving toward a trustworthy cloud computing resource "seal of approval" requires a leap of faith that global and local computing communities can create all the necessary processes.

Even if that faith proves well founded, a certification approach to cloud computing will require some potentially disruptive changes in relations between IT units and users. The most obvious one is deciding who does the certifying and through what process. Users who have discovered a cloud resource that seems to meet their needs perfectly may well resent a third party's refusal to certify it. At the innermost level of certification guidelines, central IT is probably the best candidate for overseeing the process, in part because it is the entity with the best ability to provide support to users of certified resources, and in part because of its enterprise experience. Both the realities of higher education culture and the logic of the cloud, however, would demand that certification be an open and inclusive process. In parallel with the certification process, both central and local IT units could also help users assess vendor certification claims and sort out the institutional implications of what might be a confusing tangle of competing standards. Influence of this kind could enormously reduce institutional exposure and improve the cloud computing experience for all users.

A second issue raised by a certification approach is how to enforce user accountability. Even in a fairly open "use what you want but be accountable" environment, enterprise considerations will demand some degree of user monitoring (such as usage logs and audit trails), particularly because in a cloudy environment fewer resources have the implicit controls that come with institutional ownership and physical control. Who will be in charge of monitoring the trails users leave in this environment, and who will deliver sanctions when they step out of bounds? Central IT can best influence accountability indirectly, for example, by building appropriate auditability into its resource certification processes. But enforcement responsibility and the setting of sanctions in this exceedingly sensitive area ought to lie with the authorities users are most likely to consider legitimate: themselves, their managers, and the executive hierarchies they fall under.

IT's Changing Responsibilities

It seems clear that the cloud's transformation of users into choosers will cause some power to flow "downward" in the IT federal hierarchy. Probably the greatest beneficiaries will be at the middle levels of the hierarchy, among business and academic units that gain not only IT independence but perhaps also budget dollars that are reallocated when central IT-delivered services become, in effect, business services contracted from cloud providers. Researchers, already the most independent of institutional users, will have still more opportunities to break from institutional constraints. Individual staff and student users might see radical or limited changes, depending on their needs and their willingness to venture beyond the realm of certified, supported computing.

Yet as some of the IT organization's responsibilities fade, others will remain and new ones will emerge that have no obvious "owner" other than a central IT unit. "Chooser" support is one of these, and it implies a more or less formal process of cloud resource certification that can become a potent, though indirect, protection for the enterprise. That in turn leads to perhaps the most important central IT role that will carry over into the cloud era: definition and management of institutional IT governance. The cloud's liberation of unit-level and individual users is an inherently politicizing trend that will feed demands on governance, because it means that enterprise policies once implicitly embedded in institutional service delivery will have to be negotiated (or mandated) explicitly. No one has the experience that central IT does in dealing with such enterprise IT politics. As a recent ECAR study of IT governance found, responsibility for IT governance is overwhelmingly in the hands of CIOs, and they tend to run inclusive and, by their assessment, effective governance structures.[2] IT leaders who wearily describe their role as "herding cats" may well be identifying just the sort of experience and skill that will keep central IT strategic in the age of the cloud. Likewise, today's focus on risk management and legal issues is a likely harbinger of the central IT skill set of the cloud era.

As the example of IT governance suggests, declining IT unit control over hard resources will make the ability to exercise "soft power" more and more central to the unit's existence. Additional responsibilities in this vein may include monitoring cloud resource usage across the institution, assessing the efficiency of processes that cross departmental domains, contributing to institutional information architecture and strategy, and architecting the local infrastructure (especially identity management) to permit seamless and secure access to the cloud. The common thread in these tasks will be the need to meet enterprise responsibilities through influence, negotiation, and informed risk management rather than through official enterprise authority.

Conclusion

There are, of course, many considerations that could prevent the full logic of the cloud from being realized. The cloud has not yet proved its ability to deliver cheap, scalable, virtualized computing power; still less its potential for loosely coupled integration; and least of all its radical promise of modular applications built from mix-and-match services. The decisive failure of cloud services could reinvigorate "classic" centralized enterprise computing, and even if the cloud is successful, the transition from locally hosted to cloud resources is likely to be gradual and bumpy. But in proportion to the degree that the cloud achieves its promises, it will shift power downward in the IT hierarchy, atomize enterprise IT authority, and reshape central IT's role from service provider to certifier, consultant, and arbitrator. Central IT will need to better master the arts of soft power to continue to play its vital role of articulating and protecting enterprise interests.

Endnotes

1. Garret Hardin, "The Tragedy of the Commons," *Science* 162 (1968); Elinor Ostrum, *Governing the Commons: The Evolution of Institutions for Collective Action* (Cambridge and New York: Cambridge University Press, 1990).

2. Ronald Yanosky with Jack McCredie, *Process and Politics: IT Governance in Higher Education* (Research Study, Vol. 5) (Boulder, CO: EDUCAUSE Center for Applied Research, 2008), http://connect.educause.edu/Library/ECAR/ProcessandPoliticsITGover/47101.

Bibliography

Hardin, Garret. "The Tragedy of the Commons." *Science* 162 (1968): 1243–48.

Ostrum, Elinor. *Governing the Commons: The Evolution of Institutions for Collective Action.* Cambridge and New York: Cambridge University Press, 1990.

Yanosky, Ronald, with Jack McCredie. *Process and Politics: IT Governance in Higher Education* (Research Study, Vol. 5). Boulder, CO: EDUCAUSE Center for Applied Research, 2008. http://connect.educause.edu/Library/ECAR/ProcessandPoliticsITGover/47101.

University of Melbourne

Open Information, Open Content, Open Source

Cultural and Organizational Drivers of Open Educational Content

Malcolm Read

T he purpose of this essay is to consider the cultural and organizational issues behind the creation of open educational content. In it I argue that there are many benefits to the individual, to the educational institution, and to society at large from open educational content and, further, that such educational content has to be part of a wider context of open resources across the research, education, and cultural domains.

The Open Context

The word *open* is much used as a prefix to describe an environment or process that is owned by an often diverse community of creators but available to all, usually for free. These days the concept thrives because the Internet provides an invaluable vehicle for the ready distribution of information and knowledge and the tools to manage and exploit that information. The Internet is a prime example of public benefaction; it greatly enhances the reach of information to all levels of society and countries of the world. It is not new, however; the public library movement of the 19th century was based on the "open" ethos, as were various open universities and, arguably, state-provided education, whether for children or adults. In all cases there was seen to be a clear benefit to society through ready access to educational and cultural resources.

Open educational content can help maintain a long tradition facilitated initially by public libraries and benefactors and now by the Internet and the World Wide Web. Lecturers and teachers and, indeed, anyone with expert knowledge and the skills and willingness to pass on that knowledge can now do so. The *Wikipedia* is a prime example of such open educational content albeit one where the quality of the content is variable. But first, what do we mean by *open educational content*? And how does it relate to the plethora of other *open*-prefixed terms such as *open source software, open standards, open access,* and *open science*?

Open Source Software

Open source software is probably the most well established of these concepts; the term *shareware* is sometimes used to describe some examples of open source software. Open source software is software that is made available by the authors freely, or at a very modest cost, to anyone. The software may be small, specialist applications or software tools, or large and significant products such as the Linux operating system or the Moodle learning management system. Open source software seldom comes with much support, although this is sometimes available from third-party providers, and the potential user will need adequate expertise and other resources to deploy and customize the software to meet their particular needs.

To those with the expertise, open source software can often form the basis of a bespoke solution because the source code is available in a way that the code for third-party software often is not. It may be the only affordable solution to small organizations. Thus smaller colleges and schools will often deploy mature open source software offerings where commercial solutions are too expensive. Open source software, therefore, complements commercially provided software by widening choice. Few would doubt that open source software, intelligently chosen and deployed, offers real benefits to education and society at large.

Open Standards

Open standards tend to be less visible to the practitioner. Within the world of information technology (IT), these are openly available, published standards, usually technical, for defining and managing processes and, of most interest where information is concerned, ways of exchanging data and information. Such standards can also cover operational and managerial procedures. Although some commercial software vendors would prefer a world where the user is "locked into" a particular system, open standards do provide an environment in which both open source and commercial software can prosper.

Open standards are, of course, absolutely essential in the real, not just the virtual, world; they define everything from railroad gauges (why 4' 8½"?) to electricity plugs, often at the national level. It is frequently quipped that the good things about standards is that there are so many to choose from. Defining, agreeing to, and establishing open standards is often a slow process. Nonetheless, the world would be a less convenient place without them. And in the IT world, few would doubt the benefit of open standards and, indeed, their use and development is often strongly encouraged and insisted upon by funding bodies in the education and research environment.

Open Access

Open access is a movement that started in the research area largely predicated on the argument that the outputs of publicly funded research (usually papers in scholarly journals) should be publicly (and usually freely) available.[1] The open access debate is mired in disputes with the scholarly publishing industry. The arguments for and against are not straightforward, largely due to the reward and recognition of research being heavily based on publications in prestigious journals. However, it is the research community and individual researchers who produce the research/outputs, and they should be less willing to hand over to publishers their rights to such a valuable resource when there is seldom a direct financial reward.

Proponents of open access make many, to my mind, powerful arguments in support of making their research outputs (in papers) available on the Internet, either on the web or in a repository, and either as the sole copy or more usually as a copy of the version published in a journal. Their papers are therefore more widely available to fellow researchers and, of particular importance to many, this is probably the only way the general public and much of the developing world can access them. There is also value in researchers making their peer reviews available. Further, in fast moving disciplines, such as particle physics where open access publishing is well established, the scholarly publishing process is far too slow to be an effective method of distribution.

The open access concept for research outputs is now being applied to research data, the argument being that better access to properly managed and preserved data will greatly enhance the research process. In some disciplines, such as the social sciences, this is long accepted; for example, access to population (census) data over a long time period is essential. But many disciplines can benefit from open data. However, the costs of storing data and describing the data in such a way that they can be found and used easily (known as *metadata*) can be considerable.[2] And while the benefit to a research discipline could also be considerable, the benefit to individual researchers is often less obvious; they are not usually rewarded for their data contributions.

Open Science

A final, even more ambitious, concept is open science. Under this model, researchers share their research findings while actually carrying out the research. Thus, they are in effect exposing their experiment or other research activity to review and comment and advice from their peers in real time. This could prove to be a very effective and efficient process but requires considerable intellectual bravery. The Internet makes open science possible, and this is an extension of a growing trend for collaborative research described by terms such as *virtual organizations*, *collaboratories*, and *virtual research environments*.

Open Educational Content

It is within this context of growing openness, particularly of online data and information, that the learning and teaching community should consider open educational content. The resources I have in mind are handouts and course notes that are produced primarily for use by a class; these are resources of little commercial value, compared to textbooks or more sophisticated learning materials, which can be expected to generate income. It follows, therefore, that any teachers considering making their materials readily available in an open access manner will have already determined that they have little economic value, either to themselves or their employer. This raises two considerations: Do universities and colleges regard such learning materials as conferring some competitive advantage? And, similarly, do individual teachers regard their course material as needing to be protected as a resource unique to them and as constituting a significant advantage in pursuit of their career aspirations?

There will be examples where such teaching materials do confer advantage to teacher or institution, but I would argue this is not normally the case. Such material is designed to support a particular course at a particular institution but seldom contains content that is not readily available already on the web, and few potential students will consider the quality of such course material an important criterion in deciding which university or college to attend (indeed they cannot, as such material is not usually available to them).

A number of political and policy drivers could encourage a culture of open access for learning resources. Making such resources openly available can be an important marketing tool and helps inform potential students about the quality of the academic experience they can expect from that institution.

The employing institution may have a policy to encourage or even mandate open access for such material. This will not usually be a comprehensive policy, but some universities do expect a significant proportion of handouts and course notes to be made available on the web. The MIT OpenCourseWare initiative is an obvious example, and more recently the UK Open University has built a similar library of resources called OpenLearn (see the essay by Professor Andy Lane in this volume). Even when the institution as a whole does not adopt an open access policy, many individual departments or faculties do so. Another significant driver for many teachers is the altruistic desire to share their knowledge with society, which can now be very effectively met through posting material on the web (either their own website or their employer's site), blogs, wikis, and other Web 2.0 technologies.

It is also possible to provide links between such content and online textbooks, journals, and other reading list materials. Such links are greatly facilitated in an open content environment and can provide considerable convenience for the student over current, largely library-based practice.

However, even when teachers or institutions accept that there is little or no commercial value in such resources, it does not follow that they will wish to make them openly available. It requires a great deal of work to prepare the content in such a way that it will be useful outside the class and that it will reflect well on the author and, where appropriate, the employing or hosting institution.

Issues for Universities and Colleges

These different drivers lead to different approaches and hence different "collections" of materials for users to enjoy: an institutional library or repository or a less structured and controlled user-owned Web 2.0 environment. Both are to be welcomed in that they provide free scholarly and academic material to students, potential students, lifelong learners, and society at large. This is particularly valuable to those who, for whatever reason, cannot easily benefit from higher education, especially those in the developing world. On the other hand, we must not forget that this widens the digital divide.

There are a number of reasons why a university or college may wish to make some of their learning resources openly available. Their mission may include a public-good responsibility to help educate the community other than through formal learning: many institutions regard this as a valid and useful objective within a wider role of knowledge transfer and community engagement. They may see open access to learning resources as a valuable "shop window" for attracting students and to help them understand the nature of the learning experience in higher (postcompulsory) education. It may simply be a natural extension of their open access policy for research outputs, or a relatively easy way of further exploiting their existing repository.

Many institutions will not yet be considering open access. There is an important role for policy makers and strategic thinkers in higher education to encourage this debate and help bring the issue to the attention of senior institutional management. Even if the reasons above do not motivate them, they will wish to consider where they stand in relation to other institutions locally, nationally, and internationally. They will wish to consider whether they are fully exploiting their investment in their institutional repository, and if they do not have a repository, whether they need one; they may also need to develop a policy on who owns the course material and who (the author or the employer) holds the rights to exploit and disseminate such resources. The benefits of open access can be gained regardless of who owns and exploits the rights, but in many institutions there is no clear policy. For institutions, having a clear and unambiguous policy concerning rights is more important than the specifics of the actual approach that they adopt.

Institutions must also consider the business case. Although the marginal costs of mounting learning resources may be small in terms of hardware and software, these costs will increase over time and could become significant. The major costs, however, fall to the teacher in producing high quality material. There are also costs in quality control: poorly produced or inaccurate material will reflect badly on the institution. And in many subjects the material will need to be kept up to date.

Issues for the Teacher and Author

A lot of existing course material, perhaps the majority, is not in a suitable form for making it openly available. It was written, often in a hurry, for internal consumption only. Few teachers would wish to expose such material to their peers, let alone make it more widely available.

Most handouts and similar courseware also contain some third-party materials taken from publications or other copyrighted resources.[3] To make it publicly available would require obtaining permission from the rights holder, time consuming at best and sometimes impossible, either because it is not possible to discover who the owners are (these are known as *orphan works*) or how to contact them, or because they will not reply. In some cases the author will seek financial compensation and this may well preclude the possibility of making the resource openly available. Clearing third-party rights for text materials can be expensive and time consuming; it becomes even more so for nontext materials such as photographs, moving images, and sound and can be prohibitive where performing rights (plays, dance, and so forth) are concerned.

Issues for Policy Makers Worldwide

Despite these difficulties, there is a growing interest in many countries, from national education policy and funding bodies, to encourage and facilitate the creation of an open layer of scholarly and academic content made up of research outputs and data and learning and teaching materials. This is increasingly seen more in terms of encouraging universities and colleges to build and populate reposi- tories, and less in terms of building large central libraries of learning materials. The challenge now is to join these institutional repositories not just within a country but internationally.

Such a layer of organized and quality-assured content has enormous value: it can be reused (or *repurposed*, in the jargon) by other teachers; it supplements and complements the more formal material provided to students; it provides students with resources to enable them to learn at their own pace with some freedom from time and place; it lifts the knowledge base of society as a whole. As such, it is a vision worth striving for and it helps maintain the relevance of formal education in the modern Internet age. But it is not the only model.

Web 2.0 technologies provide a more organic, and many would argue more exciting, environment for learning.. The content can be, and often is, made open to all, including students and the general public. It is not mediated by an educational organization and, in many case, is not mediated at all. This clearly places an onus on the readers to apply critical reasoning to what they read, but that is an increasingly necessary skill in using the web.

The other significant sources of open educational content on the Internet are websites (whether designed with a pedagogic intention or otherwise) and Web 2.0 technologies such as wikis, blogs, and shared multimedia resources (Flickr, YouTube, and so forth) While these are not unstructured, they are not designed or populated with education as the sole, or even main, driver, and, as a rule, they are not quality controlled. However, Web 2.0 offers a dynamic, organic, and exciting environment that empowers both teachers and learners, whether undertaking formal education or not, to contribute educationally valuable, and equally educationally misleading, content in the open domain. As such it is a valid, and on the whole valuable, part of the open content spectrum.

Although much of the content under the heading of Web 2.0 technologies, or the simple deposit of web pages, happens outside the control of formal learning, it should not be assumed that there is not a role here for the educational institution, and certainly not that the teacher is a passive contributor. Universities and colleges can, and do, embrace Web 2.0 technologies as an essential part of the learner support infrastructure; it is a powerful communication tool for peer-to-peer and student-to-teacher interaction. It is less common, however, for the institution or teacher to manage, in the sense of *organize* or *preserve*, this material. It thus can only be found, if made openly available at all, through generic search engines such as Google.

We thus have, potentially, two equally useful open content environments—one well managed and structured with quality control but expensive to create and maintain, the other more random in the reach of the content but almost free. These approaches should be thought of as complementary but obviously require different actions from institutions and teachers in order to be exploited.

Summary

There are a number of reasons why teachers and their universities or colleges might wish to add to the corpus of open content that will eventually contribute to a worldwide layer of scholarly and educational content:

- It is a marketing opportunity to attract students and to provide potential students with some insight into the higher (that is, postcompulsory) education experience, thus helping to widen access, improve retention, and reduce dropout rates.
- It adds to the body of reusable content to support the curriculum, particularly helpful for foundation courses (and remedial training).
- It provides a mechanism for recognizing one aspect of good teaching and potentially rewarding good teaching.
- It acts as a "shop window" and will be perceived, rightly in my view, as an indicator of the quality of education, not just at the individual institution but in the country as a whole; as such, it encourages more overseas students.
- In many cases it will support the ethos and mission of the institution, particularly if reaching educationally disadvantaged students and promoting distance and flexible learning are important.

◙ Finally, by being free to all and empowering students, it provides an enormous benefit to society at large, whether regional, national, or worldwide.

Building open educational content is not, however, without significant cost:

◙ It is expensive and time consuming to prepare good-quality, open access content and requires different skills from preparing normal text-based, printed handouts and course notes.

◙ It is usually necessary to prepare the resource for online dissemination and then, if required, make it available in print form (perhaps as a book); this is easier than doing it vice versa.

◙ The content must be designed to support a suitable pedagogic approach, which may be and almost certainly is very different from a traditional teaching methodology.

◙ Third-party rights must be cleared; this is often difficult and seldom speedy.

◙ In effect, the teacher and the institution become a "publisher," and they may not have these skills.

◙ Describing and cataloging (usually through appropriate metadata) are also not easy and can require specialist skills (often, but not exclusively, held by librarians); without this, the material can be hard to find. And if it cannot be found, then what is the point of making it open?

◙ A platform for storing and delivering the content is required: perhaps a repository or perhaps a leaning management system.

◙ Finally, in addition to the problems of cost and the requirement of different skills for participants, there remains the challenge of finding a sustainable business model and sustaining the necessary culture change by recognizing and rewarding high-quality and valuable (not synonymous with well-used) content.[4]

Endnotes

1. Neil Jacobs (Ed.), *Open Access: Key Strategic, Technical and Economic Aspects* (Oxford: Chandos Publishing, 2007). See also *Open Access,* a Joint Information Systems Committee (JISC) briefing paper, September 1, 2006, which also has a valuable bibliography, http://www.jisc.ac.uk/publications/publications/pub_openaccess_v2.aspx.

2. Neil Beagrie, Julia Chruszcz, and Brian Lavoie, *Keeping Research Data Safe*, a Joint Information Systems Committee (JISC) report, May 12, 2008, http://www.jisc.ac.uk/publications/publications/keepingresearchdatasafe.aspx.

3. Carol Fripp and Dennis Macnamara, "Copyright Management in the World of Learning Objects," a paper presented at EDUCAUSE in Australasia, Sydney, Australia, 2003, http://www.aesharenet.com.au/aesharenet/pdf/147educausepdf.pdf.

4. Further information and analyses of open educational content issues can be found in Guntram Geser, "Open Educational Practices and Resources: The OLCOS Roadmap 2012," *Revista de Universidad y Sociedad del Conocimiento* 4, no. 1, 2007, http://www.uoc.edu/rusc/4/1/dt/eng/geser.pdf, and in Andrew Charlesworth, Nicky Ferguson, Seb Schmoller, Neil Smith, and Rob Tice, *Sharing eLearning Content: A Synthesis and Commentary, Final Report*, a Joint Information Systems Committee (JISC) project report, September 2007, http://ie-repository.jisc.ac.uk/46.

Bibliography

Beagrie, Neil, Julia Chruszcz, and Brian Lavoie, *Keeping Research Data Safe*, a Joint Information Systems Committee (JISC) report, May 12, 2008. http://www.jisc.ac.uk/publications/publications/keepingresearchdatasafe.aspx.

Charlesworth, Andrew, Nicky Ferguson, Seb Schmoller, Neil Smith, and Rob Tice. *Sharing eLearning Content: A Synthesis and Commentary, Final Report*, a Joint Information Systems Committee (JISC) project report, September 2007. http://ie-repository.jisc.ac.uk/46.

Fripp, Carol, and Dennis Macnamara. "Copyright Management in the World of Learning Objects," a paper presented at EDUCAUSE in Australasia, Sydney, Australia, 2003. http://www.aesharenet.com.au/aesharenet/pdf/147educausepdf.pdf.

Geser, Guntram. "Open Educational Practices and Resources: The OLCOS Roadmap 2012." *Revista de Universidad y Sociedad del Conocimiento* 4, no. 1 (2007). http://www.uoc.edu/rusc/4/1/dt/eng/geser.pdf.

Jacobs, Neil (Ed.). *Open Access: Key Strategic, Technical and Economic Aspects.* Oxford: Chandos Publishing, 2007.

Joint Information Systems Committee. *Open Access*, a JISC briefing paper, September 1, 2006. http://www.jisc.ac.uk/publications/publications/pub_openaccess_v2.aspx.

Challenges and Opportunities of Open Source in Higher Education

Ira H. Fuchs

The combination of expanding demand for IT services on college and university campuses, coupled with flat or declining budgets at many institutions, is arguably the greatest systematic challenge facing higher education IT during the next several years. It puts pressure on IT organizations to juggle "keeping the lights on" with the need to provide innovative technology platforms that support new levels of collaboration and promote strategic agility for institutions as well as their faculty and students.

The pressures will only be exacerbated, for many institutions, by the arrival of federally funded, next-generation "cyberinfrastructure" that will require installation, adaptation, training, local administration, and support. If institutions do not have in place an IT infrastructure that can support these new arrivals efficiently, the cumulative burden on IT staff and budgets could be formidable, even unsustainable. Moreover, even if these cyberinfrastructure platforms are integrated, institutions face significant challenges in diffusing their islands of expertise broadly to the campus community.

One interesting potential strategy for dealing with these problems is the model of "community-source" software (CSS) production. Another is the move to a services-oriented architecture (SOA). Both strategies show significant promise, but it remains an open question as to how much of that promise can actually be achieved. The next few years will be crucial for both.

Community-Source Software (CSS)

During the last eight years, the Andrew W. Mellon Foundation's Research in Information Technology program (Mellon/RIT) has made significant investments in CSS projects to build open source IT infrastructure, particularly learning management (http://www.sakaiproject. org) and enterprise resource planning (http://www.kuali.org) systems.

These efforts are continuing: The Kuali project released the first version of its Kuali Financial System (KFS) this year; KFS has just recently gone into production at its first nonfounder institution; and the Kuali community is organizing to deliver a student information system as well. Moreover, community source initiatives have now been initiated in the academic library IT community (http://oleproject.org) and for the support, via shared technology services, of scholarship in the arts and humanities (http://www.projectbamboo.org). The premise behind these projects is that community-source approaches result in better quality, better fitted, more sustainable, and mission-critical software for higher education. Mellon/RIT and others have made the case for CSS as an alternative to proprietary commercial or home-built software in many places during the last several years. I will not repeat it here, but interested readers are invited to explore further.[1]

In a community-source project, a consortium of colleges and universities comes together to build software needed by each of them, contributing resources to a virtual organization that serves as a software development shop. As both designers and customers, they build software tailored to their own needs; the involvement of multiple, diverse institutions ensures that the product is usable by many other institutions as well, and Mellon provides support to offset the costs of collaboration and generalization. After the product is first delivered, control and governance over the project are released to the higher education community on an open source, participatory basis: Institutions contribute human and capital resources to maintain and enhance the software and govern the intellectual property of the project via participatory mechanisms. The open source nature of the project is critical: It protects institutions against vendor lock-in, allows them to share the costs of maintenance and enhancement widely, and permits widespread innovation at minimal cost.

Because CSS is designed and built by and for higher education, the "adaptation gap" between community-source software and a particular institution should be much smaller than that between commercial software (which is typically designed for the vendor's much larger, for-profit markets) and higher education. The result should be software that is cheaper to install and customize and that, because it is open source, is also far cheaper over time to maintain and enhance. Those savings may occur immediately, but it is more likely that they will only occur over time, as the software matures. Potentially even more important, the resulting software should be better fitted to the needs of higher education than its commercial competitors, both because it is newer (a transient advantage) and because it is built for and by its own customers (a durable advantage).

However, community-source software is still new, so the question of whether it is truly cheaper and/or better fitted to the needs of higher education institutions is still open. The next several years will tell if the promise can be realized—but it would be to the advantage of higher education to move up this timetable as much as possible. If CSS delivers on its promise of substantial savings and/or improved outcomes, then the sooner institutions are made aware of that fact, the more resources higher education as a whole can save; if it does not deliver those benefits, then the sooner the participating institutions know, the sooner they can either correct the problem or seek an alternative, better strategy. In either case, large sums of money can be saved, across all of higher education, by quicker, better answers to the core questions surrounding CSS. A quicker answer would require a concerted effort by an objective party to bring together the higher education community to conduct a formative and summative assessment of one or more CSS projects.

Next, assuming that CSS proves to be advantageous for at least some purposes and institutions, there is a need for some coordinating entity to assist them with the next stages of growth. CSS projects require a variety of logistical assistance, from conference planning to legal consultation on matters of tax status and intellectual property licensing. Many of these needs were detailed in the Mellon-funded EDUCORE/OOSS study (http://www.ithaka.org/strategic-services/oss/OOSS_Report_FINAL. pdf). If CSS realizes its promise, the number of CSS projects is likely to grow to the point where the proliferation of CSS governance organizations could itself become burdensome to higher education. Collecting these entities under one umbrella would make possible substantial efficiencies in service delivery; doing so proactively would further increase savings and provide other potential synergies as well.

Services-Oriented Architecture (SOA)

Many higher education institutions are excited about the promise of services-oriented architectures for increasing flexibility and cutting costs. The opportunities are real, but there are significant challenges as well. One significant opportunity is the chance to reduce the increasing burden resulting from the steadily growing number of "siloed" applications that a campus must support. Reconfiguring these applications into services running in a common environment can drastically reduce the amount of redundant software code that institutions must support, cutting costs and improving the ease of collaboration.

Another opportunity is the chance to accommodate newly arriving cyberinfrastructure in a way that is affordable and sustainable. Without SOA, each cyberinfrastructure project would need to be treated as its own silo and adapted to the campus (and to all other cyberinfrastructure projects) individually; with SOA, one can hope to integrate each new project more painlessly into the common enterprise architecture. The cost difference between the two approaches may make the difference between unsustainable and sustainable cyberinfrastructure for many higher education institutions.

Yet another opportunity is the promise SOA holds for reducing boundaries between higher education campuses. In an increasingly global higher education community, technology is too often a barrier to collaboration and the exchange of ideas. SOA holds some promise of lowering those campus boundaries.

However, even SOA enthusiasts only claim that SOA makes possible the benefits they enumerate; few would claim that SOA makes such benefits inevitable. Pursued with insufficient forethought, or even just campus by campus, SOA is less likely to deliver on its promised benefits. SOA is as much an organizational as a technological innovation and, as such, careful design, training, governance, and support are all crucial to its success. In particular, campuses that do not understand their own business models are at a significant disadvantage when implementing SOA. Without careful forethought, applying SOA locally to a single application or a single campus may simply copy the problems of the current IT infrastructure into the SOA design. Even with such forethought, SOA designed and built campus by campus is far more likely to replicate today's campus boundaries in tomorrow's technology than is SOA designed and built by institutions working together. If SOA is to provide the multi-institutional collaborative support that higher education users are demanding, it will need to be built by higher education acting as a whole. Even if individual campus efforts could be coordinated retroactively to achieve nearly the same collaborative result—which is by no means certain—that path would require resources and time that higher education can ill afford.

These opportunities and challenges suggest a role for a coordinating and educational entity around the issue of SOA in higher education. Such an entity could make it a priority to help higher education institutions equip themselves with the knowledge and skills required to make a successful transition to SOA. A combination of training and consulting services could help IT leaders with process and project management skills, as well as providing materials to educate key campus stakeholders in the costs, benefits, and skills required to make the SOA transition.

At a deeper level of engagement, the entity could assist in coordinating SOA design exercises among many higher education institutions. These exercises could be modeled on the design workshops developed by the CSS community (http://educationcommons.org/projects/display/CSSSS/Home) and could bring together diverse institutions to analyze their respective business processes and develop specifications for SOA-based higher education enterprise IT environments that could meet the needs of institutions of every size and type. Moreover, the entity could provide coordination and support for consortia and virtual organizations working to build the software according to the workshop designs. This role is also anticipated in the EDUCORE/OOSS study; it suggests that a single entity might be able to fulfill the mentoring and steering role for both CSS and SOA, going forward.

Diffusing Cyberinfrastructure

The challenge posed to campuses by incoming cyberinfrastructure is a variant of an old campus problem: how does an institution take the technological expertise concentrated in relatively small islands on campus—historically, the computer science department and perhaps one or two others—and diffuse it broadly, to provide equal support to, say, faculty and students in the arts and humanities? As one wag put it, getting technology delivered to the arts and humanities in higher education today is a little like trying to get a pizza delivered to a house in the suburbs ... in 1927.

Because of Mellon's long-standing commitment to the arts and humanities, we consider this a particularly important question. Our best current answer has two parts: Infrastructure is essential, and it must be designed for the recipients, not the donors, of the expertise. One cannot deliver technology *ad hoc*, to unsophisticated users, and expect much sustained benefit. Even if one deploys the training and support resources required to make that piece of technology a success, users wishing to grow beyond that project will still have nowhere to go. For sustainability, such projects must be embedded in an infrastructure that reduces the cost of generalizing expertise gleaned in one project for use in other projects— and that reduces the costs of mounting those other projects so that each one need not require extraordinary effort.

All this will still not be enough if the infrastructure provided does not accommodate the actual users. For example, most NSF-funded cyberinfrastructure projects are built by and for scientists. They assume a level of technical competence and programming sophistication that does not exist in arts and humanities disciplines; in some cases, even the metaphors that underlie the user interface are scientific and, as such, foreign to humanists. Even if one could strip out the scientific content of such a project and replace it with humanistic content, those platforms could never serve as an adequate infrastructure for humanists today. Consequently, Mellon/RIT is supporting initiatives to build infrastructure by and for the arts and humanities. One such project is SEASR, the Software Environment for the Advancement of Scholarly Research (http://seasr.org), which is currently in beta release. SEASR provides an analytics platform that is as capable as many of the cyberinfrastructure platforms in the physical and biological sciences but differs in two key respects: (1) It is optimized for the analysis of unstructured data (text and rich media), rather than the structured data of scientific projects, and (2) it is intended to have a humanist-friendly user interface—one that uses language, images, and metaphors that are familiar and intuitive to people with no mathematical or programming backgrounds.

SEASR is one step in a planned series of initiatives culminating in the development of a comprehensive technology platform for the arts and humanities. This platform will support the management of scholarly content and collaboration throughout the scholarly life cycle—from creation, to collaboration, to review, to publishing. Experience suggests that such a platform, if built for the least technologically sophisticated disciplines, will be just as useful and easily adopted/adapted by more sophisticated disciplines—where the reverse is far from true. That is a lesson that any higher education institution wishing to ensure parity of technology support among all its faculty would do well to remember.

CSS and SOA Together

One can use CSS models to build SOA projects; in fact, several initiatives are under way now to develop the necessary infrastructure to support SOA-based CSS projects. Mellon/RIT has funded the Kuali Student project (http://student.kuali.org/) as a "pure" SOA-based, next-generation student information system. As part of its work, Kuali Student will deliver the essential infrastructure required for an enterprise-quality, higher education–specific SOA environment. Also, the Kuali Rice initiative (http://rice.kuali.org/) is extracting essential shared technologies (including messaging, event notification, workflow, and a service bus) from the existing Kuali projects so that they can be used even by institutions that have not installed the Kuali applications; the Kuali Enterprise Workflow tool, in particular, has already achieved independent adoption in several other administrative capacities.

The SEASR project, already mentioned, is using SOA to support humanities computing projects such as MONK (text mining; http://www.monkproject.org/) and NEMA (music information retrieval; http://nema.lis.uiuc.edu/). Mellon/RIT also funds a user interface layer (http://www.fluidproject.org) and supports a data management infrastructure (for example, http://www.fedora.info, http://wiki.fluidproject.org/display/collectionspace/, http://oleproject.org). Other key pieces of SOA-based, CSS-built infrastructure, such as event and resource calendaring software, are planned. Each project uses open standards–based interfaces to permit it to be used integrally with the others—or with whatever mix of commercial and open source alternatives a particular institution might wish to employ.

One key objective of the projects that utilize a service-oriented architecture is to allow institutions maximal freedom to tailor an enterprise infrastructure that both serves their distinctive institutional needs and supports easy, standards-based collaboration within and across institutional borders. A second major objective is to provide an environment in which new demands on IT can be accommodated as they arise, in the most affordable, efficient way possible.

Conclusion: CSS and Coordination

Building a multiproject CSS environment introduces organizational and coordination challenges that are greater than those associated with any single project. The various projects must remain coordinated over time because they must continue to work together effectively. Their licensing and other requirements must be congruent, so that institutions are not caught between warring policies. Perhaps most important, their administrative overhead must be managed in such a way that it does not become burdensome to institutions to support the entire environment. Given the significant overlap among these initiatives, the current practice of creating a new organizational entity to oversee each project is a form of local optimization that may prove to be very inefficient in the long run. Worse yet, too many supporting organizations may impede the coordination that is needed if we are to realize a whole that is substantially greater than the sum of its parts.

If a single entity were already aiding CSS projects with coordination, these challenges would all be more manageable. If that same entity were also helping to educate the higher education community about SOA, then it would be ideally positioned to make intelligent decisions about how best to advance projects like MESA. The Sakai Foundation and the

Kuali Foundation are both doing an excellent job of orchestrating their respective projects (indeed, Kuali is already the home for several related efforts); however, both are also constructed by charter with missions that are domain specific rather than focused on the needs of higher education broadly. It may be time to step back and look at the bigger picture, to see if higher education can simultaneously improve efficiency while creating a new technology infrastructure that will serve our needs now and well into the future.

Endnote

1. See, for example, Bradley C. Wheeler, "Open Source 2010: Reflections on 2007," *EDUCAUSE Review* (January/February 2007): 48–67, or Christopher J. Mackie, "Open Source in Open Education: Promises and Challenges," in *Opening Up Education: The Collective Advancement of Education Through Open Technology, Open Content, and Open Knowledge,* ed. Toru Iiyoshi and Vijay Singh (Cambridge, MA. MIT Press, forthcoming).

Who Puts the Education into Open Educational Content?

Andy Lane

T he concept of open content was first mooted by David Wiley in 1998.[1] Although he was referring to all types of content, he was mainly thinking of educational content because of his interest in enabling easier construction of educational materials from a repository of learning objects. When MIT decided in 2001 to make freely available on the web, under an open license, much of the content used or produced by its faculty to support their teaching, it chose the term OpenCourseWare for that content (see http://ocw.mit.edu/OcwWeb/Global/AboutOCW/our-story.htm). In 2002, the term open educational resources (OER) was adopted at a UNESCO forum[2] and is becoming the term used most often for this phenomenon.

What Is Open Educational Content?

Whatever term may be applied to this phenomenon, open content is largely digital stuff (music, images, words, animations) created by somebody who has attached an open license to it. (I recognize that analogue versions of open content can exist and be used by people but the reuse of such content under the open license is extremely curtailed by their analogue format.) In other words, the content is openly available (it can readily be found or discovered), is openly accessible (it is in a form in which others can take it away), and is openly reusable (the user can easily modify it and is allowed under the license to do certain things with it without having to ask the creator's permission first). This is in contrast to full-rights-reserved copyright, where reuse is always closed to users unless they seek and are granted permission, and where rights holders normally restrict the content's availability and accessibility in many different ways to avoid illegal use of the material. That is almost all I will say on the rights issues around open content because I am more interested here in exploring the conditions under which any content, open or closed, may be educational, before looking at the additional implications of open content.

Who Creates Educational Content?

The creators of any digital stuff (my wider term for content) will have had in mind at least two purposes for the stuff: what they expect users of the stuff will use it for (entertainment, information, education, and so forth) and what they themselves want to achieve through creating it (personal fulfillment, reputation, income, influence, and so forth).

The users of the stuff also have at least two purposes for it: what they personally want to gain from it as it stands (entertainment, information, education, and so forth) and what else they might want to do with it for themselves or to share with others (which may be the same set of purposes that the primary creator had in mind). While this same argument applies to closed, or fully copyrighted, stuff, the effect of an open license is that users are not just primary consumers of the stuff, they are also enabled to use the stuff as feedstock for creating their own stuff (as secondary creators) without seeking the direct permission of the primary creator.

This principle of a community of users, all creators and consumers at different times, underlies the whole philosophy of the creative commons, where everyone (in theory) can build upon the work of others for the greater benefit of all by creating more stuff that helps the wider economy and is not locked away or underexploited.

It follows that open content becomes an open educational resource for which the creator, most likely a teacher in some form, had education as a major purpose or intent for that open content. It also follows that users of open content, learners or teachers, can declare it to be an open educational resource if they also are primarily using it for educational purposes, even if the primary creator did not have that in mind. In principle, all stuff can be given an educational purpose. So, what makes it effective at educating or enabling someone to learn from it as it stands—whether as a learner, to learn the subject matter, or as a teacher, to learn how that subject matter has been structured or presented as educational material?

To explore this further I will use the simple idea that content is a mediating object between a teacher and a learner, with each interacting separately with it. In many open or distance learning situations, and especially with OER, all the mediation occurs through the content as object. In face-to-face or computer-mediated-conferencing teaching and learning situations, there is the added benefit of interactions between the teacher and the learners and between fellow learners around that content as a mediating object.

Teacher–Content Interaction

The first aspect to consider is the degree of meaning associated with the content. Thus, content can be primarily concerned with simple data or information (for example, that dogs have fur), through more complex information or knowledge (for example, why dogs have fur and why different dogs have different types and amounts of fur), to the drawing out of generalizations from the particular (for example, the conceptual reasons why all mammals have fur and the general models or hypotheses that enable predictions to be made for new examples of mammals). This external knowledge, where information and experience taken from the world have already been transformed, analyzed, tested, evaluated, and stored in some form, is the basis of education.

An educational resource is one in which the creators have made sense of the existing public information and experiences of others to create something that embodies their own interpretation of that information and experiences in a structured way. An effective educational resource is one in which the structure or design of the resource is aimed at increasing the chances that inexperienced or less knowledgeable learners can both internalize that external knowledge and be able to demonstrate their own interpretation of that knowledge (I deal further with the learner's capabilities below).

The second aspect is the degree of engagement and interaction that learners are encouraged to have with the structured digital content (detailed reviews of interaction in online learning or computer-mediated higher education are given by Wallace[3] and Godwin[4]). This engagement and interaction can be achieved by the creator's inclusion of specified learning outcomes (that is, statements that set out what the creator is expecting the learner to learn from engaging with the educational resource) as well as inclusion of activities within the resource that are aimed at getting the learners to demonstrate (to themselves at least) that they have probably learned what was expected of them. This is a basic tenet of learning design that has been well explicated by Dyke and his colleagues,[5] but it is important to recognize how limited are the opportunities for creator-designed learning activities if the interaction is solely by the learner with the content, and not also by the learner with a teacher and the learner with other learners, as explained by Moore.[6] Of course, more knowledgeable and sophisticated learners are able to instantiate their own "learning activities" by which they internalize new (to them) knowledge.

The major limitation for learning activities that a teacher embeds within educational resources is that any feedback to the responses that learners make to an activity has to be either predetermined or left to the learners to judge for themselves. This is even the case with many "intelligent" computer-based systems, because such sophisticated feedback systems are still based on predetermined responses to the learner's behavior, albeit a greater range and more styles of responses. In this sense there are no direct opportunities for the learners to use dialogue with someone else to help recommunicate or negotiate their own interpretation of what they have learned. This can hinder less confident and inexperienced learners who have yet to develop their metalevel skills in learning to learn and managing their own knowledge in a specified field.

This distinction in the way educational content is structured for different purposes can be clearly seen in the differences between OpenCourseWare in the style provided by MIT (http://ocw.mit.edu/index.html), consisting largely of educational resources without pedagogic structure or learning design that require sophistication in the user (which can be expected in other educators and graduate-level students, who are their primary targets) as compared to many of the open, distance, and e-learning style resources seen on OpenLearn (http://www.open.ac.uk/openlearn) from the UK Open University (UKOU), where the resources are designed to help less sophisticated learners readily engage with them (which matches the UKOU's aims to widen participation in higher education).

The majority of OER developed so far have been of the MIT OpenCourseWare (OCW) type. These are basically resources derived from and supporting a classroom-based approach to teaching, where there is a single teacher or tutor involved in teaching a course. This approach (which I have called OER 1.0) has many entailments.

First, it is interesting to other teachers and lecturers because it relates closely to what they have to do, providing lesson plans, reading lists, and so forth from acknowledged leaders in their field.

Second, it is of interest to current MIT undergraduate students choosing their next course, prospective undergraduate students who can more clearly see what they will be signing up for, and students from other higher education institutions who can compare these resources with what their institution provides.

Third, however, OCW is not as readily accessible and understandable by those lacking confidence and formal qualifications and is not ideal for self-study unless you are a skilled self-studier or independent learner. OCW constitutes a set of resources, not pedagogically designed open learning materials.

Fourth, while OCW is translated, used, and adapted by others, it is largely on a bilateral basis between individuals and the originating institutions and between two institutions. The software support environment does not easily facilitate the collaborative development of OER because each wants to have a highly localized version rather than work on a single common version. In a similar vein, there is no supporting environment for learners to engage with each other over the study of these resources.

The second major approach to OER (OER 2.0) is that of creating self-study materials whereby the content has been designed to be more accessible to study without significant prior educational experience or qualifications in that subject and has been placed in a learning environment that does encourage some learner–learner interaction and possibly learner–teacher interaction, thus adding to the range of activities and tasks that can support learning. This approach brings in additional entailments that I deal with below.

Learner–Content Interaction

The abilities and motivations of learners are much influenced by their previous educational experiences, often measured by their success in gaining educational qualifications, the value placed on learning by their families and social/cultural group, and the amount of time and space that can be afforded to learning within their work and home commitments. Further, there is the distinction between formal learning, where achievement is recognized through assessment practices and has value in the labor market, and nonformal learning, where self-assessment is a bigger feature and provides self-gratification but where it is harder to demonstrate that "success" to others, particularly employers. All these features can influence how much time an individual learner will take to achieve the given or self-set learning goals.

With educational materials, the presumed level of understanding involved in terms of the complexity and sophistication of the ideas presented and need for prerequisite knowledge is mixed up with the form in which such material is presented to the learner, in particular the levels of interactivity and integration.[7] To some degree, where there are stated learning outcomes, these provide another measure of knowing when learning has been achieved; where there are not learning outcomes, the task becomes more open ended. Even so, different media influence the style and amount of information that can be absorbed and then processed by the learner.[8]

Learning can arise from the interaction between the learner and the content and is a property of the learner, a change in their "knowing" about the world as they interpret it. Whether the content is static (for example, text) or dynamic (for example, animation), is linear (for example, audio) or nonlinear (for example, a concept map), it becomes interactive only when a learner engages with it. It is through interaction that learners make sense of what they are interacting with, reconfiguring their mental map of how things fit together and the nature of the links between them.

The degree of sense making resulting from these interactions, whether it is surface learning or deep learning, depends on the abilities and capabilities of the learner. With content that is designed for educational purposes, then, the creator has already provided a sense making structure to the material and learners are either accepting this given sense making structure or adding new sense making structures of their own, that is, providing a new interpretation or formulation, either internally as part of their mental map or externally in the form of a new piece of content (most obviously as their own notes or as the product of a given assignment).

Teacher–Learner and Learner–Learner Interactions

It is this testing or assessment element that can most enhance the educational effectiveness of content, because it is the testing of the meaning of new knowledge against existing knowledge within a learner's mental map that is a key aspect of learning. That is why assessment activities (show me what you know and can do) need to be tied to learning outcomes (what I want you to know and do) and often why less experienced learners benefit a lot from discussion with teachers or other learners, as they test their understanding of new knowledge against the understanding of the teacher and other learners. Until recently, open educational materials tended to be print based, but the essence of digital OER is that computer- and web-based technologies provide greater scope for learners to be able to interact with more than just the content if they are informal distance learners and not part of a structured, taught course. There is a greater opportunity to shift from informal learning being a private, individual activity to a public, more social activity. Thus, a key feature of open educational resources is that they have the capability to be dynamic rather than passive in nature, are supportive of communication between users rather than simply information sharing, and move away from just individual interaction with the content to more social engagement with a shared discourse.[9]

A consequence of the increased opportunities for sharing and creating new content, whether that is new versions of existing content or new material supplementing or augmenting the existing content, is not only that the creators (teachers) need to think carefully about the learning design of their materials but also that users (learners) need to think about or be helped to understand their own learning processes as well as collaborate or cooperate in that learning design. In effect, both creators and learners need to realize that content is merely a mediating object between all those involved in education and is not itself the repository of learning. Individual learning lies in the minds of people and is demonstrated in the sense making that lies within the content they produce by themselves, but social learning[10] can be expressed through the collective, additional sense making that user–generated content by a community of practice enables.[11]

Ensuring Quality of Open Educational Content

I have articulated some basic design principles that teachers can use for creating effective educational content, but how do I know it is good quality teaching material as a (naïve) learner (or even teacher)? Building upon what I have said already, there are three main features of quality that need to be considered when answering this question:

1. Is the material academically sound in that it appropriately covers the body of knowledge and meaning for that topic?
2. Is it pedagogically robust in that the way the material has been structured matches a stated pedagogical model and sets out appropriate learning outcomes and ways of assessing those outcomes?
3. Is the way the material is presented through the chosen media helpful in enabling learners to meet the learning outcomes?

For many OER the quality assurance is carried out by the originating institution since the materials are derived from mainstream teaching activities that are already subject to quality assurance processes. Some aspects, such as academic and presentational quality, may be left to other authorities to manage, for example, publishers of textbooks. In essence, the overall quality of OER sourced from universities comes from existing procedures of small-scale peer review within the university community and the institution acting as a gatekeeper.

This is different from those OER that are derived from the efforts of either individuals (as in the Connexions site) or a broader community (as in Wikiversity), where the overall quality of such OER is judged using open peer-rating or -reviewing mechanisms. In some cases the nature and form of the authoring and publishing environment means that the presentational quality and some parts of the pedagogic quality can be reasonably assured. It is the academic quality that has to be earned, either through the existing authority of the originator or by proving oneself to be an authority by the ratings of this broader peer community.

What Makes Open Educational Content Effective (Again)?

I have argued above that the effectiveness of open educational material is usually improved where there is a clear sense making structure, a narrative that relates to explicit learning outcomes. It also helps to have formal or informal assessment tasks or learning activities linked to those learning outcomes. A single image or video clip will usually lack an explicit narrative or learning outcome and therefore places much greater demands on the users to construct their own narratives and implicit learning outcomes without the help of a mediator (teacher). Ideally, OER should be presented in an environment that allows different users (learners and creators) to communicate with each other, to develop a discourse that adds another sense making layer to that present in the original material.

Evaluating the effectiveness of just the assets cannot be done without taking into account the context in which they are used. First, OER can be a replacement for closed educational resources, that is, ones developed by teachers for their own use. Second, they can also be a supplement where educational resources are scarce.

In both cases they can make a difference to teachers because in principle, institutionally quality-assured and/or collectively developed resources should be much better than those individuals can develop on their own (the wisdom of the crowd). This will free the teacher from being a major developer of resources (teacher-centered) to devoting more time to being a supporter of learning (learner-centered). This may lead to greater levels of achievement by the learners, but a more significant measure will be teacher and student satisfaction levels with both the learning resources and the teacher support. The happier they are, the more conducive will be the learning environment.

Some learners can still achieve whatever the environment, but others need support. Open educational resources do not ensure that overall standards will be higher, that a greater proportion of students will achieve the highest grades, but they can increase the absolute numbers of people participating and provide a greater range of ways for people to learn, to give them more control of when and how they learn rather than having to fit in with selective, predetermined opportunities.

So who puts the education into open educational content? At the moment the teachers do most of this, but they also need the learners to play their part. And if we accept that there is a large informal and nonformal side to education that can be nurtured by OER, then in theory, and hopefully in practice, everyone can be a teacher as well as a learner and put the education into their own open educational content.

Endnotes

1. David Wiley, "The Current State of Open Educational Resources," Open Content Blog, posted February 3, 2006, http://opencontent.org/blog/archives/247.

2. UNESCO, *Final Report*, from the Forum on the Impact of OpenCourseWare for Higher Education in Developing Countries, Paris, July 1–3, 2002, http://unesdoc.unesco.org/images/0012/001285/128515e.pdf.

3. Raven Wallace, "Online Learning in Higher Education: A Review of Research on Interactions among Teachers and Students," *Education, Communication and Information* 3, no. 2 (2003): 241–80.

4. Steve Godwin, *A Preliminary Evaluation of the Concepts of Interaction and Interactivity in Computer Mediated Learning Environments*, The Impact of Interaction and Integration in Computer Mediated Higher Education (ICHE) Project Report 1, 2005, http://kn.open.ac.uk/public/document .cfm?docid=6083.

5. Martin Dyke, Grainne Conole, Andrew Ravenscroft, and Sara de Freitas, "Learning Theory and Its Application to E-Learning," in *Contemporary Perspectives in E-Learning Research: Themes, Methods, and Impact on Practice*, ed. Grainne Conole and Martin Oliver (Oxford, UK: Routledge-Falmer, 2007), 82–97.

6. Michael G. Moore, "Editorial: Three Types of Interaction," *The American Journal of Distance Education* 3, no. 2 (1989): 1–6, http://www.ajde.com/Contents/vol3_2.htm.

7. Mary Thorpe, *Interaction and Integration in Computer-Mediated Teaching in Higher Education: Researching the Combined Impact of Pedagogy and Technology*, The Impact of Interaction and Integration in Computer-Mediated Education (ICHE) Project Report 2, 2005, http://kn.open.ac.uk/public/document. cfm?docid=6084.

8. Mary Thorpe and Steve Godwin, *The Study Workload Implications of Computer-Mediated Interaction*, The Impact of Interaction and Integration in Computer-Mediated Education (ICHE) Project Report 4, 2006, http://kn.open.ac.uk/public/document.cfm?docid=7857.

9. Grainne Conole, "Activity Based Learning: Making the Right Choices for Successful Learning Design," invited keynote address at the Center for Learning Technology Sixth Annual E-Learning Conference, Trinity College, Dublin, May 2006, streaming video available at http://www.tcd.ie/CAPSL/clt/index.php?page=events.

10. Etienne Wenger, *Communities of Practice, Learning, Meaning, and Identity* (New York: Cambridge University Press, 1998).

11. Simon Buckingham-Shum, "From Open Content Repositories to Open Sense-Making Communities," in *Proceedings of OpenEd 2005: Advancing the Effectiveness and Sustainability of Open Education Conference*, 24–28 (Logan, UT: Center for Open Sustainable Learning, 2005), http://cosl.usu.edu/events/opened2005/docs/opened2005-proceedings.pdf.

Bibliography

Buckingham-Shum, S. "From Open Content Repositories to Open Sense-Making Communities." In *Proceedings of OpenEd 2005: Advancing the Effectiveness and Sustainability of Open Education Conference*, 24–28. Logan, UT: Center for Open Sustainable Learning, 2005. http://cosl.usu.edu/events/opened2005/docs/opened2005-proceedings.pdf.

Conole, Grainne. "Activity Based Learning: Making the Right Choices for Successful Learning Design." Invited keynote address at the Center for Learning Technology Sixth Annual E-Learning Conference, Trinity College, Dublin, May 2006. Streaming video available at http://www.tcd.ie/CAPSL/clt/index.php?page=events.

Dyke, Martin, Grainne Conole, Andrew Ravenscroft, and Sara de Freitas. "Learning Theory and Its Application to E-Learning." In *Contemporary Perspectives in E-Learning Research: Themes, Methods, and Impact on Practice,* edited by Grainne Conole and Martin Oliver, 82–97. Oxford, UK: Routledge-Falmer, 2007.

Godwin, Simon J. *A Preliminary Evaluation of the Concepts of Interaction and Interactivity in Computer Mediated Learning Environments*, ICHE Project Report 1, 2005. http://kn.open.ac.uk/document.cfm?docid=6083.

Moore, Michael. "Editorial: Three Types of Interaction." *The American Journal of Distance Education* 3, no. 2 (1989): 1–6.

Open Content Blog. http://opencontent.org.

Thorpe, Mary. *Interaction and Integration in Computer Mediated Teaching in Higher Education: Researching the Combined Impact of Pedagogy and Technology*. ICHE Project Report 2, 2005. http://kn.open.ac.uk/document.cfm?docid=6084.

Thorpe, Mary, and Simon Godwin. *The Study Workload Implications of Computer-Mediated Interaction*. ICHE Project Report 4, 2006. http://kn.open.ac.uk/document.cfm?docid=7857.

UNESCO. *Final Report*. Forum on the Impact of Open CourseWare for Higher Education in Developing Countries, Paris, July 1–3, 2002. http://unesdoc.unesco.org/images/0012/001285/128515e.pdf.

Wallace, Raven M. "Online Learning in Higher Education: A Review of Research on Interactions among Teachers and Students." *Education, Communication and Information* 3, no. 2 (2003): 241–280.

Wenger, Etienne. *Communities of Practice, Learning, Meaning, and Identity*. New York: Cambridge University Press, 1998.

Cathedral of Learning, University of Pittsburgh

Scholarship in a Cloudy World

The Tower, the Cloud, and Posterity

Richard N. Katz and Paul B. Gandel

The essays in this volume have dealt in a variety of ways with the possible impacts of ubiquitous networks, virtualization, open educational resources, open source software, social networks, and the evolving cloud of network-mediated services on the tower—the mission, programs, and services of the college and university. This essay focuses on the impact of the cloud on one critical aspect of the college or university mission—the identification and preservation of the spoken or written record of human activity.

Among other things, colleges and universities are storehouses. Gates and towers—in architecture and in metaphor—have served not only to isolate the life of the mind from the hubbub of the marketplace, but to preserve and protect scarce and sacred knowledge artifacts.[1] This is among our oldest and most precious charges. Like the monasteries and scriptoria that preceded Western universities, the modern college and university is an arbiter, transmitter, and guardian of culture and of the recorded record that comprises a great deal of humankind's shared memory. The question that arises, therefore, in the context of this volume is, Whither posterity? That is, how does the emergence of the cloud affect both the identification and preservation of society's "shared memories" and the role of the college and university in identifying and preserving this material?

This question, to a great extent, has defined the roles of college and university archivists, librarians, curators, and others for centuries. The authors believe that not only is this question of great import to the future of these noble professions, but the identification and preservation of shared memory is in fact the glue that holds culture together. Harvard University professor Chris Dede makes the case that the tacit epistemologies that underlie the technologies and behaviors characterized collectively as Web 2.0 "differ dramatically from [what Dede calls] the 'classical' perspective—the historic views of knowledge, expertise, and learning on which formal education is based." At stake, according to Dede, is a likely rethinking of the classical view of knowledge as consisting "of accurate interrelationships among facts, based on unbiased research that produces compelling evidence about systemic causes."[2] In our view, humankind's assumptions about the nature of collections—what to collect and what to preserve—are rooted in what Dede calls classical epistemology.

Record Keeping and Human Memory Sharing

To parse and address the issues of identifying and preserving shared memory that are raised by the cloud, it may be helpful to think of record keeping and human memory sharing in broad sweeps or epochs. Each epoch is defined to a very great extent by a new and disruptive technology or family of technologies.[3]

Archivy 1.0

The selection and preservation of knowledge for the purpose of creating shared memories is not only a precondition for the development of culture but a survival skill. Preliterate humans survived by documenting, on rocks and in caves, the existence and location of watering holes, dangers, religious places and objects, and hunts.

As well, many early human groups engaged in a specialized and purposeful form of storytelling. Oral speech was in many preliterate cultures the dominant instrument for preserving and sharing human memory. This memorized form "was not the vernacular of casual conversation but an artificially managed language with special rules for memorization, one of which was rhythm."[4] In the oral tradition, selecting knowledge for preservation was frequently a responsibility of a tribe or clan's religious or secular leadership. The preservation of this knowledge involved an amazing, complex, and evolving web of social relationships and responsibilities ranging from inheritance of responsibility for storytelling from father to son, to the emergence of the epic tradition in poetry in ancient Greece and elsewhere. Even after the introduction of writing, vestiges of this oral tradition persist. Official transmitters included the ancient Greek heralds, Roman stentorians, and medieval *jongleurs* and town criers who traveled the European countryside and cities. Even contemporary religious sermonizers or present-day political campaigners might be included.[5] Officially sanctioned speakers have long been employed to entertain, transmit news, or generate sanctions for contemporary and historical events.

As a process for creating shared knowledge or wisdom and of preserving this wisdom, the oral tradition was highly effective and represents an important layer of the foundation on which much prehistoric civilization was built. The "recorded" oral knowledge was remarkably durable. Individuals who were charged with transmitting socially constructed knowledge were taught things verbatim, and it was typically a responsibility that was only passed on to genetic heirs or to people who merited trust. Deviating from a script or improvisation was prohibited. Unless carriers of this knowledge died unexpectedly, the knowledge was reasonably secure and credible. Moreover, the source (provenance) of the information was also very clear. The village voice was always a designated person who was trained by his father, who had in turn been trained by his father, who had been trained by his father, and so on. The community could be really sure "where this information came from."

The durability of knowledge preserved in this fashion, however, was eroded by the emergence of writing. Some of the old stories were recorded and preserved, some morphed into folklore and legend, and some disappeared altogether as oral traditions fell into disuse in the wake of an emergent written tradition.

Archivy 2.0

Archivist Oliver W. Holmes describes this as permitting the "beginning of a passive reservoir of knowledge."[6] With this expanded capacity came (1) the need to systematize both shared memories *and* the physical artifacts that contained them and (2) the need to create a cadre of people skilled in the creation and interpretation of recorded knowledge. As well, shared memory now had physical mass and thus could not be carried from village to city in the minds of storytellers, elders, or other icons of the oral tradition. The challenge of these new realities gave rise to the emergence of libraries, like that in Alexandria, and of *bibliophylakes*, a special and influential class of officials charged with the creation, collection, care, protection, and interpretation of this precious reservoir. Central to the stature of *bibliophylakes* and their various successors such as librarians, archivists, clerks and others was trust. The oral tradition was rooted in the notion of *verbatim* transmission of information. While there were, no doubt, lapses of accuracy, the oral tradition depended to a very great extent on the shared belief that knowledge that was officially transmitted was accurate. The emergence of writing and the limited spread of literacy meant that social trust needed to be spread farther than ever and that the risk of inaccuracy would also rise. Those charged with creating, collecting, and preserving the human record occupied high positions of trust, and writing—as a representation of reality— became subject to the corruptions of memory lapse, linguistic nuance, legibility, omission, miscopying, and fraud. The rarity of human written recordings and their vulnerability to a variety of threats makes scarcity the defining characteristic of shared memory in this epoch. Other terms that characterize the period (ending around the invention of movable type) might include *durable* (but vulnerable), *instrumental* (serving largely the power elites), and *tightly controlled*.

Archivy 3.0

Archivy 2.0 centers on mediating human communications and recording knowledge through writing on portable media. The central features of Archivy 3.0 are our efforts to (1) produce repeatable verisimilitude in the printed word and images through mechanical means, (2) enlarge shared memory by proliferating recorded knowledge, and (3) expand the reach and influence of human activity through the spoken and written record. These shifts were tectonic in magnitude and shook the foundations of both how societies think about shared knowledge and how they determine what knowledge is to be preserved.

The cause of faithfulness in recorded information was aided by the emergence of the craft of printing. And, of course, the politics of information are continually changing in the face of (1) the increasing abundance of printed materials, (2) ever-expanding rates of literacy throughout the world, and (3) the emergence of English as the global language of business. The impact of printing and in particular of Gutenberg's movable type and the commercialization of abundant paper are well documented. These tectonic shifts resulted in a shift in record-keeping priorities and skills from a primary concern over protecting scarce texts to the concerns surrounding knowledge management—finding and evaluating information of value amidst an increasingly abundant documentary record. Two later technologies added to the disruptions that define this third epoch—photography and xerography. And, of course, this epoch witnessed the emergence of television and radio, whose impact on human communications cannot be minimized but which will not be examined in this essay.

In 1872, Leland Stanford hired the photographer Edward Muybridge to settle a bet about whether there was a point in a horse's gallop when all four hooves leave the ground. Four years later, Muybridge succeeded in capturing a horse in motion using a series of 50 cameras. The photographs were published in a series called *The Horse in Motion* and show quite clearly that, contrary to popular belief, a horse did indeed lift all four hooves off the ground. Muybridge continued to perfect his method of freezing motion into smaller and smaller pieces of time. He produced hundreds of thousands of frozen images of motion of people and animals, including himself.

Photography revolutionized the way we thought about the world and our notions about what we could capture and keep. Photographs rendered their subjects more faithfully than words and drawings and could be reproduced faithfully. Photographers traveled the globe capturing, and thus preserving, monuments and artifacts from faraway lands for people who would never be able to witness these scenes firsthand. And for those who did venture far from home, photography made it possible to take family and home with you in the form of the family picture album. Moreover, as Muybridge first demonstrated, photography made it possible to capture that which was seemingly invisible, such as an instant in a horse's gallop, the microscopic world, and distant galaxies. Photography unleashed a revolution and passion for capturing the world around us. It was, perhaps, an innovation that was perfectly suited to Western society that had embraced empiricism, positivism, and scientific method.

The picture, it seemed, was worth a thousand words.

Sixty-five years after Muybridge captured the collective imagination with his photographs of horses in motion (1937), American law student Chester Carlson invented "a copying process based on electrostatic energy."[7] Carlson's electrostatic process faithfully reproduced words on a page in minutes. The importance of this innovation cannot be understated. This invention simultaneously gave scaling and verisimilitude huge shots in the arm and changed fundamentally the very nature of the "posterity problem." As David Owen put it, "It gave people an extraordinary means of preserving and sharing information, and it placed the rapid exchange of complicated ideas within the reach of everyone, becoming the biggest breakthrough in written communications since Gutenberg."[8]

Photography and xerography made it possible for an enormous number of people to share *identical* knowledge in different places at roughly the same time. For those charged with preserving a meaningful record of shared memory and human experience, these innovations represented a shift from an era of scarcity to one of abundance. This shift demanded fundamental shifts in the philosophy and craft of the archivist. With the proliferation of records came attendant needs to focus on the arrangement of records and on their provenance. As well, this proliferation fostered a growing need for people and for methods that could be trusted to facilitate the appraisal of newly abundant resources and selection of those few records that would faithfully serve the need for shared memory and historical documentation.

Is the Past, Prologue?

The essence of the history of record keeping over the millennia to this point can be reduced to a series of broad concerns:

- Can esteemed and valuable information be *collected*?
- Can we *select* from among records collected those that will create meaningful and unbiased documentary record?
  - ◊ Who selects what becomes "shared memory"?
- Can this information be *protected and preserved*?
- Once collected and appraised for value, can information *be found*?
- *Who has access* to the information?
  - ◊ Under what conditions?
  - ◊ Who controls this access?
  - ◊ How easy or affordable is it to gain access?
- Can the information *be trusted*?
  - ◊ Is it credible?
  - ◊ Is it authentic?
  - ◊ Can we certify its authenticity?
  - ◊ Can we ascertain its provenance?

The shifts that we have described are truly tectonic in magnitude. They can be summarized in part as seen in Table 1.

The shifts from Archivy 1.0 to Archivy 2.0 set humankind on a fundamentally new path, and in many ways humanity's past did not in fact prepare us well for the future. The shift from information scarcity to information abundance cannot be understated in either importance or extent. And study of the history of ideas tells us that the democratization of information must be viewed as a change of enormous magnitude whose far-reaching impacts would have been hard to predict.

Table 1. From Archivy 1.0 to Archivy 2.0

FROM	TO
Human record is oral.	Human record is written.
Knowledge is scarce.	Records are abundant.
Archivists are scarce.	Archivists are scarce.
Recorded knowledge is durable.	Recorded knowledge is durable.
Recording of knowledge is representational (reasonably credible).	Recording of knowledge is literal or facsimile (highly credible).
Preoccupation with preservation.	Preoccupation with selection and appraisal.
Information is accessible by elites.	Information is accessible by many.
Information is easy to find (if extant).	Information is difficult to find.
Information is tightly controlled.	Control of information is distributed.
Provenance is clear.	Provenance is often traceable.

Archivy 4.0: The Digital Revolution

The shift from Archivy 3.0 to Archivy 4.0 is likely to be similarly potent. This is the shift to digital record keeping. While it has been only 60 years since the first electronic computers appeared in the 1940s, today virtually all information is created on computers and stored on optical, magnetic, or flash memory, tape, or other media. Digitization changes things profoundly.

New Economics

The economics of digital record keeping derive not from the ever-increasing costs associated with labor, harvesting trees and refining paper, developing dyes for ink, labor, recycling expended materials, transporting logs, pulp and paper, and so forth but from the economics of innovation we call Moore's law. The cost of computing, storing, and transmitting digital information has declined by about 50 percent each passing 18-month period since the invention of the semiconductor. Using this rule of thumb it is likely that in less than 10 years it will be possible to store the complete collection of the Library of Congress on one's personal storage device. Within 18 years, we will be able to store the Library of Congress holdings on a key fob–sized memory device.[9]

Information Is Superabundant

In 2007 computer industry analyst IDC reported that the world produced 281 exabytes of data that year.[10] This amounts to nearly 30,000 times the holdings of the Library of Congress. The amount of information published each year continues to grow. Nearly 300,000 books were published in 2006 alone, an increase of 0.5 percent from 2005 figures.[11] On July 31, 2006, *Technorati* tracked its 50 millionth blog and about 175,000 new blogs are created each day.[12] Podcasts, videos, blogs, wikis, and digital archives further expand our information sources, and 2.7 billion Google searches are performed each month. Despite the changing economics, the cost of storing all information created was estimated by one writer to approach $7 trillion annually.[13]

Everything Is Connected

Information stored digitally can be viewed or otherwise shared *simultaneously* by anyone with a computer, compatible software, a web browser, a digital display, and a network connection. The cost of transporting information has dropped to nearly nothing. Digital information can be copied infinitely, stored inexpensively, viewed at virtually no cost, and disseminated for pennies. The interconnection of everyone to everything at photonic speeds shortens the latency time needed to create shared memory and changes the behavior of those using information. These changes, of course, make other changes likely, but unpredictable.

Scientific research has already been profoundly changed by the interconnection of resources of all kinds on the network. The scale of scientific research has grown thanks to these interconnections. It is now possible to leverage the cost of enormous scientific instruments such as telescopes and particle accelerators over global scientific communities and to provide simultaneous access to primary research data anywhere on earth.

The role of place in the interconnection of people and information stores is changing and, in fact, diminishing in importance. Notwithstanding the changing role of place, the global network is overall increasing the capacity of repositories to make their collections and data available and to provide great remote support for researchers, seamless access controls, libraries of software tools, and sophisticated data management (storage, metadata, and ontology). The capacity to deliver world class remote services virtually will likely determine the fate of the modern repository in the future.

Everything Can Be Found

In the era of Archivy 2.0, recorded information was scarce and collections were precious and professionally managed. In the era of Archivy 3.0, paper-based information became abundant and the tools that were developed to produce a coherent collection and to extract value for posterity included records disposition, archival appraisal, arrangement of collections, and the production of finding aids. The outputs of these activities include magnificent collections, acres of distilled knowledge, epic backlogs of unprocessed collections acquired for preservation's sake, and finding aids that often provided detail only at the collection or record series level.

In Archivy 4.0, digitization, the emergence of the Internet and web, social tagging, and the unimaginable investment in search technology are making it possible to search at the document level or finer level of detail. These capabilities are a source of enormous private capital, lifting all boats, including that of the historical researcher. These capabilities call into question the meaning of document arrangement (for example, contextualization) in a digital context and the value of the archival appraisal function. They also raise profound questions of public policy as the dependence for discovering archival materials shifts from largely public to largely private (Google, Microsoft, and so forth) providers.

Digital Media Are Ephemeral

Until the 20th century, paper was a remarkably durable storage medium for critical information. As the records of government and business exploded in quantity, durable high-quality paper was replaced by acidic, inexpensive paper. Notwithstanding the special and very real challenges posed by the introduction and widespread use of nondurable paper stock, it is important to understand the profoundly ephemeral nature of digital media in the effort to preserve shared memory and the historical record. Digital collections can be destroyed with a keystroke and can be altered easily without a trace. The ephemerality of digital media reverses the trend toward verisimilitude enabled by photography and xerography, and efforts to lock down digital content via electronic date stamps, watermarks, and other measures are meeting only partial success. At risk is the evidentiary value in records inherent in photographs, photocopies, and other fixed, faithful-and-hard-to-tamper-with media. The ephemeral nature of digital media is also enabling changes in the very nature of the record, the nature of authorship, and the nature of provenance.

The Social Life of Information Is Undergoing Significant Change[14]

If Web 1.0 was chiefly about the posting of a great deal of the world's current information on the web, Web 2.0 refers to changes in how web developers and users use the web. Increasingly the web is shifting from a place of document discovery or a place for self-expression to a place for social interaction, including collaboration. New collaborative tools such as blogs and wikis are making it possible for people to convene around common interests and purposes. Importantly, these tools, along with open source software and open educational resources, are leveling the playing field. From an educational perspective, the web is emerging as perhaps our most open university: a virtual place where people can gather around common interests, review supporting textual resources, and engage in common cause—social, learning, commercial, or otherwise.

The unique qualities of digital media, though, are making it possible for informal groups—often characterized as "crowds"—to engage in work that had been previously individual or institutional in nature. Wikipedia is perhaps the most noteworthy example. Content cocreation is perhaps one of the most important concepts and social behaviors to emerge in Web 2.0 and a development that has the potential to rock the very foundation of archival thinking about authorship and provenance. Similarly, Web 2.0

social behaviors, such as social tagging, will also challenge longstanding professional ideas about the roles and nature of authority control in facilitating access to information.

Finally, we will need to grapple with the concept of Internet time. The rise of the collective makes it possible to witness the rapid emergence of more and more versions of information on the web. Establishing provenance is a quixotic task. Even more important will be developing and socializing methods of asserting or otherwise establishing the credibility, validity, standing, and reliability of information produced often by anonymous crowds in the "fullness" of Internet time. As Farhad Manjoo put it, "The limitless choice we now enjoy over the information we get about our world has loosened our grip on what is—and isn't—true."[15]

Establishing *Identity* Is Hard

Just as it is becoming increasingly difficult to establish the credibility, validity, standing, and reliability of information, it is increasingly difficult to establish the identity and *bona fides* of those seeking to use digital ideas and documents. Colleges, universities, and their archives have long traditions of standing apart from the bazaar, in part to place scholarly coaching and personal reflection in the service of truth seeking. The Internet and the web, however, inherently erode boundaries. The institution's ability to provide its community members with broad access rights—while at the same time mediating others' access to institutional information resources and collaborative spaces—will demand greater care and investment over time. The new media and the ease of movement across Internet territories is necessitating a rethinking of what constitutes community membership and of the rights and authorities of those who are members of a community, those who are interested stakeholders in the community, and those who are not.

Everyone Is an Archivist

As mentioned, information is now superabundant and the capacity to store it and connect to it is now widespread and inexpensive. Social forms are emerging that engage interested amateurs and professionals in tagging information to facilitate its eventual retrieval. Everyone can be a journalist, commentator, expert, and even video star on the Internet. Mundane aspects of life appear every day on sites like YouTube and Facebook, taking so-called "reality TV" to a whole new level. And take the case of George Bell, a research scientist for Microsoft, who has taken Muybridge's notion of easily recording the moment one step further—he is recording his entire life. Bell carries miniature cameras and recorders at all times to record everything he sees and hears. The sensors he carries even record changes in light and temperature. Bell, now 71, began storing his life digitally as an experiment to push the boundaries of information technology. He began by scanning books and important papers he wanted to keep. The project then mushroomed into his recording of all the details of his life, from conversations with plumbers to the scholarly papers he writes. Bell's digital database is known as "MyLifeBits" and presents an interesting challenge in determining how to manage information over a human lifetime. Perhaps even more amazing than Bell recording almost every moment of a lifetime is the fact that he is also personally storing the 1,300 videos, 5,067 sound files, 42,000 digital pictures, 100,000 e-mail messages, and 67,000 web pages that make up "MyLifeBits." The creation of such personal digital repositories is now technologically possible and Microsoft researchers believe that anticipated advances will enable most individuals to store the complete digital record of their lives.

Will the Cloud Block the Sun?

The introduction of the digital record, and the emergence of richly interconnected data communication networks, low-cost digital storage devices, search engines, and a common user interface (web), are changing how people create, retain, dispose of, value, and use information. These technical changes and these shifts in the patterns of information use may disrupt the longstanding archival community with possible serious consequences to human shared memory and to scholarship. These changes can be partly summarized as shown in Table 2. The implications of these shifts are potent and really must challenge us to ask whether knowing the past truly prepares us for the future.

There is little doubt that the digital revolution on balance is contributing in magnificent ways to world literacy, to research, and to the democratization of knowledge. There is no doubt that technologies will cut their own channels in most of our institutions, including colleges, universities, libraries, museums, archives, and others. It is hard to imagine the implications of a single scientific instrument such as the Large Hadron Collider producing nearly 100 million channels of data streaming from each of the two largest detectors and filling 100,000 CDs every second. These CDs would produce a stack to the moon in six months.[16] Or try to imagine the digital artifacts and ephemera of George Bell and the implications of the remorseless recording and storage of unedited human experience.

Table 2. From Archivy 3.0 to the Digital Revolution

FROM	TO
Information is abundant.	Information is superabundant.
Recorded knowledge is durable.	Recorded knowledge is ephemeral.
Information discovery is a public service.	Information discovery is a privately financed search engine.
Finding information is hard.	Everything can be found.
Repository is a place.	Repository is a network address.
Collections are disconnected.	Everything is connected to the network.
Archivists are scarce.	Everyone is an archivist.
Access to information is mediated by institutions.	Access to information varies widely.
Document authorship is knowable.	Document authorship cannot be easily known or reconstructed.
Archival appraisal is an art.	Archival appraisal may be an algorithm based largely on popularity.

Notwithstanding the daunting nature of the challenge, those of us charged with the collection and preservation of the human record must abide. More than this, we must advocate in the name of shared memory and assert standards for the selection and valuation of the evolving historical record. As University of Manitoba Professor Terry Cook put it, "If there is no such place in society where knowledge and meaning can be discerned, where things can be true or not true, where accountability through transparent evidence of actions and ideas by those in power can be readily achieved through good record keeping, where the records themselves in transient digital formats can be certified and locked as authentic and reliable, not tampered with, created when, where, and by whom so asserted, and trusted, then we will enter a new dark age."[17] As we all, like George Bell, create our own "presidential libraries," how many of us will withstand the temptation to "tweak" our autobiographic record so that our shared memory can be a bit rosier or more flattering? Not only do the archival and scholarly communities need to advocate for scholarly rigor and for standards, we must strive to popularize these qualities, imbed them throughout the education system, and instantiate them in search engines and throughout our presence on the Internet.

What may be the emergence of a new and superior epistemology as suggested by Professor Dede could become what Alexis de Tocqueville feared as the tyranny of the majority.[18] Will our capacity to be arbiters of our cultures be enhanced or endangered by subjecting all matters great and small to wiki-ization or to a vote? Will the "American idolization" of facts, trends, taste, and truth crush independence of thought? Will we, as Cook wonders, abandon existing professional standards or fail to construct new ones, leaving a human record possessed of "too much scrambled, meaningless trivia of information where discerning anything of value or having context-rich value statements at all becomes impossible." This state of being is guided by what philosopher Alasdair MacIntyre labeled as *emotivism*, a doctrine holding that all evaluative judgments, especially moral judgments, are merely expressions of preference, attitude, or feeling.[19] It is ironic that just as we became awash in information and wealthy in the tools of discovery, mining, and analysis, the term *truthiness* was coined.[20] Is it possible that as information becomes so voluminous, the standards of selection become so pluralistic, and the content of information becomes so nuanced, feeling will replace analysis as the social barometer of truth?

Perhaps, then, the past is prologue. Cook observes that it is possible that the cloud will envelop and overwhelm the tower, returning us to a dark age. Medieval Europe's scarcity of information and literate souls left many people in the dark. Today's superabundant but decontextualized, filtered, mashed up, Photoshopped, crowd-sourced, and opaque information environment also contains the potential for leaving people in the dark. The filtering of politically unacceptable search results by Google's China search engine is only one example of what may be possible.

What Is to Be Done?

The stakes in the game of how the tower and the cloud interact in the context of the identification and protection of the human historical record are high. Too, the issues regarding the future of those modern day *bibliophylakes* are similarly momentous. How the game will play out is completely unclear.

What is clear is that the stewards of the historical record in the past must now give voice to this great debate. We must present ourselves neither as uncritical enthusiasts of everything shiny and new nor as change-averse curmudgeons protecting a declining turf.

It seems clear, too, that the turf of the modern day *bibliophylake* is not shrinking but changing. To remain relevant and to continue to serve our great purpose, we must separate those principles that will guide our future actions from the methods and structures that have served these principles in the past. Some of the methods and structures will survive; many will not.

We must conceive of a new professional ecosystem and of our place in such a new tangle of relationships. In Archivy 2.0, the *bibliophylake* was likely a member of the religious order and a spiritual brother or sister of the scholar–scribe. In the xerographic era, records managers and archivists were linked. The new media are rendering old social and professional relations ineffectual and are opening the doors for new relations. This new ecosystem needs to be described and new professional communities and networks need to be formed.

The ephemeral nature of digital media is a vexing problem from a preservation viewpoint. Digital technologies create masses of information and conflicting goals for selection and preservation. A key question is, who determines value and for what purposes? Is it the crowd in the cloud? Furthermore, most digital media are themselves subject to easy alteration (that is part of their virtue) and are not durable. And if the storage media are durable, digital data must be readable by software to be useable. The issue of preserving digital data in forms that can be retrieved and read over centuries is enormously problematic, particularly in the sciences, where files of petabyte size are being produced and captured at the expense of billions of dollars. This is a problem of epic size that demands the attention not only of the archival community but of foundations and governments.

One of the major issues associated with preserving shared memories is the identity management issue. Substantial progress is being made in constructing a layer of middleware tools and federation practices that will help ensure that record users are who they claim to be and are authorized to do what they assert they are authorized to do. As well, this middleware infrastructure goes far in protecting the traditional privacy of the researcher. Institutions associated with preserving information need to be engaged in this work and must adapt these tools to the archival context.

Archivists will also face especially complex challenges as regards the protection of privacy. Learning management systems, for example, now make it possible to capture and preserve the classroom contributions of tomorrow's Albert Einstein or George W. Bush. Many faculty members and students might be very uncomfortable if their conversations and interactions in an online class were preserved indefinitely by their institutions. Classrooms are traditional bastions of free speech and for the testing of ideas. "Half-baked thoughts" are encouraged as part of the learning process. Knowing your every thought or proposition might be preserved forever would certainly inhibit the free-wheeling conversations associated with university and college classrooms. Similarly, health records are another area of potential conflict between archival preservation and individual privacy. It is clear that the broad standardization and sharing of digital medical records can have some significant benefits. However, this capability also raises some controversial issues about privacy and ownership, especially with regard to who can keep and use medical records of deceased individuals, which could prove to be valuable historical and medical research resources. New community standards, policies, and laws will need to be considered as social conduct in the digital context changes. The archivist needs to be engaged in this public policy debate. Otherwise, we run the risk of violating public trust or, worse, we begin to censor our history to the point where valuable records are destroyed through self-censorship in the fear that they may be used inappropriately.

And we must move closer to where history is being made. This is a reintegration, for the librarian and archivist have long been associated with those creating the shared memories. In many ways the history of archivy and librarianship is a history of shifting attention from the creators of knowledge to the artifacts themselves and to the great halls we build to house them. In a world of scarcity, those who seek knowledge must travel to the sources of knowledge. In an era of superabundance, those who wish to preserve the knowledge must now return to the wellsprings. The *bibliophylake* cannot likely remain a creature exclusively of the tower. The values we share and the standards that we must promote must be instantiated when and where the future historical record is being created and in the culture of those technology providers whose products are reshaping the landscape of shared human memory. The librarian and archivist must not simply be part of this new "cloud" of digital information artifacts. They must take a leadership role in guiding its policies and practices.

We need nothing less than a new literacy to guide ourselves and our students through the exciting and sometimes frightening new terrain. Perhaps this is the new epistemology referred to by Professor Dede and perhaps it is the scholarly literacy described by Professor Paul Courant in this volume.

Going digital may be the most significant inflection point in the history of human record keeping. Never before has so much information been available to so many people. The implications of having more than a billion people with persistent connections to the Internet and exabytes of information freely and openly available cannot be overstated. With every significant innovation comes unintended consequences and amidst the plentitude that we now enjoy in this arena are found a host of new cautions, threats, and risks. We would never turn back. The cautions, threats, risks, and other unintended consequences of going digital together comprise the challenge for the modern *bibliophylakes*. Our ancestors and we have protected the record of human achievement through wars, revolutions, fire, and flood. Our charge remains the same; the stakes remain monumentally high.

Endnotes

1. Nancy Cantor and Steven Schomberg, "Poised between Two Worlds: The University as Monastery and Marketplace," *EDUCAUSE Review* (March/April 2003), http://net.educause.edu/ir/library/pdf/ERM0320.pdf.

2. Chris Dede, "A Seismic Shift in Epistemology," *EDUCAUSE Review* (May/June 2008), 80, http://connect.educause.edu/Library/EDUCAUSE+Review/ASeismicShiftinEpistemolo/46613.

3. The authors use the term *disruptive* as used by Clayton Christensen to describe a new, low-cost, often simpler technology that displaces an existing, sustaining technology. See Clayton M. Christensen, *The Innovator's Dilemma* (Cambridge, MA: Harvard University Press, 1997).

4. Eric A. Havelock, "The Alphabetic Mind: A Gift of Ancient Greece to the Modern World," *Oral Tradition* 1, no. 1 (1986): 134.

5. Joseph J. Duggan, "The Social Function of the Medieval Epic in the Romance Literatures," *Oral Tradition* 1, no. 3 (1986): 728.

6. Oliver W. Holmes, "History and Theory of Archival Practice," in *University Archives: Papers Presented at an Institute Conducted by the University of Illinois Graduate School of Library Science, November 1–4, 1964,* ed. Rolland E. Stevens. Champaign, IL: Board of Trustees of the University of Illinois, 1965, http://www.archive.org/stream/universityarchivalstev/universityarchivalstev_djvu.txt.

7. Mary Bellis, "The History of Xerox: Xerox Photocopiers and Chester Carlson," About.com: Inventors, http://inventors.about.com/od/xyzstartinventions/a/xerox.htm.

8. David Owen, *Copies in Seconds* (New York: Simon & Schuster, 2004), 12.

9. Thom Hickey, "Entire Library of Congress," Outgoing: Library Metatdata Techniques and Trends by Thom Hickey, http://outgoing.typepad.com/outgoing/2005/06/entire_library_.html.

10. Lucas Mearian, "Study: Digital Universe and Its Impact Bigger Than We Thought," *Computerworld*, March 2008, http://www.computerworld.com/action/article.do?command=viewArticleBasic&articleId=9067639.

11. "Bowker Says Title Output Close to 300,000," *Publishers Weekly,* May 31, 2007, http://www.publishersweekly.com/article/CA6448228.html.

12. "How Many Blogs Are There? 50 Million and Counting," CyberJournalist.net, posted August 7, 2006, http://www.cyberjournalist.net/news/003674.php.

13. David Rosenthal, "Petabyte for a Century," DSHR's Blog, posted July 17, 2007, http://blog.dshr.org/2007/07/update-to-petabyte-for-century.html

14. The term *social life of information* was coined by John Seeley Brown and Paul Duguid in their book, *The Social Life of Information* (Cambridge, MA: Harvard University Press, 2000).

15. Farhad Manjoo, *True Enough: Learning to Live in a Post-Fact Society* (Hoboken, NJ: John Wiley & Sons, 2008), 4.

16. Graham P. Collins, "The Large Hadron Collider: The Discovery Machine," *Scientific American,* January 2008, http://www.sciam.com/article.cfm?id=the-discovery-machine-hadron-collider&page=2.

17. Terry Cook, letter to Richard Katz, July 3, 2008.

18. Alexis de Tocqueville, *Democracy in America* (1835), Chapter XV.

19. "Political Philosophy of Alasdair MacIntyre," The Internet Encyclopedia of Philosophy, http://www.iep.utm.edu/p/p-macint.htm#H5.

20. Dick Meyer, "The Truth of Truthiness," *CBS News*, December 12, 2006. http://www.cbsnews.com/stories/2006/12/12/opinion/meyer/main2250923.shtml. *Truthiness* is the term coined by comedian Steven Colbert in 2006 to describe things "that a person claims to know intuitively or 'from the gut' without regard to evidence, logic, intellectual examination, or facts."

Bibliography

Bellis, Mary. "The History of Xerox: Xerox Photocopiers and Chester Carlson." About.com: Inventors. http://inventors.about.com/od/xyzstartinventions/a/xerox.htm.

"Bowker Says Title Output Close to 300,000." *Publishers Weekly*, May 31, 2007. http://www.publishersweekly.com/article/CA6448228.html.

Brown, John Seeley, and Paul Duguid. *The Social Life of Information*. Cambridge, MA: Harvard University Press, 2000.

Cantor, Nancy, and Steven Schomberg. "Poised between Two Worlds: The University as Monastery and Marketplace." *EDUCAUSE Review* (March/April 2003). http://net.educause.edu/ir/library/pdf/ERM0320.pdf.

Christensen, Clayton M. *The Innovator's Dilemma*. Cambridge: Harvard Business School Press, 1997.

Collins, Graham P. "The Large Hadron Collider: The Discovery Machine." *Scientific American*, January 2008. http://www.sciam.com/article.cfm?id=the-discovery-machine-hadron-collider&page=2.

Cook, Terry. Letter to Richard Katz, July 3, 2008.

de Tocqueville, Alexis. *Democracy in America, 1835.*

Dede, Chris. "A Seismic Shift in Epistemology." *EDUCAUSE Review* (May/June 2008), http://connect.educause.edu/Library/EDUCAUSE+Review/ASeismicShiftinEpistemolo/46613.

DSHR's Blog. http://blog.dshr.org.

Duggan, Joseph J. "The Social Function of the Medieval Epic in the Romance Literatures." *Oral Tradition* 1, no. 3 (1986): 728–766.

Havelock, Eric A. "The Alphabetic Mind: A Gift of Ancient Greece to the Modern World." *Oral Tradition* 1, no. 1 (1986): 134.

Hickey, Thom. "Entire Library of Congress." Outgoing: Library Metatdata Techniques and Trends by Thom Hickey. http://outgoing.typepad.com/outgoing/2005/06/entire_library_.html.

Holmes, Oliver W. "History and Theory of Archival Practice." In *University Archives; Papers Presented at an Institute Conducted by the University of Illinois Graduate School of Library Science, November 1–4, 1964,* edited by Rolland E. Stevens. Champaign, IL: Board of Trustees of the University of Illinois, 1965. http://www.archive.org/stream/universityarchivalstev/universityarchivalstev_djvu.txt.

"How Many Blogs Are There? 50 Million and Counting." CyberJournalist.net. http://www.cyberjournalist.net/news/003674.php.

Manjoo, Farhad. *True Enough: Learning to Live in a Post-Fact Society.* Hoboken, NJ: John Wiley & Sons, 2008.

Mearian, Lucas. "Study: Digital Universe and Its Impact Bigger Than We Thought." *Computerworld*, March 2008. http://www.computerworld.com/action/article.do?command=viewArticleBasic&articleId=9067639.

Meyer, Dick. "The Truth of Truthiness." *CBS News*, December 12, 2006. http://www.cbsnews.com/stories/2006/12/12/opinion/meyer/main2250923.shtml.

Owen, David. *Copies in Seconds.* New York: Simon & Schuster, 2004.

"Political Philosophy of Alasdair MacIntyre." *The Internet Encyclopedia of Philosophy.* http://www.iep.utm.edu/p/p-macint.htm#H5.

From the Library to the Laboratory: A New Future for the Science Librarian?

Mary Marlino and Tamara Sumner

The mission of academic libraries is to support research, education, and scholarship. Historically, libraries have supported this mission by organizing and providing access to information, curating and preserving special collections, and creating physical spaces for collaboration and scholarship. While the broad mission of academic libraries is largely unchanged, transformations in technology, media, and culture are driving fundamental changes in the production and consumption of information and the practice of scholarship. As a result, academic libraries are rethinking their strategies and services to meet the challenges of the digital world and the demands of the "born digital" generation.

Science libraries, in particular, are confronting these challenges as the nature of scientific practice is being dramatically transformed by information technologies.[1] These technologies enable scientific data to be collected, distributed, and archived on an unprecedented scale. The challenge of collecting, managing, and providing access to information not traditionally curated by libraries is compounded by the sheer volume of data, issues of interoperability, documentation, acknowledgment, and authentication.

The term *e-science* is often used to describe new forms of data-driven science enabled by information technologies. Data-driven science is characterized by the analyses of increasingly large quantities of data from distributed sources. E-science methodologies include the identification and visualization of patterns, anomalies, and trends from the mining and analysis of data, coupled with the ability to share the results of analysis processes through the immediacy of the Internet. Within the United States, the term *cyberinfrastructure* is often used interchangeably with e-science.

Currently, e-science is often associated with "big science," that is, large national or international projects such as the Terragrid, the

Biomedical Informatics Research Network (BIRN), or the Linked Environments for Atmospheric Discovery (LEAD) project. These projects are developing sophisticated, distributed technical infrastructures, often based on "grid" technologies, which support domain-specific tools and services facilitating data acquisition, data analysis, and data management. This infrastructure is often housed at major research facilities or national laboratories, and user access to these advanced research services is managed by these groups and made available to individual researchers through the project portal.

For example, in the LEAD project, a scientist can examine different conditions that trigger tornados by bringing together observed weather data from various ground stations and radars. These data must be merged into a uniform data collection that is then fed into a model that simulates the atmosphere. Each time an experiment is conducted, all of the adjustments to the initialization data or model are recorded, resulting in a set of experiments that are available to be shared, rerun, and reanalyzed by others. The LEAD environment is thus making explicit and exposing what has been the more informal, intermediate stages of the scholarly lifecycle: stages that in the past may have been cryptically noted in a lab book with only the results related to a final scholarly article being documented. When the scientist publishes the final report, the primary data sources and these intermediate results can be tied to the final publication to create a richer knowledge product with the capability to be reanalyzed and replicated.

Data-driven science, however, is not confined exclusively to these large disciplinary efforts. A closer look at what is happening on university campuses and in small research labs today reveals that e-science practices are increasingly common and being applied to a wide range of scholarly endeavors in the sciences, social sciences, and humanities.[2] For instance, a master's thesis in urban planning examining the correlation between indigenous plants, property prices, and neighborhood activism may draw on diverse data sources—such as the university's special herbarium collection, the county property tax records and land use data, and records of local voting behaviors—to create an innovative geographic information visualization that can be used by policy makers debating future planning scenarios. In this case, the student is not using custom, discipline-specific e-science tools but is leveraging increasingly available Web 2.0 capabilities; that is, many organizations are now routinely exposing data through public APIs and web services. Tim O'Reilly highlights this "innovation by assembly" phenomenon as a key Web 2.0 principle, commenting that "... when commodity components are abundant, you can create value simply by assembling them in novel or effective ways."[3]

Promises and Challenges for Science Libraries

The examples above illustrate both the promises and the challenges facing e-science and libraries. The promises include the following: the potential for new scientific discoveries that are possible only through large-scale, computational analyses; a new era of transparency and replicability in scientific methods and results; and the potential for widespread democratization of scientific research, given the increasing ubiquity of open access data sources and protocols. However, hidden in these examples are several challenges for universities and their libraries.

- The first challenge concerns the sheer volume of scientific data. In the LEAD example, how does our scientist locate the required data from the various ground stations and radars? In the master's thesis example, how does the student locate the multiple data sets distributed across local government and university servers?

- The second challenge concerns data interoperability. In the LEAD example, merging data from different sources into a uniform data collection requires significant, specialized expertise in all the different data formats and a small army of graduate students. The thesis example, on the other hand, illustrates a new form of scholarly literacy: namely, students need "lightweight" programming skills to combine and remix data from multiple sources.

- The third challenge relates to preserving and documenting the intermediate products. Whose task is it to save these intermediate products for posterity and to document them so that others can find and reuse them? In the LEAD example, what is the university library's role in selecting and preserving original and derivative data sets for future reanalysis? In the thesis example, the student has created a richly annotated version of the library's special herbarium collection, adding new information about the geographic locations of particular species. How does the library incorporate this user-generated content back into its carefully managed special collection?

- Finally, the demands of digital scholarship are requiring new levels of documentation, acknowledgement, and authentication that are often beyond the immediate capabilities or interests of faculty or students. In the LEAD example, when the researcher's final report and associated data and artifacts are put into the university's institutional repository, who will be responsible for ensuring that the university has the appropriate intellectual property rights to post and disseminate this information? In the thesis example, the student's thesis consists of written documentation, software codes for the visualization, and several public data sets. Many campus libraries are tasked with preserving and archiving student theses and dissertations. Again, as in the LEAD case, the library will be challenged to develop stewardship policies and procedures to support the archival and preservation demands of multimedia forms of scholarship.

The implicit fifth challenge is the ability to address these issues at scale: in a large university setting, there could be literally hundreds of projects, theses, and dissertations that embody these characteristics at any given time. How can university libraries prepare to respond to and support these new forms of data-driven scholarship?

New Roles for University Libraries

As a first step, libraries should prioritize making the collections that they manage available to library users through open and documented web service protocols supporting programmatic access to both primary content and metadata. Currently, most libraries support individual users to access collections only through manual, query-driven interfaces. For instance, access to the herbarium collection used in the master's thesis is probably available only through a special web interface enabling users to search the metadata records using keywords and other criteria to generate a fairly traditional list of search results. However, for data-driven science, students and faculty need to be able to run computations over the entire collection and not just access individual records. The visualization created as part of the master's thesis is a relatively simple, yet still challenging, example. In this case, the student wants to construct a visualization that enables users to select a geographic area and view all of the different kinds of plant species located in that area; that is, the visualization needs to dynamically query the library's collection and repackage this information as appropriate for this special application. Today, many of the systems that libraries have put in place to enable access to collections are simply not architected to support programmatic access of any kind, thus severely limiting the usefulness of library collections for these new forms of scholarship.

Libraries are increasingly being asked to play a leadership role in helping universities capture and organize their intellectual assets, such as faculty publications, student dissertations, project reports, and scientific data sets. As illustrated in our examples, the library is often called on at the end of the scholarly process: the researcher needs to include the final report in the institutional repository, or the student has graduated and the dissertation needs to be archived. At this point in the cycle, it takes a significant amount of time, effort, and expense to examine each multimedia scholarly artifact, parse out the constituent components, and decide which of these should be preserved. Too often, libraries are called upon to make these decisions on a case-by-case basis.

Clearly, this approach will not scale to support hundreds or thousands of cases. How and when is it appropriate for the library to become involved? In the LEAD example, is it the scientist's responsibility to ensure that the intermediate products that underpin the final report are included in the institutional repository? Is it the library's responsibility to store the data sets that this work depends on, or is it the responsibility of e-science projects such as LEAD to provide this service to their disciplinary communities? Should university libraries partner with federally funded facilities such as the National Center for Atmospheric Research or San Diego Supercomputing Center to provide these archival services? In the case of the master's thesis, should the library wait until the student defends his or her dissertation and then try to acquire the software codes from the student's laptop? Or, does the library partner with academic computing to provide students with the facilities to create multimedia artifacts on campus infrastructure and develop processes for archiving these artifacts as appropriate?

E-science and Web 2.0 technologies are promoting and enabling scholars to create new works that build on data from multiple sources. As described in our examples, viewing these works and archiving these works can potentially infringe on the intellectual property rights of the creators of the original data sets. As libraries take on responsibilities for hosting and/or archiving these new works, they will also need to take on new responsibilities for rights management. Specifically, library staff must develop expertise in tracing intellectual property rights, negotiating clearances as appropriate, and communicating the rights and terms of use of digital artifacts to library users. Traditionally, these activities have been the purview of legal departments. However, as new forms of scholarship proliferate, relying on the university's legal counsel will not scale and will be very expensive.

Libraries already spend a significant amount of time and energy on patron education. In a university setting, this typically means library staff answering individual reference questions, giving presentations in departments and classes, and offering seminars to students on how to search library collections. If libraries succeed in a making their collections programmatically available through web service protocols, who is going to help faculty and students to effectively use these new capabilities? Promoting the tools and methodologies of e-science and other new forms of scholarship presents a major opportunity for libraries to play a proactive role in training the next generation of scholars.

Another important area for patron education is intellectual property rights. As more faculty and students create innovative forms of scholarship and publish these artifacts in nontraditional venues, it will become increasingly important that these artifacts are made available under appropriate licensing schemes. In short, library staff can help faculty and students to navigate the complexities of Creative Commons and other licensing schemes to make sure that scholarly work is as open as possible while balancing the rights and ownership needs of the creator and the university.

Conclusion

The discussions above illustrate many of the major challenges on the horizon for academic libraries in the years ahead. Libraries have an opportunity to build on their significant collections and content, their expertise in information management, and their historical role in supporting scholarship to become essential players in e-science in the academic enterprise. Barriers along the way include lack of leadership and vision, the more pedestrian issues of lack of technical expertise and money, the strategic pitfalls of inadequate long-term planning, and the all-too-human tendency to keep doing what you know how to do and not acknowledge that the world has changed.

The stakes for libraries are high: the last ten years have been very difficult as libraries' preeminence in supporting information seeking has been challenged by ubiquitous information on the web made easily accessible by commercial search engines. Our two scenarios illustrate the importance of data acquisition, data analysis, and data management skills for new forms of scholarship. Will librarians be able to insert themselves into the emerging processes of e-science, or will scientists and students bypass librarians and their potentially valuable services and go it alone?

It is our belief that the ramifications of "going it alone" are not in the long-term interests of either universities or science. For universities, this strategy only increases the costs and complexities of managing the institution's intellectual assets. For science, the absence of a strong partnership with libraries will hamper communication and dissemination efforts and, ultimately, scientific discovery and progress. For both universities and science, the time to lay the groundwork for this new era of collaboration and partnerships is now.

Endnotes

1. Michael Wright, Tamara Sumner, Reagan Moore, and Traugott Koch, "Connecting Digital Libraries to eScience: The Future of Scientific Scholarship," *International Journal on Digital Libraries* 7 (October 2, 2007): 1–4.

2. Gregory Crane, Alison Babeu, and David Bamman, "eScience and the Humanities," *International Journal on Digital Libraries* 7 (October 2, 2007): 117–22; Brian Lamb, "Dr. Mashup; or, Why Educators Should Learn to Stop Worrying and Love the Remix," *EDUCAUSE Review* (July/August 2007): 12–25, http://connect.educause.edu/Library/EDUCAUSE+Review/DrMash uporWhyEducatorsSho/44592.

3. Tim O'Reilly, "What Is Web 2.0: Design Patterns and Business Models for the Next Generation of Software," *O'Reilly* (September 30, 2005), http://www.oreillynet.com/pub/a/oreilly/tim/news/2005/09/30/ what-is-web-20.html.

Bibliography

Crane, Gregory, Alison Babeu, and David Bamman. "eScience and the Humanities." *International Journal on Digital Libraries* 7 (October 2, 2007): 117–22.

Lamb, Brian. "Dr. Mashup; or, Why Educators Should Learn to Stop Worrying and Love the Remix." *EDUCAUSE Review* (July/August 2007): 12–25.

O'Reilly, Tim. "What Is Web 2.0: Design Patterns and Business Models for the Next Generation of Software." *O'Reilly* (September 30, 2005). http://www. oreillynet.com/pub/a/oreilly/tim/news/2005/09/30/what-is-web-20.html.

Wright, Michael, Tamara Sumner, Reagan Moore, and Traugott Koch. "Connecting Digital Libraries to eScience: The Future of Scientific Scholarship." *International Journal on Digital Libraries* 7 (October 2, 2007): 1–4.

Social Networking in Higher Education

Bryan Alexander

The many projects and services under the Web 2.0 umbrella are now a fact of the global information world. Technorati last tracked 70 million updated blogs, a number that continues to grow.[1] *Wikipedia*, having outpaced *Encyclopedia Britannica* in number of articles and word count, has become the most famous and at the same time most disparaged encyclopedia in centuries.

Social networking services routinely enroll millions. Social music-sharing services continue to grow, as Last.fm continues to build a user base and Apple's iTunes now maintains a social function, My iTunes (http://www.apple.com/itunes/myitunes). It is no longer shocking to realize that photos are largely digital, rather than analog; it is also not surprising that they are published in active social networks, such as Flickr and Picasa. RSS feeds appear not only on most blogs and news sites, but on campus home pages and corporate intranets. Folksonomic tagging, briefly controversial, now appears in the most widely used platforms, like Amazon.com and YouTube.

Such a list can go on, but students are sometimes better positioned than older campus staff members to enumerate it. Teenagers might blog at the moment, or have either a MySpace or Facebook account, then shift to another platform as it emerges. They might not maintain wikis, but *Wikipedia* is both useful to them and perhaps slightly exciting as its notoriety grows. To post to a forum, add to a friend's wall, check out an attractive person's photos, or follow a sports figure via YouTube clips is generally unremarkable. And these are teenagers; younger children did not experience Web 1.0. These kids might play with Webkinz or Neopets (http://www.webkinz.com, http://www.neopets.com), creatures with elaborate social lives in Web browsers. Perhaps they played with other children as pirates (Puzzle Pirates, http://www.puzzlepirates.com), or fellows in Disney theme parks (Virtual Magic Kingdom, http://vmk.disney.go.com), or playful flightless waterfowl (Club Penguin, http://www.clubpenguin.com). Not yet in middle school, future college students are already participating in online social networks, consuming digital media there, and starting to create digital content. Web 2.0 is not remarkable; it describes simply the background structure of media and socialization.

How can colleges and universities respond to this world, which has erected itself around us in a very few years? As we nurture campus networks, support users in their engagement with the entire digital cosmos, how do we respond to this subtle transformation in the environment? And as we continue our investment in licensed content, licensed applications, locally accessible databases, and password-protected courseware, how do we experience this parallel universe of sometimes breathtaking openness and sociability? Several avenues are open to us and have already been trodden by some institutions: learning from successful architecture, following new and emerging technologies that are changing learning (what some call Learning 2.0), and rethinking literacy.

Identifying Successful Architecture

To begin with, we can examine what works in Web 2.0. That is, without revisiting the endlessly vexed question of defining the term, we can identify the information architecture components that have enabled the movement's quantitative success. One of those pieces is microcontent. To create a blog post, one only need write a paragraph, without using (or knowing) HTML. To create a blog from scratch, the user simply fills out a form, which is about as challenging as buying a DVD from Amazon: No knowledge of graphic design, style sheets, FTP, or web-server protocol is needed. To edit a wiki requires even less time. Adding a URL to del.icio.us means a click and a few fields. This lowering of the bar for digital publishing explains the Web 2.0 content boom.

We are already familiar with microcontent publishing in higher education. What else is uploading a syllabus to one's Moodle course or forwarding a document to be turned into an e-reserve? Higher education has also experienced a gold rush in microcontent via course management systems, with enormous amounts of class materials uploaded by faculty who would certainly "web up" less if forced to use an HTML editor and FTP client. Perhaps focusing on this homegrown microcontent process, making it easier and more visible, will grow digital teaching still further.

What our course management systems and databases do not generally offer, however, which Web 2.0 does, is the social factor. The history of social software's popularity proves that people very much want to communicate with others online. We love reading other writers, listening and commenting on their podcasts, checking their daily lives via Twitter, laughing at photos on MySpace. The two-way nature of social software, its role in the read/write web, makes this function self-reinforcing, as my comment on your blog entices a third person to comment, which grows your blog's total content still further, and so on. The openness and searchability of such content to the entire web-accessing world means content can find consumers no matter the niche, in classic long-tail fashion.

A virtual learning environment consisting solely of students and instructor, in contrast, cannot partake of these network effects. One way forward for higher education is to nudge more digital content into the open web, combining our honed wariness about privacy and security with our awareness of the full-blown social web.

Learning from Learning 2.0

Another way forward is to learn more about those who have already leaped into the web to teach, and to follow the emerging Learning 2.0. Higher education faculty have been quietly blogging for some time, and in various formats. Professors "web up" course syllabi, blog about their research interests, advocate for their field in the public sphere (as public intellectuals), require students to blog, and hold professional seminars in distributed inter-blog conversations. While *Wikipedia* takes the lion's (or vulture's) share of educational attention, faculty and their students have been creating wikis for Latin literature and Romantic poetry, spectroscopy and Karl Marx, taking advantage of what may be the world's most collaborative writing platform. Professors podcast lectures and course notes, while some students podcast right back (Swarthmore's War News Radio, for example). And those faculty have used Web 2.0 to record, share, and reflect on their experiences, participating in, while taking advantage of, the "small pieces loosely joined" style of social media conversation. One may easily read or listen to edu-bloggers, and find articles, notes, and an increasing number of print books on Web 2.0. A large body of such knowledge based on reflected practice now exists; we can draw on it to ease the way for campus explorers after such pioneers have publicly blazed sociable trails.

Pointing to such trailheads might mean not supporting Web 2.0 technologies, but getting out of the way of users. An increasing number of colleges and universities have paid Apple for iTunes U or installed blog and wiki platforms. A large number have not, or at least not at the enterprise level, for reasons ranging from LDAP integration to open source worries. Given the extensive rise in off-campus platforms, which range in cost from free to inexpensive, at times it might be a better use of staff resources to point faculty off-site, outsourcing that support. Faculty increasingly arrive on campus with off-site dependencies, which taken together constitute what a recent CIO.com article calls "the shadow IT department."[2]

Downsides can include, besides the usual outsourcing difficulties, a loss of campus branding without a negotiated host and the expending of some research time to select appropriate third parties. But as Web 2.0 continues to expand and campus IT budgets do not swell at that rate, recognizing the already existing off-campus support might be practical.

As the world becomes increasingly shaped by Web 2.0 practices, our collective experience of information is transformed. Citizens increasingly contribute content to global conversations, from pedestrians publishing mobile phone photos on the BBC site to South Korea's OhmyNews, leading to a rebirth in citizen journalism.[3] Our perceptions of YouTube videos, blog posts, and even books at Amazon.com's site are shaped by popular interventions, rankings, and responses.

Rethinking Literacy and Thinking Critically

Two responses appear to be incumbent on higher education. The first involves rethinking literacy, as colleges have taught a variety of literacies for decades (speech, writing, media). If we want our students to engage the world as critical, informed people, then we need to reshape our plans as that world changes. To an extent, teaching students to use IP-restricted databases is to prepare them for rare experiences. Universities can also draw on more than a decade of work by librarians on information literacy or information fluency.[4] Second, to the extent campus populations already contribute to Web 2.0 projects, higher education can become more deliberate in those interventions. For example, while many students arrive on campus with some degree of technological fluency, they may lack the intellectual tools to think critically about much of their experience.

Discussions of privacy and copyright, and questions about creativity and appropriation, citizenship, and governance can become grounded in years of social media experience. Such instruction and conversation is well suited to the first-year seminar and responds well to interdisciplinarity. IT professionals, librarians, faculty, and students can contribute from their specialties, traditions, and experience. Consider the case of *Wikipedia*. It cuts across disciplines, from faculty in computer science to political science to sociology. Librarians bring to bear more than a century of information retrieval and current professional discussion. IT staff can explain IP tracking, wiki structures, and markup. How much better than simply avoiding *Wikipedia* would such an intellectual and professional engagement be!

Summary

For each of the approaches suggested in this essay, intercampus collaboration is more necessary than ever. Web 2.0 projects develop with a speed considered fast even for the digital world, rippling across computing categories while developing new ones. (Just what is Twitter; microblogging? Then what is Pownce?) Sharing experiences and lessons learned with these many platforms is powerful and benefits from a large field of case studies. Approaches beyond the three outlined in this brief discussion should surface and be discussed in the best traditions of the open source world and of academe. Only then can we begin to prepare … for Web 3.0.

Endnotes

1. David Sifry, "The State of Technorati, April 2007," *Sifry's Alerts* (posted April 3, 2007), http://www.sifry.com/alerts/archives/000492.html.

2. Ben Worthen, "User Management: Users Who Know Too Much and the CIOs Who Fear Them," *CIO* (February 15, 2007), http://www.cio.com/article/28821.

3. Dan Gillmor, *We the Media: Grassroots Journalism by the People, for the People* (Sebastopol, CA: O'Reilly Media, Inc., 2004).

4. See Association of College and Research Libraries, *Presidential Committee on Information Literacy: Final Report* (Washington, DC: ACRL, 1989), http://www.ala.org/ala/acrl/acrlpubs/whitepapers/presidential.cfm, as well as the ACRL's website, *Information Literacy*, http://www.ala.org/ala/acrl/acrlissues/acrlinfolit/informationliteracy.cfm.

Bibliography

Association of College and Research Libraries. *Information Literacy* website. http://www.ala.org/ala/acrl/acrlissues/acrlinfolit/informationliteracy.cfm.

Association of College and Research Libraries. *Presidential Committee on Information Literacy: Final Report*. Washington, DC: ACRL, 1989. http://www.ala.org/ala/acrl/acrlpubs/whitepapers/presidential.cfm.

Gillmor, Dan. *We the Media: Grassroots Journalism by the People, for the People*. Sebastopol, CA: O'Reilly Media, Inc., 2004.

Sifry, David. "The State of Technorati, April 2007." *Sifry's Alerts* (posted April 3, 2007). http://www.sifry.com/alerts/archives/000492.html.

Worthen, Ben. "User Management: Users Who Know Too Much and the CIOs Who Fear Them." *CIO* (February 15, 2007). http://www.cio.com/article/28821.

Scholarship: The Wave of the Future in the Digital Age[1]

Paul N. Courant

I've been asked to write about pretty much anything I want to in the broad area of information technology (IT), the research university, and the university library. In brief, it seems to me that the most interesting and important questions center on the ways in which advances in IT change (and, equally important, don't change) what universities do and how they do it. To get to the punch line, I will argue that the defining characteristic of good universities—the production of careful scholarship in service of the creation of knowledge and understanding—is and ought to be unchanged by changes in IT. At the same time, new technologies have been disruptive and productive with regard to important aspects of the way in which scholarship is produced, made public, taught, and learned, and there is (and should be) more disruption yet to come. Thus, I take the position (as I have done before) that the response of the academy to changes in IT rightly includes both conservative and revolutionary elements—conservative in terms of mission and revolutionary in terms of how the mission is attained.[2]

The Importance of Scholarly Literacy

Research universities and liberal arts colleges have always spent a good deal of effort conveying the value of scholarly method to their students, including the great majority who will lead most of their lives outside the academy. Scholarly methods are valuable for practical work, in both the learned and less learned professions, and they are essential to the great pleasure that can be taken in understanding the world and oneself, in leading an examined life, and in being an effective member of society. Ubiquitous access to information poses a risk that the special character of scholarly work and understanding can often be skipped altogether, because it is now easy to obtain answers to questions that are "good enough," via any number of tools that are immediately, freely, and conveniently available on the web. Equally important, the process of digging through sources, grappling with ambiguity, getting confused, and finding a way out can often be avoided when one can easily find the "good enough."

Partly in response to these concerns, there has been much talk about the importance of developing "information literacy." I will argue here that our most important audience is already information literate and then some.[3] Our interest should be in ensuring the production of something that we might call "scholarly literacy," by which I mean the understanding of sources, methods, and their use that is at the heart of knowing what one knows and does not know. The problem is that the remarkable growth of information literacy has both enhanced our technical ability to produce scholarly literacy, by greatly increasing access to resources, while at the same time reducing the imperative to engage in sound scholarly practice, by making it so much easier to do work that is "good enough." The challenge that we face will not and should not be that of turning back the clock, our task is to take ubiquitous information literacy and exploit it as an asset for the development of scholarly literacy. (There would be a high payoff, by the way, to generating a phrase that is jazzier and more marketable than "scholarly literacy.")

Changes in IT—particularly the digitization of information—affect academic work of all kinds. It is important to remember that (like all technologies) IT is instrumental, rather than a goal in itself. The importance and value of IT arise from the ways it affects the use of information in the service of activities that we find to be valuable—solving partial differential equations, searching bibliographical data, enabling collaborative learning and teaching, making objects of scholarly interest available in many places at the same time, bringing music and images to consumers' homes and laptops, and, of course, many more. In the current context, what is important is how IT affects how we learn (I include research within learning) and teach.

It seems to me that the radical changes in the practice of scholarship (and many other activities) that derive from IT take place principally via two mechanisms—networking and copying. It used to be expensive to get information from one place to another, and very expensive to do so quickly. It's now cheap, indeed approximately costless at the margin, given the requisite hardware and fiber. It used to be expensive to make copies of text, images, and sound. It's now cheap, also essentially costless at the margin. (None of these activities is as inexpensive as they look to the end user, and the question of how the relevant infrastructures are to be paid for is important. But the point here is that from the perspective of literally billions of people, copying and shipping information around is essentially costless.) What is not cheap, as Joseph Esposito and others have pointed out repeatedly, is to figure out what is important and valuable in the stream of information that is now so easy to produce and make publicly available.[4] Nor is it likely to become so. In a world where there is more information than anyone can process, the traditions and methods of scholarship (which, at their best, turn information into knowledge and sometimes even into wisdom) and academic libraries should be especially useful. And new IT can help to ameliorate the problem that it has created, in that many of the tools that have been developed can be used to focus the range of material to be searched.

Fundamentally, scholarship is about learning, describing, and explaining what one has learned and how one has learned it. From the most reductionist science to the most interpretive work in the humanities, to practice the scholar's trade it is essential that we be able to provide our readers (or viewers) with accurate and reliable guides to the sources of our knowledge and understanding. Weeks, months, years, or decades from the time that a scholarly work is made public, a user of that work must be able to follow the chain of interpretation employed by the original scholar. If we are to stand on the shoulders of giants, we need to know exactly whose shoulders they are and where they can be found. Thus, when I cite a paper by Paul Samuelson[5] in my own work, a subsequent reader can reliably and accurately find Samuelson's paper, determine the accuracy of my citation, and dispute (or not) my interpretation. If things are working well, the dispute can be limited to interpretation, because we will have good bibliographic control over the sources themselves. The ability to replicate sources and methods (and thus to understand both insights and errors) across long periods of time is essential for the practice of scholarship. Without it we cannot know what our predecessors knew or thought that they knew, and hence we cannot make reliable use of their work. Put simply, it is essential that we be able to answer the question "what were they thinking," in order to make sense of what they said and did, whoever "they" may be.

In the good old days, when print was the only practical medium for communication of most scholarship, and when printing and distributing print was expensive, bibliographic control was relatively straightforward. An edition of a scholarly work (or pretty much any published work) could be well and compactly described with metadata that was natural for the publisher to produce and the librarian to collect. The second printing of the third edition of a particular book would be (almost) identical and (almost) identically described pretty much wherever it might be kept. Precision and reliability were even better for academic journals. (My colleagues who are in cataloging can go on forever, with some justice, about how it was never as good or as simple as I am making it out to be.

But I claim that for almost all scholarship, almost all of the time, the quality of bibliographic control was good enough and then some.)

The academic library, of course, has always been the keeper of the keys to this magical kingdom of reliable citation and provenance, greatly aided by the system of scholarly publishing and publishing more generally. It continues to fall to the academic library to ensure the reliable availability of scholarly works and other source material used by scholars, but this task is made much more difficult in a world where revision, copying, and making work public is trivially available to almost everyone, with no requirement for metadata or provenance and no presumption that a work with a title and URL that is available today will be available with the same title and location tomorrow, much less 40 or 100 years from now.

Scholarly work itself still comes with good metadata, and a great deal of effort has gone into ensuring that scholarly work, even when produced and distributed in digital form, can be reliably archived indefinitely. (This effort is not trivial, and it is to the credit of research libraries, scholarly publishers, and the good offices of the Andrew W. Mellon Foundation, among others, that we can reasonably expect that current and future scholarly work will be available on the terms that scholarship requires.)

But we face more serious problems, which can be well summarized by a symptom: it is much easier to search on the web, using Google or other search engines, than it is to do "proper" search and exploration of the scholarly literature on a subject. Thus, for many users, especially young people not schooled in the joys of serious bibliographic work, "good enough" threatens to replace "good."[6] There are at least three things going on here:

1. Internet-based search engines are powerful and easy to use, whereas the search tools available for the rich collections held and licensed by academic libraries are powerful only in the hands of users who are expert in both specific library resources and fairly arcane subject areas. The typical undergraduate—indeed, the typical academic working outside her own field—is likely to have much the better experience starting with Google than with federated search on library databases.[7]

2. An enormous amount of scholarly literature and other printed material is simply not findable through any electronic means, as it does not exist in digital form.

3. Even where the material is digitized and indexed, as in the case of works found in Google Book Search, material currently under copyright cannot be read online except as short snippets, and even this level of access is threatened by lawsuit.

The consequence is that scholarly method is simply not available on terms where it has any chance of competing with Internet search engines. It follows that we have a great deal to overcome if we are to ensure that our students develop scholarly literacy. Even in the best of cases, of course, good scholarly practice is far more demanding than practice that is not so good. Indeed, this was true in the days when everything was in print, and the difference was that between work that got an A and work that got a B, C, or even a D. The problem we face today is that if one is willing to settle for performance that is "good enough," it is often possible to deliver at that level without engaging in scholarly practice at all. In other words, students may get good grades for research papers that are superficially persuasive but do not embody any serious scholarship. As a result, students may never learn the difference between excellence and mere adequacy in scholarship, as they may never have attended at all to the sources and methods that scholarship requires.

I want to reemphasize here that my interest in students' learning of scholarly method does not derive from hope or expectation that more than a tiny fraction of them will become scholars. Rather, I believe that an appreciation of evidence, an ability to distinguish between persuasive and unpersuasive argument, an ability to seek and to find authoritative sources (skeptically, always skeptically), and a recognition that it is important to know "what they were thinking" will provide great benefit to our students and the societies that they comprise.

No one should be able to get away with argument by vigorous assertion backed by convenient sources. Experience of the value of scholarly method is the best defense we have against lies, laziness, and foolish ideas in essentially all domains of life where ideas and under-standing matter. Further, there is no knowledge-based process in which looking things up, knowing what one has looked up, and under-standing others' reasoning are not essential. Law, medicine, engineering, construction, agriculture, cooking, and pretty much everything else require careful records of processes and methods both for ongoing activities and for reliable innovation.

What Must the Academy Do?

In all of this, IT should be our friend. IT can and should be of enormous help in bringing ideas, evidence, and a diversity of relevant expertise to the problem at hand, whatever that problem may be. Furthermore, IT should increase accessibility to and the process of tracking the ideas that underlie attempts to solve those problems. It is the job of the education system at all levels to deliver on this promise. Doing so in higher education will require material changes within the university, in the system of scholarly publishing, and in the broader system of intellectual property and copyright. Within the academy we must do two things.

Require the Serious Practice of Scholarship

The first thing we must do is to insist that a substantial fraction of our undergraduate courses require the serious practice of scholarship. It is not sufficient to teach a course in the library on information literacy or scholarly literacy. It is probably not even useful to teach such a course if its emphasis is on teaching students to navigate the impossible maze of databases and search tools that come with the enormous power and complexity of digital resources in research libraries. [Trust me, after it is explained that one can look at only eight databases at a time in federated search,[8] and that determining which eight are best depends on the problem at hand—and oh, by the way, there are half a dozen (or is it a dozen?) broad rubrics of search and there are a thousand or more electronic resources in total in the library—the student's eyes glaze over. Indeed, the glazing starts fairly early in this process.] Rather, teaching the importance of scholarly method must be done within the context of specific learning—usually an assignment within a course—in which documenting reliable sources matters for understanding and for getting a good grade. Many faculty require such work, and many students get the benefit of doing it, but especially in big universities it is entirely possible for both faculty and students to succeed without this vital interaction. The academic library can be of enormous help here, in part by making it easy for faculty to require genuinely scholarly work via the mechanism of helping students to find good sources and cite them well and further by providing expertise both in the processes and mechanisms of good scholarship.

So far, all I have done is propose that we do what good liberal education has always done, recognizing that in the digital age it may take extra work on the part of the faculty (hence requiring extra help on the part of the library) to get the job done. That won't be enough.

Exploit IT to Facilitate Scholarly Work

The second thing that should be done within the academy is to exploit the ability of IT to facilitate collaborative work, by using the techniques of social networking (Web 2.0) to allow students to teach and learn from one other. Again, some of this goes on already, but in combination with the requirement of scholarly practice, it can be enormously valuable.

Within a few years, essentially all of the material in many academic libraries will be available in digital form. Once it is in that form (and relevant rights issues are resolved), we will be able to employ the tools of Web 2.0 in the library in support of scholarship and learning. Students can annotate and can "mashup" pretty much everything. The library becomes the bin for the mashups, with care taken to preserve both the original sources and the annotations along with the replicability and authenticity that are essential for scholarship and progress.[9]

Thus, we can use IT and the traditions of scholarship to create an environment where students get to use the academy's methods and materials to teach. We all know that teaching is the best way to learn. We can now develop a library that has digital access to an enormous amount of material and the expertise on how to find it and use it across disciplines and generations. If we can persuade our students to use the academic library, we can employ the tools of IT to learn from them (and from each other) how it can be used in the context of much broader (and less controlled) vocabularies than were imagined by the original catalogers. This is all to the good, and has the promise of improving both academic work itself and the application of scholarly method outside the academy. Moreover, enlisting the considerable intelligence and energy of our students in teaching in these ways may improve both the efficiency and efficacy of undergraduate education itself.[10]

The Rights Environment: Work to Be Done

There is one missing piece, and that is a rights environment that permits sharing and use of published work—scholarly, artistic, and more—in digital form.[11] Under current law, it is perfectly OK for a student to go into the library and read a book that is still under copyright, but it is generally not legal for the student to access a digital copy of that book via the library's web page, even in the vast majority of cases where the copyrighted book is long out of print and the publisher or author's only way of finding a copy is to go to the library. Most out-of-print works, of course, have very little street value, but in aggregate they are enormously valuable, because they constitute (with the relatively few works that are in print) the scholarly and cultural record that is essential to the academy's work of learning and teaching. These works must be available in digital and findable form. Unless the works can be easily discovered by electronic means, they simply will not be found at all.[12] Thus, the utopian vision that I have laid out here requires the widespread availability of essentially the entire corpus of published work, on reasonable terms, in the academic library.

On this last point, I am optimistic. Authors and artists care deeply about their work having an impact, and old works that are not available digitally will have almost no chance of further impact. It is plausible, both via the "long tail" logic and through increased use in college courses and elsewhere, that a modest revenue stream from out-of-print works can be generated for those who hold copyright in such works. Colleges and universities and their libraries have spent billions of dollars over the years preserving these works and will (if necessary) be willing to pay somewhat more in order to make them more usable to their communities, although it may stick in our craws to do so. To the extent that digital copies can be used for preservation, or even as the principal means of local access, libraries can save on the considerable costs of storing all of their print collections securely and accessibly. In other words, there is room to strike a deal, or set of deals, and the deal can facilitate improvement in the quality of education and the quality of discourse.

There is plenty of work to do, but the work is exactly the sort of thing that the academy ought to do well. Learning and teaching matter more than ever, in large part because in the digital age, scholarly literacy is not just for scholars.

Endnotes

1. I am grateful to Matthew Nielsen for valuable discussions and superb research assistance.

2. Paul N. Courant, "Scholarship and Academic Libraries (and Their Kin) in the World of Google," *First Monday* 11, no. 8 (2006), http://www.firstmonday.dk/issues/issue11_8/courant/index.html.

3. As Stanley Wilder has noted, "Any educational philosophy is doomed to failure if it views students as information seekers in need of information-seeking training." From Stanley Wilder, "Information Literacy Makes All the Wrong Assumptions," *The Chronicle of Higher Education* (January 7, 2005): B13.

4. See, for example, Joe Esposito, "Does More Mean More?" Liblicense: Licensing Digital Information (listserv with a searchable archive at Yale University), thread posted January 22, 2006, http://www.library.yale.edu/~llicense/ListArchives/0601/msg00066.html.

5. The particular paper I have in mind is Paul A. Samuelson's work, "The Pure Theory of Public Expenditure," *The Review of Economics and Statistics* 36, no. 4

(November 1954): 387–89. This paper provides the formalism that allows us to make economic sense of information and libraries, among other things.

6. Thomas Mann points out that good work requires tracking down the references to see if they really say what the author says that they did. One cannot automate this aspect of scholarship, and a long list of relevant citations does not substitute for engagement with the works cited. See Thomas Mann, "The Peloponnesian War and the Future of Reference, Cataloging, and Scholarship in Research Libraries" (paper prepared for the American Federation of State, County, and Municipal Employees 2910, Library of Congress Professional Guild, June 13, 2007), http:// guild2910.org/Peloponnesian%20War%20June%2013%202007.pdf.

7. Wilder notes that "if [a typical freshman] were to use her library's website, with its dozens of user interfaces, search protocols, and limitations, she might with some justification conclude that it is the library, not her, that needs help to understand the nature of electronic information retrieval." *Op. cit.*, B13.

8. This is a characteristic particular to the University of Michigan's federated search beast, but all such systems share a large set of problems in addition to having a few issues peculiar to each of them.

9. Note that the one important aspect of the current rights environment is that it may have a chilling effect on students' willingness to use existing works. The Recording Industry Association of America's (RIAA's) practice of suing its customers will surely lead at least some students to abjure entirely legitimate fair uses.

10. The terms Library 2.0 and Teaching 2.0 are already taken. A somewhat infelicitous coinage for what I have in mind would be Learning-and-Teaching-in-the-Library 2.0.

11. In an environment where the RIAA sues its own customers, students may be rightfully wary about even legitimate fair uses of existing works.

12. By reducing archiving costs, digitization also helps libraries to avoid being the arbiters of value for future generations. Historians and scholars have found great value in items considered useless in their day, just as they will of many of our artifacts today. We can potentially save much of this ephemera at much lower cost than before, providing of course that we can perfect the process of archiving the often transient content of the digital world.

Bibliography

Courant, Paul N. "Scholarship and Academic Libraries (and Their Kin) in the World of Google." *First Monday* 11, no. 8 (August 7, 2006). http://www.firstmonday.dk/issues/issue11_8/courant/index.html.

Mann, Thomas. "The Peloponnesian War and the Future of Reference, Cataloging, and Scholarship in Research Libraries." Paper prepared for the American Federation of State, County, and Municipal Employees (AFSCME) 2910, Library of Congress Professional Guild, June 13, 2007. http://guild2910 .org/Peloponnesian%20War%20June%2013%202007.pdf.

Samuelson, Paul A. "The Pure Theory of Public Expenditure." *The Review of Economics and Statistics*, 36, no. 4 (November 1954): 387–89.

Wilder, Stanley. "Information Literacy Makes All the Wrong Assumptions." *The Chronicle of Higher Education* (January 7, 2005): B13.

Where Is the New Learning?

Kristina Woolsey

In the past 20 years, the expenditures on university campuses for digital technologies have mushroomed, from millions to billions of dollars, from hundreds to thousands of support staff and system designers. At the same time, digital technologies have witnessed exponential growths themselves—in processor speeds, in transmission rates, in memory, in bandwidth. Goodwilled and generous investments in information technology units on campus have created sophisticated digital infrastructures that were hardly imagined a few decades ago.

Yet of the billions of dollars now spent on technology at universities across the country, I suggest that only a very small percentage of this resource is directed at enhancing teaching and learning. Certainly there is general technical support for teaching and learning—including administrative support, network administration, and general computer support for word processing, PowerPoint slides, and web access—but there is little specific investment in teaching and learning that attempts to take full advantage of digital opportunities in enhancing this domain. Administrative infrastructures are hungry for resources, security is critical, basic operations require attention, and professors are busy. There are few resources and little time available to focus on teaching and learning broadly defined. This means that while we may have new media, we don't necessarily have new learning.

A Little History

More than 20 years ago, in 1987, Apple Computer, Inc., introduced HyperCard to the marketplace, including it on all new Macintosh computers. It was a new kind of technology product, one that brought many ideas from research labs into the mainstream. Developed almost single-handedly by Bill Atkinson, the author of MacPaint, the basic model of HyperCard was the linking of static cards. These cards had texts or images on them that could be linked to other cards (in "stacks") with simple clicks. Clicks on texts or images could also initiate a movie, initially shown on a second screen (remember, video was an analog signal) though eventually moved onto the computer screen with the use of digitizing boards. HyperCard stacks were created using a new language, called HyperTalk, which was readily accessible to nonprogrammers.

In addition to providing a new model for off-the-shelf computing that included hyperlinked multisensory user-programmable attributes (arguably the key elements even today of new media), HyperCard introduced an even more profound capability to the mainstream computational realm—a focus on content, not calculation or analysis. And content didn't mean simple listings of texts or even images; it included experiences in pursuing ideas, doing things, and relating concepts. In a computational sense, HyperCard was rather unsubstantial. On the other hand, it provided innovative ways to present hyperlinked content materials that could be explored interactively, materials that included speeches and movies and images as well as text. It extended the palette for learning experience design.

For a number of years after the release of HyperCard, substantial activity in learning enterprises—including universities—was aimed at developing examples of new learning opportunities with HyperCard. I still remember my excitement in seeing Professor Larry Friedlander's project at Stanford—From Page to Stage—which showed a number of different performances of the same text from Shakespeare and which provided exercises in blocking out scenes in a variety of ways. Not only did my understanding and appreciation of Shakespeare increase in this viewing, I also had the intuition that I could now begin to understand and appreciate all performance arts in ways I had not before. I have similar memories of watching Professor Robert Winter of UCLA demonstrate his analyses of Beethoven's music, providing commentary on both the technical aspects of symphonies and a sense of their aesthetics as well as providing exercises for the viewer to enhance the understanding of these elements.

At the time, I directed the Apple Multimedia Lab, where our charter was to explore the implications and opportunities for HyperCard to enhance learning. Our method of exploring was to make examples of electronic environments that provided significant learning opportunities for students. We spoke of this new media-rich capability as the "new printing press." In thinking about this, we came to more explicitly appreciate the attributes of the printing press—including its abilities to create multiple copies of materials and its methodology, which focused on moving ideas beyond geographic, temporal, and personal boundaries. We imagined how excited Gutenberg would have been if he had had the capability to add sounds, pictures, movies, and interlinkages, nonlinearity, and make-your-own capabilities to his products.

We considered the opportunities to reform all of education—from kindergarten to graduate school—engaging these new capabilities, and we were very optimistic. As part of this activity, we looked to universities for collaboration in a number of contexts. One example was the establishment of the New Media Centers (NMC, now titled the New Media Consortium, given a change in concept). Acknowledging that most faculty did not have the instincts or talents to engage electronic environments for learning, we partnered with Adobe and Macromedia to support a number of centers on university campuses that would provide support to interested faculty in creating electronic learning environments for students and suggest examples of new media opportunities in the faculty member's area of interest.

We also partnered with Kinko's to provide publishing mechanisms so that materials created on one campus could be available more generally, so that faculty could move beyond their face-to-face traditions and extend their expertise to students who weren't in their classes. Our intention was to seed a new "media-rich learning enterprise"; we would provide the technical tools and universities would create new media genres for learning that would reveal new opportunities for our tool development.

Fast Forward to 2008

It has now been more than 20 years since HyperCard was introduced, and approximately 10 years since the Internet has been engaged broadly to add the powerful notion of interconnectivity to the learning experience design palette (thus enabling all sorts of revolutionary social networks and distribution opportunities). Yet I do not think that universities have contributed very much to the exploration of new media learning opportunities during these years, most certainly not in ways that go beyond local geographies, times, and individuals in the spirit of the printing press.

Those innovations that have been made have been typically limited to individual campus contexts, and often to a handful of professors. Most of the new media genres—wikis, blogs, and podcasts, IM and Facebook, virtual realities and gaming—have emerged from the popular culture, not the university culture. University publishers remain focused on research publications, not teaching materials, and these typically remain print- and paper-centric.

There have been few substantial electronic treatises developed at major universities to provide systematic understanding of new materials or to extend the reach of single-university professors. Textbooks and readers and original source materials are still the major sources of direct information for students (including Internet versions of these); face-to-face lectures are still the central methods for conveying content (although they might include PowerPoint slides); and text is still the coin of the realm. The medieval models of university education are alive and well, even as texts are now transmitted electronically instead of in conversation or on paper. Even attempts at scaling a good university experience, through distance education of a range of types, do not typically go very far beyond reenactment of lectures over distances or wider distribution of print materials.

New Media Can Support New Learning

One could logically argue that this situation has emerged because new media do not offer anything for learning, that their capabilities are fundamentally suited for pop culture and commercial enterprises, that they have no relevance to the serious abstract theoretical thoughtful domain of the university. Yet, although it is the case that some of the uses of new media are mindless, this position is countered by countless examples of situations where new media have been shown to provide important insights and significant learning:

- Simulations and games can provide high levels of engagement, providing opportunities for what-if reasoning explorations as well as direct experience over extended periods of time for direct interactions with phenomena.
- Movies and stills of historic interviews or events and of historical artifacts and reconstructions provide original evidence as well as elements for research explanations.
- Media-rich field observations of biological phenomena can provide important materials for later analysis, as well as powerful elements for encouraging conversations.
- Connections between experts spread around the world and aggregations of data gathered from sensors also spread globally can enhance collaborations and explanations.
- Distributed blogs can provide multiple interpretations of events that are not possible with a limited number of professional media outlets.

And, contrary to 20 years ago, most of us have had direct experience with a number of examples like these.

In addition, a number of arguments for these new media representations have been set forth in the past two decades to encourage the serious consideration of their incorporation in learning. Many arguments focus on learning style; these arguments suggest that new media representations are very important to certain learners, such as visual and acoustic learners and others who struggle with texts. Other arguments are based on representational appropriateness; these arguments suggest that certain materials require new media for their core development, be it the interlinking of original source materials in the humanities or the economic simulations of large data sets or the acoustic readings of poetry to lend focus to the sound of the poetry. There is also a popular set of "fashion" arguments emerging; these suggest that this is the way the world is going, hence it is important for students to gain currency in this world.

At first glance this last argument might be considered faddish, and in some sense it is. Just because everyone is doing it, why should new media be incorporated into the university learning enterprise? However, this argument becomes very powerful once one acknowledges that the youth of today are being brought up in a world that is densely packed with new media experiences; interactions with television, video games, and the computer take up a substantial amount of a youth's life by the time he or she enters the university. It seems quite reasonable to take advantage of the perspectives and skills developed by these individuals, and it becomes important to acknowledge their backgrounds as one designs learning environments for these digital youth, providing them with knowledge and experiences to allow them to move from their status of digital natives to responsible digital citizens.

Yet, few universities have developed sustained programs to investigate new media opportunities systematically, to identify where they are effective and where they are not. Nor have faculty broadly embraced new media opportunities in extending new learning opportunities for their students. There are few university groups that address the interdisciplinary field of new media learning, and no emergent "new media rhetoric" departments to investigate opportunities in this arena.

Obstacles to New Learning

There does not seem to be any strong intellectual argument about this, but instead the inertia to stay with the familiar is routinely overcoming the instinct to try to improve, in a system that has few established metrics that might identify a need for improvement in the learning enterprise. There are frequent blips in the learning landscape, as something exciting emerges, but then, unfortunately, the promising developments typically disappear or are replaced by something even more exciting for the moment.

Administrative organizational structures, even those initiated to support learning, tend to focus on meeting the insatiable demands of the changing technologies, and the invention of new learning approaches (or the sustenance of approaches that were new 5 years ago) is put aside. Brave faculty who embrace the new media opportunities typically burn out after a couple of years of experimentation, or they come to their senses and focus on their research and the demands of their institutions for promotion.

Some argue that the reason faculty cannot create great learning experiences for their students is that they don't have the financial resources that commercial enterprises have. Video games require millions of dollars to create, for example, establishing quite a high bar for visual design and interactivity that seems by many to be impossible to match. Of course, the reason video game companies can invest this much in their games is that they plan to sell the games and recoup their investments (and more). And yet universities, which are themselves multimillion-dollar businesses receiving direct payment from their "customers" for "learning services" (for example, tuition), have not organized themselves to invest directly in the development of new learning materials and environments.

The core investment that universities do make in the learning enterprise is to hire great faculty, and then give them almost complete freedom and autonomy in carrying out their teaching responsibilities. Great faculty are obviously central to great universities and can be very important for student learning, but, almost by definition in most academic fields, these great faculty are extremely immersed in print representations of their expertise. Few university faculty claim to be expert in nontextual, nonlinear distributed explanations, and if they do, they are not typically provided stimulating environments in which they can extend their expertise with colleagues.

The new media resource groups that have emerged on campuses struggle to collaborate with faculty. The hierarchies that divide faculty and staff prevent equal collaborations between form and content, and so the assistance that staff can provide faculty is typically limited to technical assistance rather than to significant experimentation and imaginative explorations of explanations and learning activities in a content domain. Collaborations between faculty and new media experts and craftsmen more often than not disintegrate, as an equal footing for "form and content" in a design activity is very difficult to maintain.

Outside of the university there are few economic drivers for the exploration and development of new media learning opportunities, especially to pursue implementation at scale after an initial idea has been articulated and demonstrated. Resources on the Internet are expected to be available at no cost (except for the viewing of some distracting advertisements) and the technical updating of electronic products has proved too expensive for most publishers. No new publishers have emerged to support the "new media textbook" (acknowledging that both the words *text* and *book* are metaphoric), so there are not even the traditional venues for the development of teaching materials in collaboration with an outside publisher available for new media materials.

Without university support or organization or outside resources, faculty are then very unlikely to commit substantial resources to develop new media environments for their students. Many media support facilities then go ahead and develop new media materials without faculty involvement; yet without faculty participation in creation and a broad faculty commitment to use, the impact on the students and the institutions is typically not very significant or long lasting.

Summary

At the end of the day, we are committing billions of dollars to digital technologies on our campuses, and we are not impacting the fundamental competencies of the academy as a place of learning. Research has advanced significantly in its engagement of new technologies—to model new phenomena, to gather new data, to visualize new results in ways not possible without the technologies—but the general mission of learning at universities has not typically followed this successful model.

We are supporting lots of computers and many tools for individual expression and information gathering. We are extending infrastructures to support the newest digital technologies that are introduced by industry. However, at the core, we are not focused on learning with technologies. We are supporting students with computers so that they can better take advantage of an educational system that is at its heart still an idiosyncratic face-to-face, text-based enterprise. All the exponential trends we are riding in technology development and computer use simply do not add up to significant advances in new learning paradigms.

Oh, well. Many students at great universities are doing just fine. The revolution is still just around the next corner.

Teaching and Learning Unleashed with Web 2.0 and Open Educational Resources

Christine Geith

At a meeting of the OpenCourseWare Consortium, Dr. Richard Rowe, former president of the One Laptop per Child Foundation and founding partner of the Open Learning Exchange, challenged us to change the frame through which we view the world: to perceive our world based on abundance and not on scarcity.[1] Looking at education, how can we create abundance, and what would it look like? Though Rowe was focusing on education in developing countries, his frame is also useful for viewing education systems for formal and informal learning in developed countries.

Taking up Rowe's challenge, this essay examines how the latest web capabilities (Web 2.0), in combination with open educational resources (OER), are creating abundance for teaching and learning.[2] Let's consider this abundance by looking at Gwyn's story and exploring what this might mean for formal education.

Gwyn's Story

Meet Gwyn, a typical adult in her early 30s in the United States. She is involved in one of the nation's leading hobbies and shares many of the characteristics of web users described by the Pew Internet and American Life research.[3]

Gwyn is passionate about horses—she rides a friend's horse every weekend, has been taking riding lessons for two years, and attends many local horse shows with the dream of being a competitor herself. She is planning to buy two horses of her own. Gwyn owns a house and enough land for horses, but needs to build the horse barn and set up her pasture before her dream of being a horse owner can become a reality.

Gwyn's Network Activities

Gwyn shares the progress on her plans for setting up her horse farm on her blog, where she regularly gets advice and feedback from other horse lovers. Some of the feedback is from people she knows, including friends, new acquaintances from horse shows, a local riding instructor, and a growing number of like-minded people who are either looking to do what she's doing or have already done it and are giving advice.

She says that writing in her blog helps her pull her ideas together and that when she gets comments back, it really makes her feel as though she's getting it and that she can really do what she plans. She also talks about how people in online groups have helped her decide what kind of equipment to look for when she sets up her barn and have her thinking about using wind energy to power her farm. She's starting to gather resources and make contact with people on that topic in order to incorporate it into her planning. At least two of the groups she's found in her social network applications are sharing helpful resources, and she plans to attend some of their local events.

Gwyn is continuously trying to learn all she can about what horse to buy. She reads online articles on horses and has downloaded many educational horse posters on topics such as horse breeds and colors. She also found a free and open horse breeding textbook online. She seeks advice from horse professionals using an online ask-the-expert service and in the leading discussion forum for horse breeders.

Gwyn stays up to the minute on the latest happenings in the horse world with the custom page she set up for horses. Right now it displays horse news from the leading publishers, horse photos, the latest postings from her two online groups, the latest links in her social bookmark site, and the latest feeds from the 50 horse blogs she subscribes to. She checks her site every time she's at her computer throughout the day. She also has daily photos and blog headlines sent to her PDA.

She's starting to use her PDA to send short video blog posts when she rides on weekends. It's show season now, so she's been getting lots of photos and text messages from friends about what they are wearing and who is winning at the shows. She likes to take lots of photos, too, which she shares online, and has had a few used by others on their sites, which makes her want to take even more and better pictures.

When asked how she's figuring out how to set up her farm, Gwyn says she seeks advice mostly from her friend who shares her horse and some of the people she's gotten to know from riding, such as her riding instructor. She says she's been able to go deeper into details and options through what she's learned on the web and that her website and social bookmark site have really helped her organize her resources and even find a lot more.

Gwyn reports that some of the free web tools she's found have really helped her plan. She found a landscape planning tool she's used to diagram her farm and share it in her blog; she's used the map coupled with site data to prepare her land use permit; and she found a pasture management calculator and a nutrition calculator.

Gwyn also found a number of online courses that could help her; some were free and some were not. She went through a free OpenCourseWare (OCW) university course on pasture management that she said helped her a great deal, even without the instructor. Since it was licensed using Creative Commons, she copied parts of it, combined it with her photos, and shared it on her blog. Other open educational resources have provided her with valuable information about caring for and managing horses. Next, she's planning to enroll in a noncredit online course in horse management offered by Michigan State University's My Horse University (http://www.myhorseuniversity.com). She'd like to make sure she knows what she's doing for her new horse and she trusts the university will have the best research-based information.

Next month, Gwyn breaks ground on her farm. Then, she'll update her goals on 43 Things (http://www.43things.com) and start working on her next goal.

Gwyn's Personal Learning Environment

Gwyn's story describes today's web-enabled environment for informal, personalized learning. Let's look at the kinds of learning activities in which Gwyn is engaged.

Gwyn is discovering, selecting, and assembling resources; doing analysis and data visualization; engaging in both local and global communities of novices and experts; creating and publishing content; writing to reflect, synthesize, and apply; receiving feedback on her progress from experienced peers; and setting and publicly stating learning and performance goals for herself. Gwyn is also engaged in formal learning with a trusted, reliable source to achieve a particular level of expertise.

The breadth, depth, and volume of resources on the topic, the high level of engagement with a global community of interest, and the ability to create and publish resources as part of the community set this experience apart from any other form of informal learning prior to Web 2.0. The speed, scope, scale, and personal control of what Gwyn is able to do in this environment is unlike anything that has existed before for individuals. With the growing number of open educational resources and tools, personal learning environments are growing faster, richer, more individualized, and even more socially connected and complex.

Teaching and Learning Unleashed

Fortunately, networked environments thrive on abundance and complexity. The more people use them, tag them, mash them up, and remix them, the more useful they become. In many ways this is the opposite of what happens in institutional environments trying to manage scarce resources. For example, lectures enable one expert to teach many; office hours schedule scarce faculty time; curriculum and course syllabi standardize content; class schedules pace interactions; and credit hours standardize outcomes. OER and Web 2.0 are creating an abundance of what has been scarce in the past while enabling us to manage the growing complexity.

Open Educational Resources

What happens when universities make their structured educational content available via the web? It leads to even more resources and increases our chances of finding things that are useful, or can be made useful, in our own context. From MIT's pioneering OCW project (http://ocw.mit.edu) to the United Kingdom Open University's OpenLearn project (http://www.open.ac.uk/openlearn/home.php) to the more than 120 universities worldwide that are publishing open resources through the OCW Consortium, the OER Commons site (http://oercommons.org) shows 24,000 such resources, and there are thousands more in other portal and repository sites. From computer literacy to irrigation to biotechnology, resources range from course presentations and readings to videos and animations. Moreover, there are hundreds of schools and organizations around the world translating materials into multiple languages and making them available as open resources (for an example, see http://oops.editme.com).

A growing number of these resources use licensing such as the Creative Commons license (see http://creativecommons.org) that enables free use and reuse of the resources. The increasing recognition of this license around the world is one of the enablers of the rapid growth in OER.

Anything can be used as a resource for learning, but an "educational" resource is intended to facilitate learning. The OCW Consortium defines it as having a planned structure to achieve defined learning outcomes. Jon Dron defines it, from the learner's perspective, as being "… sufficient to encapsulate a learning need that may be experienced as a choice in a learning trajectory."[4] As educational resources become open and available, learners have the freedom to utilize the information they need to construct their own learning as well as create new resources that may be useful to others. Open educational resources take knowledge out of the hands of few into the minds of many.

Abundance of Active, Constructive, Collaborative Interaction

Making resources available is only the beginning. As resources proliferate, more tools are emerging to find them, remix them, mash them up, and cocreate them in social networks. Finding educational resources is being made easier by the ccLearn project of Creative Commons (http://learn.creativecommons.org). Tools such as wikis enable people to contribute, edit, and discuss resources in an environment of shared creation. Wikiversity (http://en.wikiversity.org), WikiEducator (http://wikieducator.org), and Curriki (http://www.curriki.org) are examples of open educational resource wikis for teaching and learning. Remix and mashup tools include Rice University Connexions (http://cnx.org), which enables custom textbooks. If you have access to the software that created the original resources, and if they are licensed in a way that enables derivative works, you can download and edit resource files such as those on Teachers' Domain (http://www.teachersdomain.org). For this reason, open file formats, such as OpenOffice (http://www.openoffice.org) and Kaltura (http://www.kaltura.com) are used to enable global access.

Freedom of Time and Place

One of the important legacies of distance and online learning is growing acceptance that learning online can be as good as, and even better than, learning face to face. The No Significant Difference research phenomenon (http://www.nosignificantdifference.org) has matured to the extent that the majority of academic officers in U.S. institutions agree that online is as good as face to face and getting better. Online learning is offered by more than two-thirds of U.S. higher education institutions and the rate of compound annual growth in online enrollment has been 21.5 percent during the past five years.[5] Clearly, we know how to create effective learning experiences that are available anytime, all the time, and anywhere.

Access to Expertise

While it is still not easy to fill faculty positions in institutions, the web is making it easier to tap into a range of people from novice to expert. Self-publishing in blogs, podcasts, video, and image archives does not make anyone an expert, but reputation systems certainly start to provide information useful in making judgments about someone's level of expertise. Finding peers, mentors, coaches, and experts—people who play key roles in learning experiences—is enabled by services such as Tutor.com (http://www.tutor.com) and social learning sites such as Livemocha (http://www.livemocha.com), eHow (http://www.ehow.com), and LearnHub (http://learnhub.com). Gwyn, for example, could have asked questions of university equine experts at Extension.com (see http://www.extension.org/expert/ask_an_expert) or of peers at EquiSearch.com's community site (http://forum.equisearch.com). She also could have used ChaCha (http://www.chacha.com) for quick answers to her horse questions on her mobile phone.

Additional Credentialing

One of the constraints in the new environment is a lack of credentialing mechanisms. Curriculum standards, unit skill standards, and knowledge and skill competency definitions are growing open resources. Open self-diagnostic tests and the ability for learners to organize their e-portfolios around standards are here now. Yet measuring, valuing, and recognizing learner performance remains an exclusive function inside formal education systems.

Quality is traditionally tied closely to the brand of the institution. The brand has many factors that influence its perceived value, including price and exclusiveness, alumni network, job placement rate, and much more. Another view of quality comes from a focus on the performance of the learner. Direct-assessment universities such as Western Governors and a number of adult competency–based institutions place the assessment of learning outcomes at the center of their quality brands.

It is possible that we'll see growth in credentialing bodies such as formal organizations, institutions, and communities of practice that will endorse various assessments and value them within their communities. We may see the emergence of performance records aggregated and maintained by individuals independent of their service providers. Today's search tools enable an informal record of contributions to communities—blog posts, the contribution of resources, and the participation in communities—which are all means of creating a reputation, a measure of expertise in context. It has yet to be seen if, or in what ways, Web 2.0 and OER will trigger the emergence of an abundance of credentialing options focused on the performance of the learner outside the walls of formal education.

Conclusion

Gwyn's story illustrates how Web 2.0 and OER are creating an abundance of resources and emergent structures that enable a rich environment to support individual, personalized learning:

- an environment organized by the learner to define and achieve their learning goals;
- learning where "learners" and "teachers" are freed from constraints imposed by a scarcity of expertise and a scarcity of learning resources; and
- learning where learners choose and cocreate their resources and support services.

This gives us a glimpse into what is becoming possible using an ever-growing abundance of digital, socially networked resources and systems that thrive on complexity and self-organization. There is still a long way to go, and critical issues to be worked out, from these pioneering efforts to widespread adoption. Yet, it is already becoming clear that Web 2.0, OER, and the legacy of online learning hold the potential to help us create education systems that thrive on large-scale abundance to enable individual performance.

Endnotes

1. For information about the OpenCourseWare Consortium, see http://www .ocwconsortium.org; for the One Laptop per Child Foundation, see http:// laptopfoundation.org; for the Open Learning Exchange, see http://ole.org; for the agenda of the OCW Consortium Santander 2007 meeting, see http:// ohana.mit.edu/ocwc/display/Meetings/Santander+07+Agenda.

2. Open educational resources (OER) is a global social movement to provide free-to-use and reuse teaching and learning resources— from K–12 lesson plans to college courseware—for anyone to use, reuse, tag, rate, and review. For examples, see http://www.oercommons.org. Also see the OECD 2007 report, *Giving Knowledge for Free: The Emergence of Open Educational Resources*, at http:// www.oecd.org/dataoecd/35/7/38654317.pdf.

3. Pew Internet and American Life Project, "Hobbyists Online," September 19, 2007, http://www.pewinternet.org/pdfs/PIP_Hobbies_2007.pdf.

4. Jon Dron, *Control and Constraint in E-Learning: Choosing When to Choose* (Hershey, PA: Information Science Publishing, 2007), 134.

5. I. Elaine Allen and Jeff Seaman, *Online Nation: Five Years of Growth in Online Learning* (Needham, MA: Sloan Consortium, 2007), 5, http://www.sloan-c .org/publications/survey/pdf/online_nation.pdf.

Bibliography

Allen, I. Elaine, and Jeff Seaman. *Online Nation: Five Years of Growth in Online Learning.* Needham, MA: Sloan Consortium, 2007. http://www.sloan-c.org/ publications/survey/pdf/online_nation.pdf.

Dron, Jon. *Control and Constraint in E-Learning: Choosing When to Choose.* Hershey, PA: Information Science Publishing, 2007.

Pew Internet and American Life Project. "Hobbyists Online." September 19, 2007. http://www.pewinternet.org/pdfs/PIP_Hobbies_2007.pdf.

University 2.0

John Unsworth

One of the major challenges facing universities in the next decade is to reinvent themselves as information organizations. Universities are, at their core, organizations that cultivate knowledge, seeking both to create new knowledge and to preserve and convey existing knowledge, but they are remarkably inefficient and therefore ineffective in the way that they leverage their own information resources to advance that core activity. In what follows, I will explore some of the ways that the university could learn from what is now widely called "Web 2.0"—a term that is meant to identify a shift in emphasis from the computer as platform to the network as platform, from hardware to data, from the wisdom of the expert to the wisdom of crowds, and from fixity to remixability.

The Information Railroad

In approaching this topic, I would like to begin with a summary of a very interesting article on what will seem like a very different topic: "The Transportation Revolution and Antebellum Book Distribution Reconsidered," by Ronald J. Zboray. This article was published back in the spring of 1986, well before Web 1.0.[1]

As is customary in academic writing, Zboray begins by recapitulating the accepted understanding that his article is meant to modify. He writes,

> The transportation revolution has generally been credited with nationalizing—some may even say homogenizing—literary life in the antebellum United States. Prior to improvements in modes of transport, book production was highly decentralized, with numerous secondary cities supplying reading matter to their immediate hinterlands. The regional orientation of production inspired by this decentralization was, according to the traditional view, disrupted early in the nineteenth century by the first wave of the transportation revolution. A truly

national reading public came into being and with it,
presumably, a truly American literature.[2]

Zboray's second paragraph then summarizes the modification he
proposes to that view:

> While this view certainly does hold a great deal of
> truth it contains much oversimplification as well.
> The broad concept of the "transportation revolution"
> obscures the special role the railroad played in changing
> patterns of literary dissemination in antebellum America.
> The improvements in road and water transport that
> characterized the early transportation revolution did little
> to facilitate the circulation of literature on a national
> scale. Books continued to move along many of the
> same avenues and in the same tenuous, seasonal manner
> as they had in the days of the colonial book peddlers.
> But it was the railroad that improved the regularity of
> communications upon which the emergent discount/
> commission relationship between central publisher and
> local bookseller depended. Also, the year-round regularity
> of rail communication permitted a national periodical
> literature in which publishers could advertise their books.[3]

So, while the railroad was important in moving books more easily, it
was (Zboray argues) at least as important as a communications technology
that lowered what we would now call the transaction costs of publishing,
and that allowed advance marketing to reach a broad audience. Moving
the stuff, moving the money, moving the marketing: each of these was
made easier by a single technology—the railroad. But if we assume that
railroad service was the same in all parts of the country, then our railroad-
based understanding of the changes in publishing would fail by assuming
homogeneity instead of understanding heterogeneity and its effects. On
that last point, Zboray says:

> ... the regional orientation of book dissemination did
> not diminish as much as the traditional view would
> have it. Instead, the coming of rail transformed the
> regional orientation of literature, so that it conformed
> to the different levels of rail development in the North,
> South, and West. With conditions of literary distribution
> differing in each of the three regions, the very idea of a
> truly national reading public in antebellum America may
> itself be an oversimplification.[4]

Information Friction

The Zboray article is a nuanced discussion of what I would call "information friction" in the 19th century—the factors impeding the movement of information in various forms from one place to another, and the lubricating effect of a new technology on the coefficient of friction for different materials interacting in a system.[5]

Now I would like to focus on information friction in the present, and in a system that, like the one Zboray discussed, includes publishing but also has other important components. And while for Zboray the larger frame in which publishing existed was the American reading public, for my purposes that larger frame is something more concrete, though perhaps no more homogeneous, namely, the 21st century university. My argument will be that universities, out of which the Internet (and its low-friction protocols) originally emerged, seem in their own information practices to gravitate to monolithic information systems that promise to be seamless but in practice prove to be less flexible and ultimately less innovative and interesting than the granular and remixable information services now often called Web 2.0. And while these monolithic systems may offer more control to administrators, they prevent innovation by faculty, staff, and students, and they ultimately make the university comparatively inefficient as an information organization.[6]

I will admit that, as an administrator, I have sometimes thought that universities, like religious orthodoxies, may be designed to inhibit change in order to ensure the perpetuation of the values they represent, in which case what I'm discussing here would be a feature, not a bug. But be that as it may, it is demonstrably true that universities exhibit relatively high information friction, and it seems worth asking what would be different if that friction were reduced.

Most faculty, I think, have had the experience of going to a conference in some faraway place, only to discover that they share a research interest with someone else at their own university—but at the same time, are any two disciplines' conference abstracts prepared in the same way, and could we actually cross-reference them? That's anecdotal evidence that we need better information exchange within and across universities. So is the fact that as interdisciplinary educational programs become more important, it is surprisingly difficult to inventory courses and collocate syllabi in a given topic area across colleges, schools, and departments. For that matter, could our students import their class schedules into their personal calendars? And how many of us work on campuses where there are multiple incompatible calendaring systems in use? And how often can we actually follow citations in online journals to articles in other online journals as reliably as we could, with print, by trudging through the stacks? What methods do we have of understanding the intellectual heritage of those around us (who was my colleague's dissertation adviser?) and how can we know who else is connected to them in that heritage? Where is the RSS (Really Simple Syndication) for CVs? What tools do we have for assessing the nature, extent, and value of informal collaborations and coauthorship? What tools do we have for actually managing the threads and throes of our e-mail lives, now so totally out of control?

I have been a part of a community-based standards development process, in the Text Encoding Initiative (TEI), and I am familiar with both the value and the shortcomings of that approach to solving the kinds of problems I have just enumerated. Certainly there is a very real value in having the discussions that inform such standards, and in embodying the outcomes of those discussions in guidelines, at least when the subject matter is of central disciplinary and intellectual interest to scholars (so, in the case of TEI, the ontology of literary and linguistic texts), but there are well-known problems with approaching information integration as a matter of uniformity in metadata or markup—beginning with the problem that in the real world, even when you aim for uniformity, you do not achieve it, so tools and techniques that depend on it will break. Beyond that problem, there is the fact that there will not always be intrinsic intellectual interest in ontological debates around all of the data types that are important to universities as information organizations (calendars? CVs? syllabi?).

Sometimes, in these cases, there are other imperatives that drive, or try to drive, integration—usually administrative ones. In the two universities where I have worked in the last 15 years, hundreds of millions of dollars, quite literally, have been spent to license, customize, and deploy enterprise resource systems that aim to integrate all of the administrative functions of the university under one schema, one ontology, one monolithic information infrastructure.

Searching for "information friction" on Google, I actually found one such system, though not one aimed at universities: "ComFrame removes the friction that inhibits smooth operations, seamless communications, and optimal productivity. We create solutions that break down enterprise information processing barriers, helping you move forward" (see http://www.comframe.com/why/why_ops_01.htm). Even in this brief description, "seamless" is a red flag: the promise of "seamlessness" is premised on uniformity, on total control over the generation and use of information resources. The notion is that you run an empire, and your problem is unruly principalities—if you could only subjugate them all to one information regime, then the emperor's new clothes would be...seamless.

However, the reality of our information ecosystems today is that they are not closed systems but open ones: no university, for example, generates and controls all of the information that is important to its faculty, its students, or its staff. That is a simple and undeniable fact, and from that follows the observation that a seamless information management environment can only be some kind of terrarium, artificially closed off from the world around it.

Needed: "Seamy" Systems

What we need instead, I would argue, are "seamy" information systems, designed for cobbling together new information services, showing (even foregrounding) their discontinuities, but doing so in ways that encourage people to think about new ways to draw this or that bit of information into this or that information context and provide this or that information service.

BibApp

An excellent example of this kind of flexible and innovative information service in a university context is something from the University of Wisconsin–Madison's library, now also being adopted at my university, called BibApp. Strictly speaking, BibApp involves more prefetched and preprocessed data than mashups usually do, but it is certainly in the spirit of mashups in that it cobbles together a number of information sources to do something interesting and new. Here's a brief sketch of what it does and what you can do with the result.

BibApp starts by using the Rails framework to build a generic bibliographic database for storing information about publications. Next, you pull in faculty information from the campus LDAP (Lightweight Directory Access Protocol) server, and you sort those individuals into generic groups (representing things like departments) using information that also comes from LDAP. Next, using the names of faculty and what a human being knows about the standard online publications or disciplinary databases for the departments in which those faculty work, you get their published papers and the subject headings under which those papers are listed in the disciplinary database. Using the published papers, you parse citation records, look for coauthors, go to Sherpa, and get archival data for authors.

Having assembled and stored this information, here are some of the things you can do. With subject headings, you can generate tag clouds showing you what are prominent topics for individuals, research groups, or departments; since you have publication dates as well, you can actually show an evolving timeline of topics of interest for an individual, research group, or department, and you can show what journals commonly publish research from a given individual or group. With publisher-supplied DOIs (Digital Object Identifiers) you can generate URLs, get the file, or link to the citation. You can search for a subject and find faculty members who work in that area; zeroing in on one faculty member, you can follow a link to his or her home page (listed in LDAP) and see his or her types of publications (80 percent journal articles, 20 percent conference presentations, what subjects are of interest lately). You can expand out from one faculty member to the department, the college, or the campus, to see who that person is publishing with at the university, and you can then see what groups those people are in and what those groups are doing. If you wanted to, you could use that information to generate network graphs of publishing patterns. Presumably, you could also have RSS newsfeeds for people or for groups (if those were listed in LDAP), or the BibApp host could serve them up (or, for that matter, provide RSS feeds for subjects of interest).

In their YouTube-style presentation on code4lib.org (at http://code4lib.org/2007/larson), the developers of BibApp, Eric Larson and Nate Vack, admit that this is still experimental code, but part of the point here is that it will always be that, and it should always be that. BibApp is not a "seamless, enterprise-wide solution," it is a seamy, stitched-together mashup. On the other hand, it didn't take three to five years to put in place, nor did it cost a hundred million dollars: BibApp represents work done in less than a year with a $10,000 grant and a few people "willing to work weekends."

One of the challenges for a project like BibApp, as its developers freely admit, is that apparently simple things like names of persons are not simple in practice, especially when you want an automated process to use them as identifiers or disambiguators. You may have a lot of Michael Smiths on your campus, and when these Michaels publish, their names may look exactly alike or—at least as often—the problem may be that the same Michael Smith sometimes publishes as Michael Smith, sometimes as Michael J. Smith, sometimes as M. J. Smith, and so forth. Likewise, citations are not always marked off from other text in a way that would make them easy to pull out, nor are they formatted consistently across books, journals, or disciplines. Real data are messy, in other words.

These are problems that people doing bibliometrics have been dealing with for a long time, and there are contextual strategies for mitigating some of the mess, but you could also allow authors or other users to suggest corrections, and you could use visualization techniques to spot outliers (the one article by Michael Smith about veterinary medicine among a host of others on mechanical engineering) and examine them. In the monolithic systems approach, or the top-down classification and encoding approach, the usefulness of the system depends on the accuracy of the data or the data representation, but in a mashup, people are willing to trade some of that accuracy for increased functionality and the flexibility to extend that functionality when interesting new opportunities present themselves. Perhaps most important is that the application itself be fault tolerant and not require highly structured data.

BRAIN

I have another example, conceptually related in some ways to BibApp, and possibly even a service that could be tacked onto it. This example is a project of my own, currently in mothballs, called BRAIN, which stands for Better Repositories Are Information Networks (see http://brain.lis. uiuc.edu). BRAIN is a peer finder for institutional repositories, and it was designed to provide an incentive for faculty to deposit their materials in those repositories.

Here's how that incentive scheme works. When a scholar deposits a document in an institutional repository that participates in BRAIN, he or she gets back a list of documents from any open-access repository or journal that best match the material deposited, based on several relevance measures (coincidence of citations, overlapping vocabulary, plus a variety of full-text clustering techniques). Because data mining can be time consuming, we serve up the relevance information to participants by e-mail, rather than as a real-time web service, but we can format that e-mail to provide links directly to full-text content of relevant open-access materials. BRAIN itself would not republish any of the material it aggregates, beyond the metadata.

We have built a prototype system for BRAIN, mostly from open-source software, with some key pieces contributed by other academic software developers, and plenty of glue code written by students at UIUC, again in under a year, with a small grant. You can try it online, though you'll find that relevance is problematic, depending on how well the subject area of your submission matches what is in the repository, and particularly so in the measures that depend on citation extraction, which needs more work.

Making Seamy Systems a Reality

Even this small experiment exposed some interesting problems, though, in the real world of institutional repositories. Two in particular come to mind.

The first problem BRAIN had with the real world was that institutional repositories are a largely undifferentiated mix of primary materials from library holdings and scholarship or research findings from current faculty. There is no attempt made to separate or distinguish the two, which means that if you go out to hoover up everything you can find in open-access institutional repositories, which we did, you get a lot of stuff, but only a relatively small amount of it is scholarly or scientific literature of recent vintage.

The second problem BRAIN had with the real world was that a lot of people apparently put image-only pdf files in their repositories. To do vocabulary comparisons, citation extraction, and full-text clustering, BRAIN wants to use PDFBox to extract the text from PDF files, but that doesn't work if the PDF is a picture of a text rather than a text.

These are the sorts of problems that will probably decrease over time, but the first one might only decrease if there were information services for which it was important to distinguish recent scholarship from older library holdings, and the second might only decrease if the percentage of recent scholarship in institutional repositories increased. Both depend to a significant extent on the end user—as a source of demand in the first case and as a supplier of content in the second. The kind of information services that are going to get that end user involved, and that are going to make demand felt and encourage contributions, are likely to look more like mashups than like traditional library catalog systems, or enterprise resource programs of any kind.

Increasing the motivation to deposit materials in institutional repositories may be especially important in the humanities: recent surveys indicate that "the number of humanities documents in institutional repositories is currently far lower than that in STM disciplines" (see http://eprints.rclis.org/archive/00005180/). That may be because scholars in those disciplines are still considerably less wired than their colleagues in science and engineering, on almost any campus I know.

To return for a moment to Zboray and to the differential effect of the railroad on publishing in more and less "railed" communities in antebellum America, the fact that there is still significantly higher information friction in humanities and, to some extent, social science departments than in science and engineering departments on the very same campuses is, I would argue, producing a digital divide within those campuses. The humanities are the equivalent of the underindustrialized South with its devalued currency and its genteel poverty, steadily losing ground to other parts of the campus, where the trade is in gigabits and petabytes. At the University of Illinois, Green Street is the Mason–Dixon line: north of it are the many mansions of the engineering campus, south of it are the hamlets of the humanities and social sciences.

Happily, though, the cost of deploying University 2.0 does not need to be great, and even the poor can participate. What we need more than big science or big servers are good ideas about interesting things that faculty, staff, and students could do with the information produced in, by, and about universities: WhoShouldIHaveLunchWith.app, perhaps, or SixDegreesOfMyAdviser.app, or ShowEmergingFields.app, or WhatConferenceShouldIAttend.app, or WhatJournalsPublishOnMyTopic. app, and so on, and on.

If the university makes its information accessible in the right way, people will build these things—sometimes people in the library, but also people elsewhere on campus, or simply elsewhere. There are issues of privacy, copyright, and all the usual sources of information friction, but even partial information could be useful, even metadata could serve many of these purposes. It would help, of course, if universities promoted some basic kinds of interoperability, not overfitted, but very simple: a standard calendar event expressed as an RSS feed; a recommended rdf tag or two for CV or syllabi. These would not have to be monolithic systems or all-encompassing standards, but they could be functional requirements for vendors who want to sell things like calendar systems to campuses, and they could be recommended to faculty and departments on the basis of the effort-to-utility ratio that can be demonstrated even with imperfect data.

Conclusion

I want to close by repeating something I said a couple of years ago, in a lecture on vernacular computing that I gave as the Vodaphone Fellow at Kings College, London. When I wrote this, I wasn't thinking of Web 2.0, which hadn't become a buzzword at that point, but now that it is here, this passage seems more true than when I wrote it. I said,

> Fifteen years ago, the challenge before us was to imagine
> how new technology might provide a new platform for
> the practice of scholarship in the humanities, but today
> our challenge is the reverse. It is no longer about opening
> the university and inviting the public in: it's about getting
> out where they already live, and meeting the public in the

information commons, on the same terms that everyone
else does. In fact, it's almost too late for us. We will find
that hard to believe, ensconced (as we all are) in solid-
seeming residential universities, with long histories and
the expectation of a long future—but older institutions
on more solid foundations have been swept away or
radically transformed in cultural upheavals of the past.
In spite of the inertia of these institutions, which we all
know so well, the forces of change outside the institution
have much greater inertia, and all of the practical
furniture of our daily academic lives could easily be gone,
or changed beyond recognition, in a generation.[7]

So, while I recognize and give full weight to the inertia of universities,
inertia doesn't necessarily mean that you remain in place, especially when
the friction between you and the world around you suddenly decreases.
We are at such a moment today, and it should be possible, with just a small
push, to move the university forward into University 2.0.

Endnotes

1. Ronald J. Zboray, "The Transportation Revolution and Antebellum Book
Distribution Reconsidered," *American Quarterly* 38 (1986). Today, you can find
this article on JSTOR, and its first page is also on Google.

2. Ibid., 53.

3. Ibid., 53.

4. Ibid., 54.

5. "Information friction" is also discussed by David Glazer in an entry in his
blog, at http://dglazer.blogspot.com/2005/11/coefficient-of-information-
friction.html. When writing this, Glazer was the unemployed former CTO at
Open Text; he is now director of engineering for Google.

6. By "comparatively" here I mean compared to other kinds of information
organizations—for example, Amazon, eBay, Facebook, FedEx, Flickr, Garmin,
Google, the Internet Archive, NASA, the National Oceanic and Atmospheric
Administration, PayPal, Random House, Second Life, UPS, the U.S. Postal
Service, the Weather Channel, Yahoo, YouTube, and so forth. At http://
programmableweb.com, you can track a "mashup" timeline: the number they
knew about increased from 1,800 to 2,400 in a recent six-month period,
and the "mashup matrix" is 125 APIs long on each axis as of October 2007.
Google alone has 27 APIs for mashups; Yahoo has 24; how many does your
university have?

7. John Unsworth, "Public Networks, Vernacular Computing," presented as the Second Biennial Wisbey Lecture at King's College London, March 23, 2005. http://www3.isrl.uiuc.edu/~unsworth/Wisbey.html.

Bibliography

little d big G. The David Glazer Blog. http://dglazer.blogspot.com/.

Unsworth, John. "Public Networks, Vernacular Computing." A paper presented as the Second Biennial Wisbey Lecture at King's College London, March 23, 2005. http://www3.isrl.uiuc.edu/~unsworth/Wisbey.html.

Zboray, Ronald J. "The Transportation Revolution and Antebellum Book Distribution Reconsidered." *American Quarterly* 38 (1986): 53–71.

The Tower, the Cloud, and the IT Leader and Workforce[1]

Philip Goldstein

Higher education technology leadership is in the midst of a changing of the guard. Many of the community's pioneers have either retired or will retire shortly. These individuals were often their institutions' first or second senior information technology (IT) leader. They presided over the development of both the technological and organizational foundations on which higher education IT rests. Findings of the IT leadership and workforce study conducted by the EDUCAUSE Center for Applied Research (ECAR) in 2007–2008 indicate that the role will be in equally good hands as it passes to the next generation.

The survey on which the ECAR study was based found many of the ingredients for success among respondents. Leaders and aspirants alike hold advanced degrees, exhibit positive leadership styles, and share with their predecessors a commitment to higher education. No doubt as individuals and as a community they will bring new perspectives and ideas born from their unique experiences and the changing world in which they work.

But how will the CIO role that the next generation occupies be different? More specifically, will it be diminished in its authority and importance? *IT Leadership in Higher Education: The Condition of the Community*, a 2004 ECAR study,[2] looked back on the most recent generation of IT leaders as having led higher education through an amazing set of transitions. In a relatively short period of time, leaders helped to create the modern Internet and initiated an explosion of communication, collaboration, and access to information that today's students take for granted. That study discussed how these leaders ushered in a new era of computing that has touched all aspects of higher education.

Will we look back on that time as the golden era for IT leaders? Despite the many positive signs that respondents reported in 2004, the study raised a cautionary question as to whether we were headed for a period of decline. In 2003, an article in *CIO Magazine* spoke of the "incredible shrinking CIO" whose resources were being cut, influence being diminished, and organization being eroded by outsourcing.[3] In 2004, these issues were seen as warning signs on the horizon, but it was not clear whether they were by-products of a cyclical downturn in the economy, a knee-jerk reaction to the "irrational exuberance" for technology created by the dot-com boom, or something more permanent.

From Prophets to Plumbers

Today, questions about the future of the IT leader's role are being drawn with even sharper distinction than in 2003. The discussion has moved beyond whether declining finances or the unrealized promises of the past will diminish the role of the CIO, focusing instead on how technology change itself will alter what it means to be a CIO. The rise of "cloud computing" in the minds of some will completely alter how organizations deliver IT services. In theory, organizations will be able to reach into the Internet cloud to access all of their computing services, from basic storage to more advanced functions such as computational computing and advanced business applications. Evidence of the cloud can be seen on campuses today. Institutions are turning to Google or Microsoft to provide e-mail. Others are using software as service models from vendors such as Salesforce.com as part of their administrative applications. Some are even looking at the possibility of buying computing cycles or storage on demand from external providers such as Amazon.

Rise of the Cloud

In the view of some and taken to the extreme, the potential of the cloud is to completely supplant the need for an IT organization or at the very least radically alter its role. Perhaps the most outspoken proponent of this vision of the future is Nicholas Carr. In 2003 Carr grabbed attention with his article "IT Doesn't Matter."[4] In it, Carr argued that technology was becoming so commoditized that it no longer served as a source of competitive differentiation. By extension, Carr argued that a CIO was therefore the manager of commodity technologies and less important to his or her organization's future success. Technology was a necessary evil, not a source of distinction. More recently, Carr has further evolved his argument to suggest that not even this commodity role will last for much longer. In his latest book, *The Big Switch: Rewiring the World from Edison to Google*, Carr equates the rising computing cloud to mass electrification. He foresees a world in which mass data centers and high-speed networks render obsolete the technical infrastructures of individual organizations. He says, "In the long run, the IT department is unlikely to survive, at least not in its familiar form. It will have little left to do once the bulk of business computing shifts out of private data centers and into the cloud."[5]

Where will the CIO be left in Carr's vision of the future? Not in a very exciting place. Those who share his view of the future seem to suggest that the Internet cloud will shift services outside the institution and shift power from central IT groups to individuals and departments. No longer will institutions need to create organizations to broker technology services on their behalf. Rather, each department or individual will be able to turn to the cloud to assemble the services they need.

Whither CIO Influence?

From Carr's point of view, the CIO is either headed to the backroom to manage commodity infrastructure or will be responsible for overseeing the transition of that infrastructure to the Internet cloud. What would be left is a hollowed organization and a role that concerns itself with information security, local technical support (which also could be outsourced), and a small number of new innovation services that have not been adopted by the cloud.

Carr certainly offers a provocative view of the future. And his expectations about the ability of the Internet to enable the aggregation of commodity IT services may be dead-on. But does it have to necessitate the demise in importance of the CIO and the IT organization? Being freed of the need to continuously invest and operate commodity services may be incredibly liberating for CIOs and offer a completely different way to conceive of their roles.

Could the rise of the cloud in fact enhance the influence of the CIO? Might a new breed of CIOs be able to shift the conversation from the provisioning of technology services back to how their institution can take advantage of technology? In fact, a 2007 survey of corporate CIOs by the IBM Center for CIO Leadership suggested that CIOs believe their influence in the corporate sector is on the upswing.[6] The survey revealed several promising results, including these:

- 80 percent of CIOs believe they are valued members of the senior leadership team;
- 69 percent reported significant involvement in strategic decision making; and
- 86 percent of respondents believe their industry leaders are using IT to a large or great extent to create competitive advantage.

According to the survey report, respondents reported greater confidence in their influence and strategic importance in 2007 than they had in the prior year.[7]

Among respondents to ECAR's IT leadership and workforce survey, the majority of senior-most IT leaders also reported relatively positive assessments of their influence. The findings showed that:

- 74.1 percent were engaged often in discussing the IT implications of institutional decisions;
- 62.6 percent participated often in decisions related to the administrative directions of the institution; and
- 69.2 percent participated at least sometimes in decisions pertaining to the academic direction of the institution, including 36.2 percent who participated often.[8]

Organizationally, many respondents were in positions that provided them access and authority to influence broad decision making. In this ECAR survey, 47.8 percent of the senior-most IT leaders were members of the president's or chancellor's cabinet at their institution. In the 2004 ECAR study, 50.6 percent of respondents were members of the president's cabinet; thus, it appears that the organizational authority of the senior IT leader in higher education has neither diminished nor expanded in the past four years. It is possible, however, that the number of senior-most IT leaders with cabinet membership has reached the high-water mark in higher education.

Carr's view envisions that the cloud will have a dramatic and uniform impact on IT organizations, but inevitably there will be variations in adoption of the cloud among higher education institutions. Institutions will likely move services to the cloud at varying paces depending on their resources, their strategy, and the uniformity of their requirements. It seems likely that institutions with smaller IT organizations will gravitate toward the cloud to take advantage of the economies of scale and increased capabilities that vendors can offer in service areas that the IT organizations themselves cannot match. On the other hand, institutions with diverse user requirements and larger resource bases will likely embrace cloud services in more opportunistic and targeted manners. They may move services to the cloud for a portion of the population they serve, but continue to operate the same service themselves for another constituent group. Or, they may only embrace the cloud in areas that free up resources that can move quickly into offering a new, more strategic service. Still other, likely large IT groups may try to become the cloud themselves. They may choose to leverage the same technologies and economics to offer services to other campuses.

The overall point here is that institutions are likely to fall along a broad continuum of adoption practices. It seems unlikely that there will be rapid, dramatic movements of services outside of the IT organization.

Rather than preside over the inevitable transition of their organizations to the cloud, it seems that CIOs will have much to say and do to determine where and how best to capitalize on its potential.

Perhaps the closest analogy is the library. The library in the higher education community has long provisioned library services in a variety of ways. Nearly all libraries, for example, have forsworn cataloging services in favor of centralized services that provide scale and scope economies. Nearly all libraries acquire digital serials and other periodical publications under license from commercial suppliers. Nearly all libraries participate in the shared service of interlibrary loan and in a variety of open source and open content initiatives. Still others have partnered with Google or others to render their collections digital. Under the range of options that present themselves in this richly interconnected environment, academic libraries are simultaneously seeking scale and differentiation, serving their communities by becoming either large repositories of print holdings, hybrids, or deft consumers of materials licensed from others.

Some Alternative Conceptualizations of the Role

To ignore Carr's predictions would be unwise. The long-term potential to completely transform the set of services that IT organizations provide is very real. Financial pressures alone are likely to lead many IT organizations to turn services over to the cloud out of necessity. Shortages in the labor market may be another driver. However, this need not signal the demise of the CIO role in importance or influence. As described earlier, IT organizations will likely make a range of choices regarding their pace of adoption of the outsourcing of IT services. Most organizations are likely to end up with a mosaic of sources for their services including internally provided, externally provided, and collaboratively provided (for example, open source) models.

On the other hand, the movement of services to the cloud is a force for change. Many of the services that are the likely candidates for this form of outsourcing (e-mail, storage, data centers, application software) are the "meat and potatoes" of what IT organizations do today. Many IT leaders derive their power, authority, and seat at the table from their responsibility for the budgets and staffing that deliver these services. While the outsourcing of these services does not have to mean the diminishment of importance of the CIO, it will introduce significant change. If CIOs are not proactive in defining new roles, sources of influence, and authority, it could lead to the eventual hollowing of the job that Carr and others have predicted.

The CIO who performs the role well is much more than manager of the central IT organization. He or she wears several other hats including strategic adviser to institutional leadership, technology consultant to academic and administrative departments, advocate for technology and technology adoption, risk manager, and steward of the institution's information assets. The potential is there for CIOs to stake out new roles and sources of influence. However, these changes will challenge CIOs to think and prepare differently to define these new roles and will challenge institutions to be open to accepting them. The possible added or enhanced dimensions of the role are described next.

Services Architect

The rise of the cloud may diminish the set of traditional services that an institution's IT organization must provide on its own. However, it also presents that institution with a more complex set of options to weigh. Increasingly, choices for provisioning technology services are not limited to a binary decision of make or buy. In fact, there is a more complex set of sourcing options that includes make, buy, collaborate, consolidate, or eliminate the service altogether.

We see this complexity playing out in the area of e-mail. After many years of facing rather simple choices of first building their own e-mail or implementing a commercially vended package, institutions now have broader options to sort through. The historical make-or-buy choice is still there. In addition, institutions can also choose to outsource to a provider such as Google, but continue to act as the intermediary arranging for the provision of the service. Or, they can choose to step aside completely and enable each individual student or faculty member to choose their own e-mail provider. Some still face the challenge of weighing whether there should be one uniform approach to the service (consolidate) or if parts of the institution should be able to elect their own service solution. Each option brings with it a complex set of pros and cons that must be weighed from multiple perspectives. The CIO and by extension the IT leadership team should be both the conveners of and major contributors to these discussions.

Complex services-sourcing options are increasingly available for each discrete technology service. The fluid nature of the environment also suggests that the decisions may not have terribly long shelf lives. Increasingly, the role of the CIO will be to proactively identify the sourcing options for various services and to be the convener of the appropriate stakeholders to weigh the options. The CIO of the future will also need to be the convener and orchestrator of a more complex set of governance practices and relationships. Historically, IT governance has been mainly focused internally. With increasing numbers of services provided by the cloud, governance will have to extend to include the providers of these outside services, whether they are corporations, consortia, or multi-institutional collaborations. CIOs may find themselves at the nexus of interwoven governance structures. In fact, the ability to convene, facilitate, and manage these internal and external relationships may replace control over dollars as the source of CIO power in the future.

Data Evangelist

Most institutions are only scratching the surface when it comes to leveraging their data to improve decision making.[9] Technology is rarely the limiting force. Rather, the challenge is to create a culture that demands analysis and requires evidence to support decision making. It requires leaders who ask for data and staff who are skilled at analysis. As institutions face increasing external pressure to measure outcomes and increasingly competitive markets for resources, their appetite for analysis will likely increase. CIOs are well positioned to be the bridge between the technology, the data, and the decision makers within the institution.

The CIO and his or her staff can work in the cabinet room to demonstrate to the leadership the potential to use data. They can also work across the organization to forge alliances with administrative units that are already inclined toward analysis such as institutional research, admissions, or the registrar. CIOs can jointly sponsor proof-of-concept projects that raise the visibility of analytical decision making. They can develop capabilities within their own organization to design metrics and measurement systems at the process, unit, and organizational levels. In fact, analytical design or strategic measurement consulting could become a new service line within some IT organizations.

CIOs must also be leaders at their institutions in conversations about the preservation and protection of data. Information security is just one important part of this role. The CIO is also uniquely positioned to educate the campus about the need for effective data governance including policies to define access rights, processes to preserve common definitions of data, and mechanisms to improve the accuracy of data at the point of capture. The CIO is also the natural leader of initiatives to design and implement technologies and processes that enable the ongoing integration of data across multiple applications and application providers.

The CIO and the IT organization will not be the only potential source of leadership in this area. The library, institutional research, and planning offices are all important stakeholders as well, and rivalry and competition for leadership among these officers and the CIO are inevitable. The topic is broad enough to accommodate multiple leaders, each of whom brings the unique expertise of his or her own organization to the conversation. Many CIOs are already accustomed to leading by influence in areas in which they have little or shared direct authority (for example, shared governance of administrative systems). The data evangelist role is another opportunity for CIOs to gain stature and authority by serving as conveners and facilitators who work effectively across the organization.

Innovation Incubator

The development of the web has no doubt placed more technology and information directly in the hands of individuals. The barriers to technological innovation keep lowering, and individuals need to turn less often to professional IT groups to help them develop solutions. Research labs, individual faculty, and staff have access to comparatively powerful technology tools that enable them to innovate.

As innovation capacity spreads throughout the institution, it presents the central IT organization and the CIO with difficult choices. Does the CIO try to hold back the innovators in order to control risk and the costs and complexity of technology support? Does the CIO take a hands-off approach and hope that a thousand flowers will bloom and the institution will see a return on the multitude of investments made by individual innovators? Or, is there a way that the CIO can influence and support innovation to the benefit of both institution and individual?

These are challenging questions and each CIO will need to find the right balance for his or her institution. However, the solution is not likely to be found at either of the extremes. Clamping down on innovation is unrealistic and counterproductive. Allowing anyone to do anything is too risky and costly an approach for any responsible CIO to take.

One conceptual model that may be useful to adopt is that of the business incubators. Although most incubators of the 1990s failed to live up to the unrealistic expectations placed on them as sources of new business and economic development, they succeeded as physical and virtual places where ideas, money, and expertise were brought together to further an innovation. Rather than build physical business incubators, however, CIOs can embrace the incubator concept of convener of the ingredients of innovation.

For example, a CIO and the IT organization can position themselves as resources that enable individuals to experiment with technology. The IT group can work with academic leadership to provide seed grants, equipment, and technical expertise to support individuals experimenting with new ways to use technologies in areas that are important to the institution. Much like a small business incubator advises and coaches entrepreneurs, they can support and influence individual technology innovators. The CIO role could evolve to be like that of a venture capitalist who makes connections among innovators, helps to secure resources, and works on behalf of the institution to find and promulgate the most successful experiments.

Process Architect

It is quite possible that developments such as software as a service (SaaS) will increasingly remove the IT organization from the day-to-day operations of administrative systems. To the extent this does occur, IT organizations should respond like any other business that sees a portion of its operation become commoditized. CIOs must respond by shifting resources to other activities that deliver higher levels of value to the institution. For example, SaaS may make applying updates to software a commodity service best done outside of the institution. However, configuring business processes to leverage the capabilities of technology to best support the needs of the institution is a unique and valued service that IT groups can move into. Few institutions have expertise in this area and even fewer have designated a senior leadership position to worry about the effective design and deployment of processes.

CIOs can position themselves and their organization to fill this void. This is not to suggest that the IT organization would dictate to financial or student services groups how to conduct their business. Rather, the opportunity would be to create a collaborative service that specializes in the analysis of processes to find opportunities to make the best use of technology. These services can be delivered in the context of technology implementation projects or as part of ongoing improvements to leverage already acquired technology. The CIO can become the primary spokesperson to the campus on how to build the capacity to measure and improve processes across the institution.

Some CIOs may be understandably reluctant to take on this role. As a community, IT leaders have appropriately pointed out the need for functional managers to take more ownership for their systems and processes. Perhaps the time has come to alter that approach. Is it sufficient to call on functional owners of processes to improve? Or, might more progress be made if IT organizations refocus a portion of their capabilities to facilitate these improvements? At the end of the day, the lack of process change or the inability to maximize benefits from technology inevitably becomes the CIO's issue. Process shortcomings erode confidence in the value of technology and make it that much harder to build support for the next investment.

Orchestrator

Closely related to the role of process architect is the role of services orchestrator. More than ever, tomorrow's higher education IT leader will need to translate an architecture into a legal, technical, and service web that appears to all as an integrated whole. And the creation of a holistic presence must, of course, convey—in a virtual context—the sense of place and self-conception the institution wishes to manifest. This will be extraordinarily difficult. The core skills of tomorrow's IT leaders in this guise will be:

A sourcer of services. This role will include the crafting of a sourcing strategy; the identification, integration, and testing of services to be acquired; the negotiation of license terms; and the establishment of service level agreements and performance standards and liabilities.

An integrator of systems. While the promise of standards–based architectures suggests that some day software will "snap" together, the reality of this promise remains far in the distance. Today's CIO struggles with the rising complexity of large heterogeneous hardware and software that need to interoperate seamlessly while producing transaction logs and other trails that are both transparent and repeatable. This complexity is only likely to increase in the near term as CIOs of the future strive to integrate vended solutions with homegrown solutions and with open source solutions, and so forth. Integration and coordination tasks will for some get even more complex as some IT leaders attempt to achieve advantage by sourcing labor in other locations, including abroad. In such cases, orchestration of time zones, intellectual property laws, national laws governing privacy, access, and e-discovery, and other issues will add to the challenge.

A brand manager. While formal responsibility for managing the college or university's image rests typically with a public affairs organization, the CIO today and increasingly in the future will have a great deal of influence over how the institution is positioned in the cloud. While the institution's cyber presence will likely embody software, services, and processes that have been sourced, distinguished, and integrated "at home," that presence must appear to the user to have a consistency and feel that says: "Oh, I am now at UC Berkeley." In addition, the evolution of the cloud means that the college and university will need to extend its presence into the cloud. Increasingly, for example, higher education institutions are establishing beachheads in Facebook, MySpace, YouTube, and other places where students and prospective students are found. The task of managing that presence in ways that complement the myriad strategies for managing an institution's presence in bricks and mortar will be daunting.

Information Policy Manager

The promise of the Internet cloud hinges on the proposition that technology is becoming a utility that—like many commodities—can be produced more effectively when aggregated at scale. Moving services outside of the institution enables a shift from managing technology to managing information. Discussion about the data evangelist role already advanced some of these arguments and suggested an opportunity for CIOs to become a leading voice for the use and stewardship of data at their institutions. The information management role extends that argument into the realm of information policy and strategy.

The increased presence of the institution and its individual faculty and staff on the web introduces a broad spectrum of policy issues. The definition and protection of intellectual property rights, the conduct of members of the campus community in cyberspace, and management of the institution's brand and image on the web are just a few examples. As the institution's intellectual property goes digital, it also creates a new realm of policies and procedures that must be developed around access rights and privacy. The CIO must be prepared to lead and participate in the policy discussions that will govern this new world of interconnectedness.

From a strategic perspective, the institution must make decisions about its presence on the web. Colleges and universities are very protective of their reputation (with good reason) in the physical world. The world of the web offers much less ability to control image and brand. When any individual can create a video of an event (positive or negative) on campus and put it on the web for all to see, it changes the extent to which any institution can manage its message and control the flow of information. Institutions must be prepared to think about how they can use the tools of Web 2.0 to defend and enhance their images even while these very same tools could be used by individuals to the detriment of the institution.

Institutions must also make decisions about how to invest in their own web presence. What is the value of an institutional island in Second Life? Do alumni want to subscribe to a portal provided by their alma mater?

These are obviously issues that are much broader than technology adoption decisions. But because the CIO will have deep knowledge of how the technology is being used, she or he will have the opportunity to become a part of these strategic discussions.

Proactive Strategist

IT leaders and researchers have long spoken of the need to align technology projects and priorities with institutional strategies and priorities. Alignment is clearly important, but is it enough? University of Wisconsin–Milwaukee Chief Information Officer Bruce Maas argues that "the alignment concept is long outdated as it implies passivity. CIOs need to be proactive and help identify how to help the university respond with technology to reach its markets and provide more effective business processes. The CIO has the opportunity to work with the president and provost to really dig in and find solutions." The payback, according to Maas, is a change in perception of how IT contributes: "IT has been characterized as a utility, but it is not a utility only. It is better to think of IT and treat it as an investment opportunity that creates innovation."[10]

Contributing more proactively to strategy will be more easily accomplished in some institutions than in others. Institutions differ in their degree of openness to thinking about technology as a strategic asset or the access they provide the senior IT leader to strategic decision making. However, it is likely that everyone can make more progress toward the repositioning of IT as an investment opportunity. Maas's challenge is also not an invitation to overpromise the benefits of technology as a transformative force. The path from being viewed as a cost center to an area that yields benefit in return for investment is likely through the accomplishment of numerous small demonstration projects rather than overly ambitious claims.

In some institutions the opportunity to contribute to strategy will be a top-down one for the CIO. He or she will have entree to the upper echelon of the institution and will be able to contribute to strategic discussions alongside other institutional academic and administrative leaders. In fact, CIOs may experience the locus of the discussion shifting toward their involvement as institutions try to make meaning of Web 2.0 phenomena and changing student expectations.

For others, the opportunity will lie in developing richer partnerships with individual units. Presenting to an organization ideas to further fundraising success through data mining or partnering with a dean to improve retention by embedding technology in the advising process are equally valid ways to demonstrate the strategic value of technology. Becoming an indispensable partner to more and more members of the administration will transform IT and the CIO into strategic assets to the institution.

Getting from Here to There

Many of the potential areas of new responsibility described envision the CIO more in the position of influencer than chief. While it would be naïve to think that there is not some level of risk of loss of stature in this transition, the findings of the ECAR IT leadership and workforce study suggest that for many, trying to hold onto direct control over many aspects of technology and its application is a losing proposition. In the future, it is likely that CIOs will increasingly gather power, authority, and stature from their ability to be agile, knowledgeable conveners of stakeholders around a host of issues related to the application and management of technology. It is growing less and less likely that CIOs will be granted seats at the leadership table merely by virtue of running a large organization. This will challenge CIOs to develop different and better relationship-management skills and broader knowledge of the academy. It will challenge the institution to acknowledge, reward, and empower leaders who contribute as much through their ability to influence as through direct command and control.

Interestingly, corporate CIOs appear to be moving in the direction of creating value through influence. In the IBM Center for CIO Leadership's 2007 CIO survey, 53 percent of respondents considered "promoting collaboration between IT and lines of business" to be their highest priority. Further, only 15 percent of the respondents thought their organizations were good at it today.[11] Perhaps higher education can emulate what corporations are doing and move the relationship between central IT organizations and colleges and administrative divisions to a higher plane. Rather than seeing their capital consumed in wrestling for control over commodity IT services, CIOs can instead go over the local IT organization to find ways to directly contribute to the strategic agenda of the dean. The political capital and trust gained through such relationships will no doubt make it much easier to rationalize service delivery models and achieve greater influence over decentralized IT spending.

Achieving these somewhat idealized conceptualizations of the CIO role will not be easy. There are many hurdles to be overcome. Time is one obvious problem. The time and energy of most CIOs are easily consumed with concerns of execution: managing projects, fighting service crises, and sustaining the reliability of the infrastructure—all the more reason to look carefully at opportunities to shed some commodity services as the cloud matures. Similarly, CIOs need to find leverage in their own organization. The only way to have the time to focus on the more strategic agenda is to develop trusted lieutenants who can contribute to both the day-to-day operations and the strategic agenda.

Skills themselves are another potential hurdle. While many respondents professed proficiency in critical skill areas such as influence, negotiation, and communication, that is largely in relation to what today's CIO job requires. The roles described above require CIOs to exert considerable influence through their powers of persuasion and the strengths of their relationships. CIOs will likely need to take their communication skills and their ability to manage internal relationships to even higher levels of proficiency. Likewise, skill areas that were evaluated by respondents as areas of relatively less proficiency, such as managing external relationships, will become even more important in the future. If the CIO is to become the services architect of the future, she or he will need to become skilled in evaluating and managing collaborations with corporations and other institutions.

The CIO will also need to take steps to build new capabilities within the IT organization. To fully realize the roles of data evangelist or process architect, the IT leader will need to be backed up by organizational capabilities. As IT organizations find opportunities to transfer commodity services to the cloud, they will need deliberate people strategies to transform the skills of existing staff or add new staff in these emerging service areas.

Relationships will be critical to the ongoing transformation of the CIO's role. As described in the preceding section, CIOs will rarely obtain mandates to play these roles. Just as their predecessors were pioneers who had to establish the initial contours of the CIO role, the next generation of leaders will have to lead the refinement and extension of the role. IT leaders will need to nurture relationships at all levels and with all parts of the institution. They will need to be conversant in the strategic issues confronting a diverse set of organizational areas. They will need to build trust that encourages other units to invite them into their inner planning discussions. In particular, because of the evolving role of the IT leader, the proximity and importance of some relationships are likely to shift. As the skills and demands of IT leadership shift toward contract administration, services orchestration, architecting, and so forth, the new best friends of the CIO may be found in unlikely spots. Such future friends include the general counsel, risk manager, institutional auditor, librarian, and chief research officer.

The Workforce

The preceding section, which described a reconceptualization of the role of the CIO, could have just as easily been describing new roles for the entire IT leadership team. The impact of cloud computing on the skill sets required of IT leaders will not be limited to just the CIO. The potential new roles for the CIO in many cases represent new or extended lines of service for the IT organization as well. The transition to this new model of IT and IT leadership may evolve incrementally, but it will transform the skill mix required in the entire organization.

New IT Worker Skill Sets Needed

To move IT organizations into some of the areas described above will require not only strong technical staff, but also staff with excellent communication and political skills. More staff will be required who are skilled at process analysis, group facilitation, data analysis, and data management. New professional positions that focus on these skill sets may need to be created in IT organizations. Such positions, in fact, likely exist already in some organizations in their project management offices or in business analyst groups.

As these new skill sets are emphasized, there will be a congruent diminishment in importance within the IT organization for other skill sets. As the cloud realizes its full potential, IT organizations will have a diminished need for staff to manage servers, databases, and perhaps some applications.

As the role of the CIO changes, so will the role of managers and directors. Whether they aspire to be CIOs or would prefer to remain as leaders of specialty areas within IT, they too will need to evolve their skills. It seems likely the future will place a premium on leaders who demonstrate understanding of the broader institution, are skilled at managing internal and external relationships, and are skilled at articulating as well as demonstrating how technology can be applied to address higher education's most strategic needs. What those needs are will evolve over time, but if staff are looking for some places to bet their careers, there are several promising candidates. It seems inevitable that institutions will continue to need specialists who can work with faculty to integrate technology and learning. Likewise, the management of data for research or institutional decision making seems promising. For leaders with more technical interests, integration and architecture seem likely to be high-demand areas as well. The cloud may remove the need for the IT organization to provide some services, but the institution will still expect someone (the IT group) to be able to blend these disparate systems and services into a cohesive user experience. Gazing deeply into a crystal ball, one might foresee the rise of specialists in cyber marketing. These might be individuals with expertise in plotting how institutions position themselves in virtual worlds.

Will There Be a Shortage of IT Workers?

While we manage this transition in the composition of the IT organization, will we also be experiencing a shortage of skilled IT workers? The data examined as part of the ECAR leadership and workforce research were inconclusive. Demographic projections suggest that the size of the population leaving the workforce due to retirement will be larger than the number of workers coming in to replace them. Further, there has been a reported decline in the numbers of individuals who have pursued degrees in areas such as computer science that often have provided the supply of skilled IT workers. However, other factors play into determining whether we will indeed face an absolute shortage in numbers of skilled workers. A prolonged slowdown in economic growth could mute some of the demand for labor. A decision by baby boomers to defer retirement out of necessity or preference could also mute the impact of the projected shortage of workers.

Among the senior-most IT leaders surveyed in the ECAR study, the majority were concerned that higher education would see a shortage of skilled IT workers and that their institutions would face significant challenges recruiting adequate numbers of skilled IT staff. In light of this concern, it seems prudent that CIOs take steps to prepare for a possible shortage of skilled workers or at the very least a more competitive labor market. To do so requires a much more focused and deliberate commitment to a series of people-management strategies targeted at recruiting, retention, and productivity.

First, institutions need to decide what they are selling to prospective recruits. It is likely no longer realistic or practical to compete against the compensation advantages held by the corporate sector by promising that higher education offers less pressure, reduced work hours, and an idyllic campus setting. Too many of our staffs now work long hours, feel the pressure of major projects and growing workloads, and have been moved to office space off the main campus to make this claim. Higher education needs to identify and capitalize on other areas of potential competitive advantages. The opportunity to stay within the employee's preferred geographic location could be one important factor. Certainly, at most institutions you can build your career without fear of being transferred from the New York to the Hong Kong office (although some institutions' globalization strategies may change this, too). The relatively smaller nature of some higher education IT organizations may provide them with an opportunity to offer staff environments in which they can take on broader responsibilities and accelerate their career growth.

Sharpening the recruiting message needs to be coupled with a strengthened infrastructure to source talent. More competitive labor markets will require more thoughtful strategies to find the best candidates, in some cases before they are needed. Using the alumni network as a source of candidate referrals and more formally cultivating students as future employees are two strategies that are within reach of most IT organizations. Hiring dedicated IT recruiters to maintain a list of potential job applicants and to help manage the recruiting process is another.

To aid both recruitment and retention, higher education IT organizations must pay more attention to developing career paths for their staffs that tie together growth in skills and growth in compensation. The lack of sufficient career-path and skill-building opportunities seemed to be an area of concern for some of the respondents to the ECAR IT leadership and workforce survey. Those who were less satisfied with career-path and skill-building opportunities reported that they were more likely to leave their current institutions in the near future (less than five years). The study suggests that business continuity planning seems to be spurring a focus on developing succession plans and career paths that focus on building skills several layers down into the organization. This is a positive development that would benefit all institutions. Perhaps the dual pressures of business continuity planning and the possibility of a labor shortage can become twin forces that enable CIOs and human resources leaders to work collaboratively on programs that define multiple career paths for IT professionals and encourage experimentation with compensation programs that reward skill building as well as promotion.

Higher education IT can also become a leader at adopting strategies such as job sharing or flex time to make it easier for staff to balance work and life. A willingness to experiment with these strategies could help mitigate the disadvantage of lower compensation. There also seems to be a potential intersection between "green" initiatives such as telecommuting and strategies to provide flexible work arrangements that may promote improved retention.[12]

It would also behoove IT leaders to focus more on raising the quality of management and supervision in their organizations. Results of the ECAR IT leadership and workforce survey document the detrimental effects on motivation and retention that poor supervisory interactions can create. The higher education literature has long acknowledged that technical staff are not necessarily taught how to lead and manage people as they rise in their careers and are not always prepared for this aspect of their positions. Acknowledging the problem will not be good enough as we move forward. If we do face a labor shortage, staff are not likely to remain working for a boss who is not a good manager. IT organizations also need the gains in productivity that presumably come from a workforce that is motivated because it is well led and managed. Whether through community-wide initiatives, the efforts of regional consortia of institutions, or intra-institutional partnerships with the human resources department or the business school, the IT community needs to invest more in building the management skills of IT professionals before, during, and after they rise into the ranks of management.

Advice to Leaders

Achieving the transition to a new conceptualization of the CIO role will take time. ECAR research does not suggest either an imminent or a revolutionary change. Rather, change is likely to take hold through a series of smaller evolutionary steps that alter the perceptions and expectations of the role. What is important is that the IT leadership community articulates a point of view on the future of the CIO leader. Leaders need to be secure enough to let go of the past. While IT organizations must make responsible decisions about how and when to turn services over to the cloud, they cannot deny its existence. They should not fear that moving services out of the IT organization will make them less relevant or less secure in their institutions.

Paradoxically, the very fact that IT leaders demonstrate willingness to experiment and leverage alternative service delivery models can hasten their transition to a new and more strategic role. It can free up resources within IT that can be repositioned. It demonstrates an openness to change, which can serve as a model for others. It enables CIOs to more forcefully insert themselves in conversations about leveraging technology, rather than arguments about who provides it.

What else should leaders do to prepare for the future? On the top of the leaders' to-do list should be taking steps to broaden and deepen their understanding of the institution. As seen among the survey respondents, experience outside the IT organization bears a relationship to the IT leaders' sense of their influence, especially on academic issues. IT leaders cannot go back and redo their career paths to gain these experiences, but they can take steps to develop deeper familiarity with the various parts of their institution. Actions leaders can take include the following:

- Allocate more time to meet with deans or department chairs to better understand their priorities (as opposed to their superficial technology needs).
- Seek roles on institutional planning committees.
- Offer to periodically attend staff meetings in other divisions to learn more about the issues they face.
- Seek professional development opportunities in areas outside of technology, or offer to go with other campus leaders to their professional conferences.

It is important for IT leaders to take these actions for themselves and to encourage (or require) their managers and directors to do the same. The relationship-building job is too large for one person to do alone. It must become the responsibility of the whole IT leadership team.

There are also institutional actions that leaders can take that will secure their future roles. For example, many aspects of the strategic role of a CIO will be greatly facilitated by IT governance. CIOs need to create effective mechanisms to learn about the needs and interests of stakeholders and to establish mechanisms to weigh competing priorities across the institution. These aspects of governance will help cement the CIO's responsibility to maximize the leverage the institution creates from its technology investments.

IT leaders must also begin to educate their institutions about the coming opportunities and challenges. Initiating a dialogue of the potential challenges and opportunities presented by the cloud or the impending workforce shortage also provides the leader with an opportunity to start a conversation about the changing role of central IT and his or her own role. It is always better to define your future than to have someone else do it for you.

Lastly, all of the secondary and primary study data urge all IT leaders to focus more on the workforce. As evidenced by the respondents to the ECAR survey, there is significant opportunity to improve staff-management practices. Leaders should require their managers and directors to join with them to provide more frequent communications to staff about the goals and priorities of the organization, become more skilled at providing effective feedback, and demonstrate tangible interest in the career goals and skill development of all staff.

Of course, leaders need to lead by example. They must take the time to understand the career goals and skill-development needs of their own direct reports. Leaders can't wait for a staff member to self-identify as a future leader. They need to reach out to rising managers and directors and provide them with opportunities to build the knowledge and experiences that will prepare them to lead in the future. Not everyone will want to be a CIO. Some will aspire to lead smaller teams or departments. Others will want to be better individual contributors. Regardless of ultimate career goal, it appears that all staff will benefit from opportunities to broaden their skills and perspectives.

More institutions must become proactive in putting in place strategies to meet the challenges of a shrinking pool of skilled workers. As we learned from the ECAR study's qualitative interviews, a multifaceted strategy is required. Change takes time and institutions need to begin now to take steps to make themselves more attractive employers and less people dependent. IT leaders need to build complementary service strategies and human resource strategies that seek opportunities to leverage skill sets of other organizations in areas of common need and to create new skills and positions in areas of uniqueness.

As a community, IT leaders need to look for strategies to build diversity in their organizations. It is in institutions' collective and individual interests to ensure that they have deep pools of qualified candidates for every position in their organizations. With so much to accomplish, organizations must know that every member of their team feels they are in an environment that is taking maximum advantage of their talents. We cannot afford for any of our organizations to become inhospitable to staff based on race, gender, ethnicity, or any other factor.

Advice to Aspirants

There is much that should encourage an aspiring leader to keep working toward the CIO role. Demographics alone suggest that there should be ample opportunities for aspiring leaders to fill. Aspirants can also take heart in the fact that there will be no shortage of challenges for them to address once they arrive in a leadership position. The CIO role is still maturing and as this essay suggests there is room for the next generation to put its own stamp on it. The first generations of IT leaders had to professionalize the role and fight to establish their seat at the table. The next generation will have the opportunity to demonstrate how CIOs should use the seat that they have earned.

On many fronts, aspirants appear to be taking the right steps. The ECAR survey respondents who aspired to the CIO position were much like the current crop of leaders in terms of their skills, educational attainment, and leadership styles. Given our assertions about the future of the CIO role, it would be in the best interests of aspirants to gain as much exposure as they can outside of the IT organization. Gaining experience managing institutional IT governance groups, serving in leadership roles in multi-institutional collaborations, and building experience managing external partnerships all seem like must-have experiences. These experiences will help equip them to step into a role that is becoming more about the application of technology across the diverse aspects of an institution. If aspirants are fortunate enough to become IT leaders at their present institutions, the relationships they build outside of IT will be invaluable as they step into a role that is as much about influence as it is authority.

Maintaining technical knowledge is important. An IT leader must have enough technical skills to be able to earn the respect of his or her organization and be a facile translator of technology's capabilities and constraints to academic and administrative leaders. However, aspirants should not build their technical résumé to the exclusion of all else. Leaders are increasingly valued for their ability to communicate, plan, and manage and develop staff. In addition to focusing on the skills and areas of specialization already discussed, aspirants should also give serious consideration to obtaining a doctorate. As the leadership job becomes one increasingly of influence rather than authority, the need for the PhD credential will likely grow.

In the ECAR study, aspirants to top college and university IT jobs and nonaspirants alike recognized the demands of the job. The question for many came down to whether they thought they could make a difference. If a CIO role is incrementally more time consuming and requires more sacrifice of work–life balance, then respondents wanted to feel that they would be able to make an incrementally larger contribution. In this regard there is cause for optimism. It is unlikely that the CIO role will shrink in responsibility or influence. Neither the talents of the individuals in the CIO roles or the needs of our institutions will likely allow that to happen. Rising CIOs have every reason to believe that they can make a difference.

Summary

ECAR's 2004 study concluded that the condition of the IT leadership community was strong and its prospects for the future were good. The 2008 ECAR study found nothing that would refute that conclusion. Institutions are served by an IT workforce that is dedicated to both technology and higher education. It is a community in transition that will no doubt see waves of retirement that will alter its makeup. Fortunately, there appears to be another generation of leaders and workers willing to step into their places.

There is reason to be optimistic for the future. Our institutions are still discovering the many ways in which technology and information can enable them to achieve new things. The cliché that higher education IT's best days may still be ahead need not be a hollow promise. However, higher education's IT practitioners cannot afford to be passive about the future. IT leaders will need to take action to define it for themselves and their institutions.

Higher education must also heed the warning signs about our organizations and workforce. Individual and collective action is required to improve the quality of management, mentorship, and skill-development available to our staffs. As labor markets contract, advantages will accrue to organizations that can create environments in which staff want to work through compensation, communication, and opportunities to build a long-term career. The CIO job will not be the right destination for everyone. Our human resources programs need to respect alternative career aspirations and create mechanisms for individuals to be recognized for their contributions in ways other than just promotion to management.

In 2002, Gary Augustson, former vice provost for information technology at Penn State, wrote about the challenges faced by IT leaders. His article acknowledged the many reasons why leading IT is hard but also described why it is so vitally important. Whether you are an IT leader, an aspiring leader, or a member of an IT workforce, the article offers much to validate the efforts you put forth. There is no better way to close this essay than to quote the conclusion of that article:

> The information technology efforts within higher
> education form a key part of the underlying national
> infrastructure that supports the ability of the United
> States to be a global leader—whether in driving global
> economic success or making the world safe for our
> children and grandchildren. The effective leadership
> of these efforts is immensely important. The job is
> not already done. In fact, the job has just begun. IT
> leadership in the twenty-first century will be the
> ultimate challenge.[13]

Endnotes

1. This essay is derived from Philip Goldstein, *Leading the IT Workforce in Higher Education* (Research Study, Vol. 6) (Boulder, CO: ECAR, 2008, in press). Throughout this essay, reference is made to the 2008 ECAR IT leadership and workforce study and the survey on which the study was based. *Leading the IT Workforce in Higher Education: Survey Instrument* may be found online at http://connect.educause.edu/Library/ECAR/LeadingtheITWorkforceinHi/45192.

2. Richard N. Katz, Robert B. Kvavik, James I. Penrod, Judith A. Pirani, Mark R. Nelson, and Gail Salaway, *IT Leadership in Higher Education: The Condition of the Community* (Research Study, Vol. 1) (Boulder, CO: ECAR, 2004), available from http://net.educause.edu/ir/library/pdf/ers0401/rs/ers0401w.pdf.

3. Stephanie Overby, "The Incredible Shrinking CIO," *CIO Magazine* (October 15, 2003).

4. Nicholas Carr, "IT Doesn't Matter," *Harvard Business Review* (May 2003).

5. Quoted in Edward Cone, "Nicholas Carr: Why IT Will Change," *CIO Insight*, January 9, 2008, http://www.cioinsight.com/c/a/Expert-Voices/Nicholas-Carr-Why-IT-Will-Change.

6. The survey was conducted jointly by the IBM Center for CIO Leadership in collaboration with the MIT Sloan Center for Information System Research and Harvard Business School.

7. *The CIO Profession: Driving Innovation and Competitive Advantage* (IBM Center for CIO Leadership, October 2007), http://whitepapers.zdnet.com/abstract.aspx?docid=352948.

8. Goldstein, *Leading the IT Workforce in Higher Education*, op. cit.

9. Philip Goldstein with Richard N. Katz, *Academic Analytics: The Uses of Management Information and Technology in Higher Education* (Research Study, Vol. 8) (Boulder, CO: ECAR, 2005), available from http://www.educause.edu/ecar.

10. From an interview conducted by the author with Bruce Maas of the University of Wisconsin–Milwaukee as part of the 2008 ECAR IT leadership and workforce study.

11. *The CIO Profession: Driving Innovation and Competitive Advantage*, op cit., 12.

12. Ted Dodds and Richard N. Katz, *Developing the IT Workforce at the University of South Australia* (Case Study 2) (Boulder, CO: ECAR, 2008), available at http://connect.educause.edu/Library/ECAR/DevelopingtheITWorkforcea/46813.

13. J. Gary Augustson, "Leading the IT Team: Ultimate Oxymoron or Ultimate Challenge?" *EDUCAUSE Review* (March/April 2002): 18, http://connect.educause.edu/Library/EDUCAUSE+Review/LeadingtheITTeamTheUltima/40319.

Bibliography

Augustson, J. Gary. "Leading the IT Team: Ultimate Oxymoron or Ultimate Challenge?" *EDUCAUSE Review* (March/April 2002): 12–18, http://connect.educause.edu/Library/EDUCAUSE+Review/LeadingtheITTeamTheUltima/40319.

Carr, Nicholas. "IT Doesn't Matter." *Harvard Business Review* (May 2003).

The CIO Profession: Driving Innovation and Competitive Advantage. IBM Center for CIO Leadership, October 2007.

Cone, Edward. "Nicholas Carr: Why IT Will Change." *CIO Insight*, January 9, 2008. http://www.cioinsight.com/c/a/Expert-Voices/Nicholas-Carr-Why-IT-Will-Change.

Dodds, Ted, and Richard N. Katz. *Developing the IT Workforce at the University of South Australia* (Case Study 2). Boulder, CO: EDUCAUSE Center for Applied Research, 2008, available from http://www.educause.edu/ecar.

Goldstein, Philip. *Leading the IT Workforce in Higher Education* (Research Study, Vol. 6). Boulder, CO: EDUCAUSE Center for Applied Research, 2008, in press, available from http://www.educause.edu/ecar.

Goldstein, Philip, with Richard N. Katz. *Academic Analytics: The Uses of Management Information and Technology in Higher Education* (Research Study, Vol. 8). Boulder, CO: EDUCAUSE Center for Applied Research, 2005, available from http://www.educause.edu/ecar.

Katz, Richard N., Robert B. Kvavik, James I. Penrod, Judith A. Pirani, Mark R. Nelson, and Gail Salaway. *IT Leadership in Higher Education: The Condition of the Community* (Research Study, Vol. 1). Boulder, CO: EDUCAUSE Center for Applied Research, 2004, 107–108, available from http://www.educause.edu/ecar.

Overby, Stephanie. "The Incredible Shrinking CIO." *CIO Magazine* (October 15, 2003): 66–76.

Afterword

Charles Darwin observed that it's not the strongest of the species that survive, nor the most intelligent, but those most adaptive to change. For humankind, the pace of change has been accelerating, and never as rapidly as in the past century. One hundred years ago, our body of knowledge doubled only once every century. Today, our body of knowledge doubles every few years. In our digitized, microchipped world there is virtually no subject that cannot be Googled, downloaded, and consumed. In higher education the challenge is clear. How can we analyze and apply that information in ways that will help our learning institutions thrive? How do we turn that ubiquitous cloud of information into real knowledge?

In his remarks elsewhere in this book, Richard N. Katz talks about the 10 threads that have influenced the tapestry of higher education since the inception of the academy. In this new millennium, technology is the bright new strand that weaves through our institutions and binds them to one another, enabling an unprecedented degree of collaboration and learning. That digital thread connects us to something more than information. It connects us to the world of ideas.

And those ideas are changing the practice of education. Classroom instruction has been augmented and sometimes replaced with online learning. Traditional office hours are increasingly supplemented with e-mail and online conversations. What lies ahead? What will the classrooms of tomorrow be like? Will there even be classrooms? How will the relationship between teacher and learner change? And how will technology affect that change?

We are pleased to serve as a sponsor of *The Tower and the Cloud*, a collection of essays that asks us all to imagine that future together. At SunGard Higher Education, we imagine a future where the lines blur between institutions and organizations, between consumers of technology and solution providers, between learners and teachers. In this future, new ways of knowing, more creative platforms for learning, and better forums for understanding will create new opportunities for those of us who share a passion for education.

We hope to see you there.

Andy Cooley
Senior Vice President, Marketing
SunGard Higher Education

Campanile, University of California, Berkeley

Index